PARAGON ISSUES IN PHILOSOPHY

PARAGON ISSUES IN PHILOSOPHY

African Philosophy: The Essential Readings
Tsenay Serequeberhan, Editor
Critical Theory and Philosophy
David Ingram
Critical Theory: The Essential Readings
David Ingram and Julia Simon-Ingram, Editors
Foundations of Cognitive Science: The Essential Readings
Jay L. Garfield, Editor
Foundations of Philosophy of Science: Recent Developments
James H. Fetzer, Editor
Living the Good Life: An Introduction to Moral Philosophy
Gordon Graham
Meaning and Truth: Essential Readings in Modern Semantics
Jay L. Garfield and Murray Kiteley, Editors
Metaphysics: A Contemporary Introduction
John Post
Philosophy and Cognitive Science
James H. Fetzer
Philosophy of Science
James H. Fetzer
Philosophy of Human Rights
Patrick Hayden
Philosophy of Sex and Love: An Introduction
Alan Soble
Philosophy of Sport
Drew Hyland
Philosophy of Technology: An Introduction
Don Ihde
Problems in Personal Identity
James Baillie
Self-Interest and Beyond
David Holley
Social and Political Philosophy
William McBride
Undressing Feminism
Ellen R. Klein
Woman and the History of Philosophy
Nancy Tuana

THE PARAGON ISSUES IN PHILOSOPHY SERIES

At colleges and universities, interest in the traditional areas of philosophy remains strong. Many new currents flow within them, too, but until recently many of these—the rise of cognitive science, for example, or feminist philosophy—often went largely unnoticed in undergraduate philosophy courses. The Paragon Issues in Philosophy Series responds to both perennial and newly influential concerns by bringing together a team of able philosophers to address the fundamental issues in philosophy today and to outline the state of contemporary discussion about them.

More than twenty volumes are scheduled; they are organized into three major categories. The first covers the standard topics—metaphysics, theory of knowledge, ethics, and political philosophy—stressing innovative developments in those disciplines. The second focuses on more specialized but still vital concerns in the philosophies of science, religion, history, sport, and other areas. The third category explores new work that relates philosophy and fields such as feminist criticism, medicine, economics, technology, and literature.

The level of writing is aimed at undergraduate students who have little previous experience studying philosophy. The books provide brief but accurate introductions that appraise the state of the art in their fields and show how the history of thought about their topics has developed. Each volume is complete in itself but also aims to complement others in the series.

Traumatic change characterized the twentieth century, and the twenty-first will be no different in that regard. All of its pivotal issues will involve philosophical questions. As the editors at Paragon House continue to work with us, we hope that this series will help to encourage the understanding needed in a new millennium whose times will be as complicated and problematic as they are promising.

John K. Roth
Claremont McKenna College

Frederick Sontag
Pomona College

UNDRESSING FEMINISM

A Philosophical Exposé

ELLEN R. KLEIN

UNDRESSING FEMINISM

A Philosophical Exposé

PARAGON HOUSE ✦ ST. PAUL

PARAGON ISSUES IN PHILOSOPHY

First Edition 2002

Published in the United States by
Paragon House
2700 University Avenue West
St. Paul, MN 55114

Library of Congress Cataloging-in-Publication Data

Klein, Ellen R.
Undressing feminism : a philosophical expose / Ellen R. Klein.
p. cm.
Includes bibliographical references and index.
ISBN 1-55778-811-1 (pbk. : alk. paper)
1. Feminism—United States. 2. Feminism—United States—History. 3. Women's rights—United States. 4. Equality—United States. 5. Anti-feminism—United States. I. Title.
HQ1421 .K54 2002
305.42'0973—dc21
2002011913

For current information about all releases from Paragon House, visit the web site at http://www.paragonhouse.com

For my sister: She always knew the empress had no clothes.

CONTENTS

Preface xiii

Chapter One: *Whither Feminism?* 1
- The One and the Many 3
- Gender Feminism 9
- The Equality Question in Feminism 20
- Summary 25

Chapter Two: *The First Generation* 29
- In the Beginning 29
- The Civil War 36
- The Thirteenth, Fourteenth, and Fifteenth Amendments 38
- Toward the Twentieth Century 40
- WWI 44
- The Nineteenth Amendment 45

Chapter Three: *The Second Generation—Its "First Wave"* 47
- Sex, Prohibition, and the Charleston 47
- Depression Years 50
- WWII 52
- Happy Days 56
- The Sixties 58

Chapter Four: *The Second Generation—Its "Second Wave"* 71
- Sex, Politics and Sexual Politics 73
- The ERA Era 77
- The Personal is the Political 83
- Equality as Difference 88
- The Patriarchy Inherent in Western Culture 98

Chapter Five: *Third Generation—Looking "Back to the Future"* 105
- Women as Victims 107
- Paglia: Broad Social Criticism 112
- Sommers: Debunking Education 114
- Klein: The "Date Rape" Question in Feminism 122
- Masculism 130

Chapter Six: *The Next Generation* 137
Backlash and Separation 138
Sluts, Girlie Girls, Bitches and Cunts 143
Feminism as PAC and Globalization 153

Chapter Seven: *Is Feminism Dead?* 163
Warrior Women 165
The Myth 169
Feminism's Voice 178
The Un-Dead 181

Notes 182

Index 209

PREFACE

Undressing Feminism offers the reader an opportunity to view feminism's history and philosophy through the eyes of an "outsider"—that is, someone who has not bought in to its political agenda. Although the text is not intended to be fundamentally polemical, my commitment to what I have called "first generation" feminism will be obvious. As such, the content of this text will be unique for the genre.

The form of this text will also be unique. For I do not simply present the development of feminism chronologically, but rather chronicle the most fundamental kinds and stages of feminism through an analysis of the philosophical notion of *equality* and its operational and legalistic notion of *equity*. The latter notion is assumed simply to mean impartial justice or fairness under the law. With respect to this text, the law will be taken to mean the federal and state laws of the United States of America.

The issue of equality is not so easily defined. Hence, it is the object of this text both to discover and analyze just what is meant by equality at different stages in the lifetime of feminism. Whether one views such changes over the last century or so of feminism's history as important or trivial, just or unjust, harmful or helpful will be left to the reader.

At times, especially in the book's sixth and seventh chapters, my discussion of feminism requires the use of coarse terminology. I intend no offense to any reader when this is the case, but, from time to time, scholarly accuracy necessitates the use of provocative words. Without these words, the aspects of feminism under discussion can neither be identified nor described properly.

I would like to acknowledge my eternal indebtedness to my former professor and friend, Dr. James Fetzer, for believing in me through the years. Thank you so much for giving me the opportunity to do this project.

A special "thank you" is extended to Ms. Peggy Dyess, from the Flagler College Library for all of her expert assistance and advice with collecting important resources—I could not have done this without her. Also from Flagler Library I would like to thank the Director of the Library, Mr. Michael Gallen, and his assistants Mr. Brian Nesselrode, Mr. John Daniels, Ms. Grace Engelstadter, and Ms. Catherine Norwood. From the mailroom at Flagler I would like to thank Mr. Terry Bennett and Mr. Jerry Teater, whose technical assistance was invaluable. I would like to also give special thanks to the administrators at Flagler for their continued support of my scholarly work, especially Chancellor William Proctor, President William Abare, and Dean Paula Miller. I would like to also thank my colleagues Dr. Timothy Johnson, Dr. Thomas Graham, Judge Richard Poland, and Dr. Arthur Vanden Houden for their scholarly advice and daily inspiration. Finally, from Flagler College, I would like to thank the students from the 2001 summer course entitled: *Feminism and Masculism*—Ms. Cheryl Fitzgerald, Mr. Jeremy Fowler, Ms. Tamara Moore, Ms. Valerie Wishneski, and Mr. Jude Wright for helping me formulate and polish some of my ideas, and Hannah Messler for her editorial assistance.

Of course, no manuscript could be written without the love and support of family and friends. Thank you Lynnie and Freddie, thank you Athena, thank you Margaret and Gelman. And thank you Lori and Sig Brody and Diana Martin.

To my parents—Dr. Ronald and Mrs. Lillian Klein, my sister, Dr. Carole Klein, and her son Austen Mitchell Bolitho, thank you so much for your time, attention and support.

Thanks for special editorial assistance must be given to my lifelong friend Mr. Phillip James Perea and, of course, my editors at Paragon House, Ms. Laureen Enright, Ms. Rosemary Byrne Yokoi, and Dr. John K. Roth.

Finally, for loving and nurturing me, though I'm always working, extra special thanks go to my husband Mr. Timothy J. Kotsis.

CHAPTER ONE

WHITHER FEMINISM?

"Forget feminism," were the first words out of the mouth of one of my former students when I told her that I had been honored with the task of writing this text. Her tone was not one of anger or disgust, but simply of disinterest, akin to the groans students emote when they have to hear some stuffy old professor rehash ancient notes on a topic no one is interested in anymore. She added, "Pleeeaaasse, I need feminism like I need a hole in my head."

I must admit I was taken aback. I knew that an earlier *Time/*CNN Poll found that 58 percent of women did not call themselves feminists;[1] that *Time* had recently declared feminism dead; and that 43 percent of the respondents of the 1998 Poll said they "had an unfavorable opinion of feminists";[2] and that many people see feminism as being "marginal and benign."[3] What I did not know was that it had managed to be wiped from the minds of the twenty-something generation of college women without so much as a whimper. How was this possible? How did feminism go from being a legal trailblazer in the 1800s to a major political powerhouse in the 1900s to a hackneyed and superfluous ideal in the new millennium?

One reason for the above response, we are told by unsympathetic elders,[4] is that today's young women take feminism for granted. These "Neanderthal feminists"[5] saw every act of sexuality—the showing of a bit of cleavage or leg—as a symbol of oppression. Contemporary women, women who "dress to kill," are simply prodigal children. Born from generations of women who had been voting and working on their careers for years, these young women see such privileges as nothing new or special. Feminism, according to its old matrons, can offer nothing to such a spoiled daughter. According to such feminists, the ungrateful little brats should be, nonetheless, scared feminist, or at least shamed into taking up the cause.

More sympathetic elders, however, argue that it is only natural that old-fashioned feminism has nothing to offer those so inundated with their mothers' ideologies that even the mention of the term 'feminism' makes them cringe. Today's young woman is justifiably tired of hearing about how her mother walked the proverbial ten miles to school in the snow just to find that she was being short-changed on her education by so-called patriarchy. The seemingly ungrateful daughter is simply asserting her individuality by being more interested in the height of her heels than in marching for some tired feminist cause. And who blames her? After all, she is just a girl. (Although it is important to note that even a dead, or dying, feminism is trying to win the hearts of the latest generation of daughters by simply repackaging itself in a new, definitely pink,[6] outfit.)

Although the above scenarios are palatable, I think that a better explanation for the *ennui* of the younger generation is that they responsibly recognize that everything must pass. Feminism, from the perspective of today's young women, is, frankly, old, and old things inevitably fade away. Mourning is unnecessary; eulogizing absurdly overdramatic. Today's youth resist "labeling" of any kind from anyone from any generation.

Of course, there is another possible cause for this malaise, if not downright apathy. It may be that the contemporary woman sees all too well that feminism's death be not a proud one. The exaggerated claims of sexist oppression by men (e.g., the trio of exaggerated beliefs—that all men are rapists, that all heterosexual sex is rape, and that any sex with a man is rape[7]), the unjust behavior of feminists toward men (e.g., with respect to paternity and child support[8]), and the lowering of the bar of human excellence (e.g., standards for gaining entry into military service[9]), have all lent a hand in the distaste and distrust of feminism by today's young women.

Take, for example, the following cases, which portray the seemingly unequal way in which men and women have been treated with respect to violence, sex, evidence and testimony.

> In Maryland in the 1980s, Mark Bowles served thirteen months of his sentence for raping his ex-girlfriend Kathryn Tucci before she confessed that she lied.
>
> In 1991, James Liggett of Everett, Washington was convicted of raping a woman he had met through a dating service, and spent a year in prison before her story fell apart—not only because she reported an eerily similar rape by another man from the same dating service (a navy serviceman who was investigated by military authorities and cleared after he passed a lie detector test), but because a private detective Liggett hired found out that she had a history of unstable behavior, including dubious claims of rape.[10]
>
> In a 1998 column, writer/professor Elayne Clift describes persuading her fellow jurors to convict a man of stalking on ambiguous evidence because she thought of "the Clothesline Project" commemorating women who died at the hands of men. Around the same time, the trial of Virginia politician and developer Ruthann Aron charged with plotting to kill her husband and another man ended in a hung jury, despite damning evidence, because a female juror insisted on seeing Aron as a victim of mistreatment by men.[11]

In the wake of feminist theorizing, such absurd consequences are becoming more common.[12]

THE ONE AND THE MANY

However plausible the above reasons for such a response are, one thing is for certain—feminism has aided and abetted in its own reputation.

As the social/political/philosophical/sexual/literary/artistic/etc. movement known as "feminism" ages, it becomes more and more difficult to actually define the term 'feminism' itself. According to those inside the club no definition of 'feminism' "is completely satisfactory because the term is amorphous and ever changing and because there are so many schools of thought with widely varying views."[13] It has made itself a "moving target," exempting itself from criticism and critique.

Regardless of one's political position, however, everyone agrees that these last five years have seen a surfeit of claims and beliefs that have been loosely organized under the rubric of feminism to where "the definition of 'feminism' has become ideologically overloaded."[14] "Recently the different meanings of feminism for different feminists have manifested themselves as a sort of sclerosis of the movement;"[15] a splitting of the movement into many factions, specialized agendas that seem incompatible.

The first attempt to systematically categorize and explain the variety of existing *forms* of feminism was documented by Rosemary Tong.[16] In the late 1980s, Tong identified the following—liberal feminism, Marxist feminism, socialist feminism, radical feminism, psychoanalytic feminism, existentialist feminism and postmodern feminism.

The first form, *liberal feminism*, according to Tong, focuses on the idea that "female subordination is rooted in a set of customary and legal constraints that blocks women's entrance and/or success in the so-called public world."[17] In other words, notions of equality and fairness are assumed to be meaningful, but there are certain discriminatory blocks in our social/legal system that prevent women from being viewed fairly or equally with men. "Only when society grants women the same educational and occupational opportunities it grants men will women become men's equals."[18]

This form of feminism is still viewed to be alive and well in contemporary feminist circles whose primary focus is to work on changing law, specifically workplace harassment, comparable worth, family, and rape laws.

The second original form, *Marxist feminism*, is defined by Tong to be a feminism that understands "women's oppression not so much as the result of the intentional actions of individuals but as the product of the political, social, and economic structures associated with capitalism."[19] To embrace such an account, one needed to first embrace Marx's social/political materialism[20] and then superimpose that ideology on one's understanding of sexism within a given capitalistic society.

This form of feminism *per se* seems to have gone out of style. For one thing, many feminists became dissatisfied with the "essentially gender-blind character of Marxist thought—that is, with the tendency of Marxist patriarchs to dismiss women's oppression as not nearly as important as worker's oppression."[21] *Socialist feminism* was then formed.

Like their Marxist sisters, socialist feminists argue that the only way to bring about gender equality is through the massive reorganization of wealth and property.

> But even more profoundly, socialist feminists lament the social and psychological consequences of living in a culture which rewards 'beating out the competition', 'killing off the other guy', and 'coming out on top'.... socialist feminists argue that the very concept of community is undermined by these aspects of capitalism; community requires shared concerns, a sense of cooperation rather than competition, and some sense of relatedness and collectivity.[22]

Eventually, Marxist and socialist feminism were paired into one ideology.

What is known today as *Marxist/socialist feminism* claims not that women deserve "equal pay for equal work" in the marketplace, but that because the gap between the wages of men and women is so great, it must be that the marketplace is, itself, fundamentally sexist. "As many socialist feminists see it, the ultimate aim of the so-called 'comparable worth movement' is not simply to make women the economic equals of men but to break down what is an increasingly scandalous hierarchy of wages..."[23] Marx's overly scholarly, cumbersome, and inherently masculine critiques of capitalism (as well as his scientifically problematic commitments to materialism), are forsaken by many contemporary feminists for a simpler and more direct socialistic criticism of American male culture.

Radical feminism may have still been "evolving" during the time Tong first chronicled the movement, but today it is, at best, devolving into what is now known in the popular press as either *lesbian feminists*, *Feminazis*,[24] or both. The focus of all three is that what is most essential to feminism is womanness, that womanness is essentially biological, and that biology is essentially sexual. Therefore, the focus of such feminists has been to examine the relationship between women's sexuality and the widespread oppression by men.

At the beginning of this movement, women's bodies were believed to be the cause of their disempowerment and many lesbian feminists and Feminazis turned to attacking the notion of sex with men, and then men in general, as being inherently dubious. The act of penetration, and therefore the penis itself, were viewed to be essentially tyrannical and evil.[25] The *Red Stocking Manifesto*,[26] for example, which claims that men are the source of all oppression, or the now infamous claims by Susan Brownmiller,[27] Catherine MacKinnon,[28] and Andrea Dworkin[29]—"that all men are rapists," "that all heterosexual sex is rape" and that "all intercourse is rape" respectively, as well as the myriad of web sites[30] professing the hatred of men, all attest to this unfortunate development. Despite protestations to the contrary, there are many feminists who hate men and several who have publicly claimed and/or advocated such passion. Some women have even claimed that "'You can hate sexism and not hate men'—I hadn't ever heard of that."[31]

Interestingly, and ironically, many of these feminists no longer view the female body and its vaginal-centered sexuality as a source of "penetratable" weakness and oppression, but rather as a fundamental source of power and, ultimately, liberation.[32] However, this 180 degree turn may have been too little too late. Radical feminism, due to its fundamental commitment to biological essentialism,[33] has had a difficult time staying alive in the academy and an even more difficult time recruiting new young women from outside. Moreover, its often mean spirited interpretation of such essentialism with respect to male biology has been blamed for making feminism sickly, if not terminal.

Psychoanalytic feminism and *existentialist feminism* have become unpopular for an entirely different reason. The former turned to Freud[34] for inspiration. This love/hate relationship with Freud's often very sexist theories—specifically that of "penis envy"—led feminists to deny that biology determined personhood. Such feminists shied away from the radical commitment to bodies as being either good or bad, and "emphasized instead the experiential and cultural influences that shape woman's gender identity and behavior."[35] Any particular woman, in order to be truly free, must realize that what was holding her back was not her biology but her psyche. With such a realization a woman can then begin to actually think for herself.

In order to think *for* oneself, however, one must first learn how to think *about* oneself. Thus *existentialist feminism* was born.

By way of the philosophies of Jean-Paul Sartre[36] and Simone de Beauvoir,[37] feminists were told to focus on a new understanding of self and self-consciousness if they wanted to achieve true liberation. Through esoteric and philosophically problematic notions of 'self', 'other,' 'being' and 'nothingness', existentialist feminists try to liberate women by reminding them that the goal of life is to be all one can possibly be as an individual, i.e., to be free. Such "freedom" may be more difficult for women given their biology and the present social order, but overcoming such obstacles is certainly not impossible.

However, de Beauvoir reminds us that even though we can (and must) shape ourselves, there will be limits on where and when such shaping can take place. "Just as a sculptor's creativity is limited by the marble block at hand, our freedom is limited by our society. If we want to be all that we can possibly be as individuals, we must first clear the social space for this project."[38]

If it is a "deep truth about us"[39] that we begin in society, then it is a mistake to begin one's journey to freedom from an isolated position.

Feminism, via its numerous approaches, had come full circle. From liberal feminism and its commitment to a societally based equality with men, to Marxist feminism and its rejection of the material bases for societal injustice (i.e., the workplace), to radical feminism's embracing of the body, to psychoanalytic feminism's embracing of the primacy of the psyche, and finally to existentialist feminism's recognition that one must first gain social/political equality with men in order to escape bondage. It is no wonder that today's young women are at least confused by, if not simply tired of, feminism's lack of direction.

And these distinctions are only the tip of the theme and variation iceberg. Overarching all of the above forms of feminism is what has been, and still is, called *postmodern feminism.*

> Postmodern feminists worry that because feminism purports to be an explanatory theory, it, too, is in danger of trying to

> provide the explanation for why women are oppressed or the ten steps all women must take in order to achieve true liberation. Because postmodern feminists reject traditional assumptions about truth and reality, they wish to avoid in their writings any and all reinstantiations of phallologocentric thought, which is thought ordered around an absolute word (*logos*) that is "male" in style (hence the phallus).[40]

In other words, given that all of the above forms of feminism require that one think within certain constraints given to us by Western *male* culture—e.g., ideas such as oneness, justice, rightness, fairness, freedom, truth, reality, objectivity, self, other, liberation, etc.—there will be no way to really break free from the chains of male domination without breaking down these constructions. Even the very act of trying to fit feminists, any specific feminists, into any of the above categories at some level buys into male bias. Therefore, "by refusing to center, congeal, and cement separate thoughts into a unified and inflexible truth, postmodern feminists claim to resist patriarchal dogma."[41]

Unfortunately for these feminists, this radical turn to undermine all previous philosophical, political, and scientific paradigms led them to embrace a postmodernism that was more deconstructive[42] than feminist. Having made such "important intellectual currency of the insight that social identity is multiply fragmented,"[43] feminism was split into yet even more feminisms including *cultural feminism*, *ecological feminism*, *multicultural feminism* and *gender-inclusive* (*anti-sexist man inclusion*) *feminism* to name just a few of the more popular forms.

What became central to the feminist project was to "respect difference by treating the subject (or self) so that she is represented as socially situated in many dimensions of power and identity besides gender."[44] No one was content to be a part of anyone else's feminism. Ultimately, what is now known as *lifestyle feminism* "ushered in the notion that there could be as many versions of feminism as there were women."[45]

Many feminists even began to claim that this is the most serious problem facing contemporary feminism(s).

> At the crux of the current debates about politics and political activities, among feminists today, is the question of whether it is possible, or desirable, to maintain a unified force of 'women' and their different perspective(s) in order to resist the historical oppression of women, as women, while simultaneously incorporating, in a serious way, the 'differences' among women in both theory and practice.[46]

Given the present state of feminism, then, proponents lament that "no one could have predicted that so many uncontainable divisions would arise between and within women's groups."[47] Even more sadly, it was the women themselves who became "feminism's greatest problem."[48]

GENDER FEMINISM

Nonetheless, what seemed to have turned into total chaos bore some threads of similarity. In the light of the above factioning and infighting there was a ray of hope. Some even proudly proclaimed that it is "certainly possible to construct a base-line definition of feminism and feminist which can be shared by feminists and non-feminists alike."[49] "One such thread might be the search for a male-oriented bias in any already well-established discipline."[50] And with this I agree. That is, I believe that there exists at present at least one major commitment which joins all forms of contemporary feminism: the commitment to the construct of *gender*. When feminism *post* postmodern feminism concerned itself with not merely subverting, mocking, reappropriating, or even eventually reforming, all of language, but focused on deconstructing particularly feminist terms such as 'woman', 'sex' and 'gender', this ushered in the next category of feminism. In at least a loose sense, all of the above factions intersect, at some point or other within their theorizing, with what is now called *gender feminism.*[51]

Although gender feminists vary according to their specific political agenda—everything from concerns about sex, family, and children to concerns about multinational corporate ethics or environmental issues—in the final analysis, almost every kind of feminism that remains today can be, at least broadly, classified as part of gender feminism.[52]

Gender feminism claims that the construct of 'gender' is essential to every aspect of one's political and personal lives. As such, unless one puts on "gender colored" glasses, one will be unable to see, let alone rise above, the fact that "the problems of women are not all from within, but are largely externally imposed; much of the "condition of women" can be explained by those things which are precisely sociological—institutions, roles, norms, values, and processes of socialization.[53] Gender feminism finds oppression everywhere.

'Gender' is a term that was "introduced by feminists in order that the social aspects of sexual difference should not be ignored."[54] Learning how to use the "gender lens" to "properly" view every political construct, every legal construct, every social construct, and every personal action performed by both men and women in all venues of life as gendered is what is known as raising one's *consciousness*. According to gender feminism, having achieved "consciousness" has become the only necessary and sufficient condition for entry into the sisterhood.

Unfortunately, determining who has and who has not achieved "consciousness" has become very problematic. Traditionally, at one end of the "consciousness" spectrum are the obvious cases of the Martha Stewartesque housewife who has never been self-conscious at all, let alone conscious of the social and political forces which control her life up to and including the very products she places on her family's dinner table. It's not that such women wouldn't understand or enjoy "consciousness." It's just that they have yet to be exposed to their true selves. Although today such women seem to exist only in theory, it is claimed by many feminists that within certain minority populations in the United States, as well as all over the Third World, such women are the norm.[55]

At the other end of the spectrum is, of course, the feminist academic who works solely within the scope of gender feminism. She is a woman who researches, publishes, teaches courses, grades papers, interacts with students, deals with her colleagues, and conducts her personal life, most especially her sex life, all without ever removing the "lens." For such women, the insidiousness of patriarchy lurks everywhere. Everything from the price of one's dry cleaning to works of art to space exploration is infused with gender and gender bias. Such women litter the halls of most academic institutions in the United States.[56]

But what of the rest of the population, those who fall within the gray area between definitely having and definitely not having gender "consciousness"? Most importantly, what of those individuals, male or female, who not only understand what "consciousness" is, but have had every opportunity to gain "consciousness," and yet have refused to accept the legitimacy of the "lens"? Can such individuals be said to be "conscious"?

In other words, two serious metaproblems arise: can one consciously reject gender feminism?, and is gender feminism immune to criticism?

The first brings to mind the Pauline Reage novel *The Story of O*,[57] in which a very beautiful and wealthy woman chooses to become a sex slave to a man. Is this an example of "sexual submission as good, and, in fact, life-affirming"[58] or something oppressive and horribly sexist? Feminists seem to be of one mind. "Any clear-headed appraisal of O will show the situation, O's condition, her behavior, and most importantly her attitude toward her oppressor as a logical scenario demonstrating the psychology of submission and self-hatred found in all oppressed peoples."[59]

The second question asks the readers to consider the fact that any and all statistics which do not favor feminist agendas are ignored[60] and that any serious arguments against their philosophical theories are either discredited or never debated head on.[61]

It is important to note, however, that such metaproblems are not the only serious issues gender feminism faces. Another concerns the term 'gender' itself. The term 'gender' may have been invented for political reasons,[62] but it seems to have been brought into common practice solely due to the politeness of our society.[63] Given that the term 'sex' has been appropriated to mean the activity of engaging in foreplay and copulation, another term needed to be adopted to mean that which biologically distinguishes little boy babies from little girl babies, men from women. The fact that these two terms are often interchanged in our society can be seen by the way the term is used on certain standardized forms. For example, governmental documents, medical records, and even consumer surveys ask for one's gender and then label the boxes "M" for male or "F" for female. It is clear from such examples that what such forms are interested in is nothing more complicated than the sex of the client or consumer.

But while it seems that the overall convention is that sex and gender are simply two different terms with the same meaning, most gender feminists argue that it is important to distinguish between the biological aspect of the sexual center of meaning and its socially and psychologically determined aspects. In other words, in academic circles, the term 'gender' is used to mean something different from sex *because* "gender is not as simple as the biological difference between women and men,"[64] "'women' and 'men' are not simply biological categories,"[65] or because "masculine (e.g., independent, aggressive, competitive, rational and physically strong) and feminine (e.g., passive, nurturant, cooperative, emotional, and physically weak) gender characteristics are distinct from male and female sex characteristics."[66]

Unfortunately, not all gender feminists agree with just how "fundamental" or "distinct" such characteristics are. Some take a moderate position claiming that "a gender system bases itself on sex by treating sex difference as important...but by feminine being and masculine being I will mean not women and men simply, but women or men or other beings to the extent that they are feminine or masculine."[67]

More radical theories abound. For example, some gender feminists claim that the distinction between the two is so *fundamental* that it yields the odd and potentially problematic possibility that "*man* and *masculine* might just as easily signify a female body as a male one, and *woman* and *feminine* a male body as easily as a female one."[68] Such a move would make claims of sexism toward women both odd and politically problematic. For it would not be clear just what it is about a woman, if it is not her body, that makes women *visible* targets of discrimination.

Also problematic is the claim that the distinction is simply *arbitrary*, imposed completely independent of sex by social forces which are merely culturally relative.

> The sex-gender distinction merely takes an essentially arbitrary set of role assignments—roles that happen to be assigned by sex, for greater or lesser utility—for the ideal

> gender domain in which roles belong to beings by virtue of a center, sex-related meaning that they participate in. Because sex role is not the same as gender role, Margaret Mead could intelligibly claim that the Arapesh and Mundugumor tribes have sex-role systems, in that they divide activities by sex, but not gender systems in the sense of a sexual division of personality types.[69]

Sex, according to some gender feminists, though a "biological given" was "elided into gender, a social construct, so that it could be deconstructed."[70]

Such a move, however, is problematic. If the "deconstruction" of social constructs is so simple, if women and men can easily and completely switch gender roles, then the gender feminist charges of sexism are merely hysterical dramatizations. This is why gender should not be mistaken for "lifestyle," something that can be "adopted or discarded as one chooses…not a carte blanche to differentiate men's and women's lives in any old way."[71]

In the final analysis, then, most gender feminists are forced to claim that while gender must remain distinct from sex, it is nonetheless to be constructed in such a way that it is no less "real." "Like race and class, gender cannot be renounced voluntarily."[72]

We are then back where we started, realizing that gender feminism insists there must be a distinction between sex and gender—one that, like Goldilock's porridge, is not too hot, and not too cold, but just right[73]—but still not really knowing what "just right" is. And, unfortunately, gender feminists have yet to be forthcoming about their central construct: *gender*. This, I believe, should make contemporary scholars at least a little bit suspicious. Even at the *1995 United Nation's World Congress on Women in Beijing*, it was reported that "not one of the participants knew how to define 'gender'."[74]

However, not only is there no hint of suspicion in academic circles, the distinction between sex and gender is so much a part of everyday academic life that gender feminists simply assume the presence and importance of gender in all arenas of their scholarly and pedagogical lives. And such assumptions now go completely unquestioned. This mindset, however, not only affects theorizing, but sometimes dangerously controls the lives of individuals both in and outside the academy.

For example, one set of gender feminists claims that it is simply a "fact" that biological sex has little, if anything, to do with social gender, a "fact" supported by empirical evidence. "Studies of hermaphrodite babies, whose sex is difficult to determine at birth, also provide some evidence that sex and gender are separable phenomena."[75]

Of course such evidence is itself quite problematic. For one thing, once it is presupposed that sex and gender are separable *phenomena* that were not created but rather discovered, it is difficult to imagine just what kind of "phenomenon" gender actually is. Is it an empirically testable phenomenon, something that can be seen, smelled, tasted or touched? If so, I am hard pressed to see how any empirically testable biological phenomena within a specific organism could be, in principle, fully separable from any other within that same organism. Modern biology tells us that everything on the planet is inextricably connected with everything else; certainly any attempt to disentangle the interconnection of "phenomena" within a given individual organism must be, at least, an extremely elaborate and difficult task. Furthermore, modern medicine states that most of our chromosomes are intricately linked. Certain traits that seem to be totally separable from one's sex traits, e.g., red-green color blindness, is in fact sex-linked. It may be that the difference in DNA between male and female humans is only 3 percent, but that small percentage shows itself in every single cell of our bodies.[76]

Perhaps the "phenomenon" of gender is fully "separable" because it is conceived to be non-empirically testable, albeit nonetheless phenomenal, similar to one's soul. If so, then I find it hard to believe that the existence of true hermaphrodites who have acclimated to an arbitrarily assigned gender designation could count as evidence either for or against the existence of, let alone separable existence of, gender.

Of course it may be that the "phenomenon" of gender is empirically testable, but does not actually reside in any particular individual. Instead, the "phenomenon" would be part of (in? supervene on?) a group of individuals, a specific community, or the entire species. Although this would make its "separableness" relatively more reasonable, it would make the link between specific individuals and *their* gender characteristics difficult at best.

The most straightforward attack on the above connection between the evidence from hermaphrodites and the theoretical separation of gender phenomena and sex is that there is a much simpler explanation for the result. The most reasonable explanation for what seems to be a certain amount of success with the arbitrary dubbing of gender is not that gender and sex are fundamentally distinct phenomena, but that given the truly hermaphroditic nature of the person (someone who may actually be biologically both sexes), acclimation to one supposed "gender" identity as opposed to the other becomes essentially irrelevant. That is, even if "gender" were not merely *invented* by gender feminists but a phenomenon actually *discovered* by science, it's "separableness" from sex could not be said to be demonstrated by such cases. Furthermore, even if it were true that such test cases actually revealed some "separable phenomenon" known as gender, it does not follow that this phenomenon should be assumed to contain the evolutionary strength to ever be viewed on par with, let alone override, the biological phenomenon of sex. As a matter of fact, the evidence from empirical psychology seems to claim that sex traits rule.[77]

Nonetheless, researchers continue to treat one's *gender role* and even sexual *gender preference*, if not personal *gender identity*, as something that can be manipulated by one's nurture—the social construction of one's familial and community environments—*alone.*

Both the empirical weakness of the belief, as well as the professional and political dangers of such hubris, became obvious in the tragic case of a man-made hermaphrodite. In this well documented case, one of two twin boys suffered a botched circumcision. He was then further surgically altered through total castration, chemically treated with estrogen and forced by his parents and physicians into living his young life as a girl until, at puberty, he insisted on knowing what was wrong with him.[78] For many years this case was cited in numerous sociology and women's studies texts as the definitive evidence of the sovereignty of nurture over nature. After all, the boys were biological twins! And now one's a boy and one's a girl! Gender feminists lauded the experiment and frequently cited it as having demonstrated the empirical strength of their construction. However, after the publication of the Reimer case, "some feminist scholars quietly dropped the twins case from new editions of their women's studies textbooks."[79] For gender feminists to claim that "whether gender is able to keep biological sex at bay permanently remains controversial"[80] seems to be an understatement indeed.

Not as dramatic, but nonetheless potentially dangerous, is the fact that although "gender" was invented by feminists with the noble intention of empowering women, it might be having quite the opposite effect. There are two interconnected ways in which the political insidiousness of a commitment to gender exposes itself in contemporary culture. The first is through the popular press.

Although the degree is up for grabs, there is no doubt that the media, especially advertising, affects us, to some extent or other. And the media, across the board in all venues—for example, television and magazines—seem to be telling us that the feminist construct of gender is doing its job precisely wrong.

Gender images[81] in our culture divide into three major forms: *gender neutral*, *gender bending*, and *gender denying*. While the first form (represented, e.g., by "Calvin Klein" ads) is the most innocuous, it does tell us something about young women of today; that is that they are attracted by persons (models), who, whether male or female, appear to be neither.

When gender is "bent" away from center, the preferred move seems to be to those models who look and dress like men. Even some lesbians have claimed that they:

> refuse to conform to a straight society's rules for dictating what is normal for women. Men try to claim all the fun personality characteristics for themselves; being dynamic, being a hero, being strong, brave, independent, active, even wearing trousers.[82]

Finally, when women do choose to be ultra feminine, for example, sexy starlets such as Nicole Kidman and Sharon Stone who have been known to pose in magazines such as *Vanity Fair* or *Glamour* wrapped in feather boas, such women are viewed to be traitors to feminist ideals. In one *Life* article, a photo of just this type is censured by feminists.

> We become confused, even disoriented, in the presence of glamour. We sense its power over us, even as we recognize its illusion; its triviality embarrasses us, our surrender to it disturbs us. The pinup photo is cruel to its subject as well. The very essence of the model's person—her privacy, her femininity, her spirit—is being offered up for the pleasure of strangers who possess the power to think about her what they choose.... The cruelest message in this kind of picture is that the women viewing it are inferior, the men looking at it inadequate: "Look at me, you can't *be* me. Look at me, you can't *have* me."[83]

It seems that when the gender of femininity is being at best subtly rejected, at worst overtly vilified by feminists,[84] the question of its political usefulness needs to be readdressed.

What may even be more interesting than the attacks by feminists on women who are ultra feminine is the fact that effeminate gender expression is accepted in men. Both straight and gay men are, of course, viewed as natural in their masculine, or even hyper masculine roles, but, interestingly, gay men are accepted, at least by most feminists, in their hyper feminine roles as well. Rue Paul's femininity, for example, is not only not revered by feminists, but claimed that such men actually play an "influential role in defining the feminine."[85]

Considering the power of the media, especially on the youth, feminism's commitment to the construct of gender seems to be, at best, problematic. At the very least, it is not clear that pop-culture's tastes reflect well on feminism as a political movement designed, to some degree or other, to empower women.

More problematic than pop culture's interpretation of gender feminism is the trouble gender feminists have caused themselves through their own theorizing about gender itself. Conventionally, the meaning of gender depended on representing it as something that allows for women to be different from men in a way that is substantial but not essential. Again, however, there was dissention among the ranks. Two contradictory notions of gender arose.

> One that sees considerable similarity between males and females and another that sees profound difference.... Some feminists believe that affirming difference affirms women's value and special nature. Others believe that insisting on no difference is necessary for social change and the redistribution of power and privilege. Both ways involve paradox.[86]

Actually, it is only when the two are viewed to be goals that must be achieved simultaneously that an actual paradox appears.

That is, if gender is so fundamental as to ensure difference between men and women, it seems to simply conflate the notion back into the static and essentialist construct of sex. If the sexes are fundamentally different then it is reasonable that at least in some circumstances sexism is justified. After all, if men are, in fact physically stronger than women, then with respect to jobs or positions that require strength women need not apply. Of course, if difference is overemphasized then gender feminism may lose its political muscle.

Parenthetically, one could build in the gender feminist caveat that "difference" can never be interpreted to mean "lack,"[87] but then it becomes unclear just what "difference" means if every venue of adjudication renders men and women to be equal.

On the other hand, "difference" qua sameness is also sticky. If difference is underemphasized, then it becomes unclear just what the political project of gender feminism could be. If men and women are the same, how could it be that "women are innocents and men are beasts?"[88] That is, if men and women are not at least a little bit different, then what's the problem, i.e., what is at the heart of the feminist beef about male bias and sexist oppression? If it's not to "end sexism, sexist exploitation, and oppression"[89] of *women*, then what is it? At the very least gender feminists must believe both of the following claims:

> The Descriptive Claim: *Women are oppressed,*
> and
> The Normative Claim: *They ought not be.*

When difference from men is undervalued, feminists lose their *raison d'être.*

Thus the paradox. Enough sex/gender difference between men and women must be sustained to give feminism[90] a legitimate reason for fighting; but difference cannot be overemphasized without losing the battle before they have even begun to fight.

THE EQUALITY QUESTION IN FEMINISM

The paradoxical battle with "difference" (in all its forms) has been a long and serious one for feminists.

> Even where difference is not in the foreground of feminist thinking and writing, it remains in the background as a point of contention that can be used against any empirical or theoretical generalizations that may be advanced.... Feminists have reflected on three kinds of difference: first, their own difference as women in relation to men, usually taken as a socially constructed gender difference; secondly, social difference between women; and thirdly, theoretical differences between feminists. The second and third types of difference have been seen as threatening the very possibility of feminist theory.[91]

But the "first type" is no less troubling. And nowhere is this paradoxical tension concerning the "difference as women in relation to men" more obvious than in the feminist desire for *equity* and *equality*.

Equity is defined, first and foremost as the simple act of impartiality, i.e., fairness and justice. It is a "type of justice that developed separately from the common law and which tends to compliment it...under modern rules of civil procedure, law and equity have been unified."[92] Thus, although theorists often use the term 'equity' it seems that for the most part they are simply using it to mean what has come to be known through the years as *legal equality*. Where "equality under the law" is

> defined under the equal protection clause of the 14th Amendment stating that 'no state shall...deny to any person within its jurisdiction the equal protection of the laws.' This clause ensures that no law will be enacted that discriminates

> against a particular group of people. It also ensures that laws will not be enforced in a discriminatory manner.[93]

Unfortunately, however, legal equality is only one of many forms of equality now recognized in social and political circles. According to Stanley Benn, for example, "there are three ways of ascribing equality—descriptive, evaluative, and distributive—and they are not, of course independent of one another."[94] With respect to feminism, the term seems to have as many different meanings as there are feminists themselves. Nonetheless, all of them have a common history.

The classical (Western) history of the ideal of equality begins with *The Old Testament*, the first five books of which contain the story of a people, the Jews, "chosen" or picked out to be unequal. The later *Psalms* and *Proverbs* go on to make yet further distinctions, namely between the good from the bad man. Plato too believed it most important to recognize difference (with respect to degrees of human excellence) rather than similarity between individuals. Thus, his maxim of equality, which was later stated directly by Aristotle, was simply: "Equals are to be treated equally and unequals unequally.... Injustice arises when equals are treated unequally and also when unequals are treated equally."[95] This has come to be known as "formal"[96] equality.

And although the notion of formal equality held supreme for a very long time, the colonization of the "new" world was the perfect impetus for social and political philosophers to at least theorize about, if not put into practice, new constructions of equality. For Hobbes, for example, men, all men, come into the world selfish, brutish, and in constant danger. There is no question that everyone is, basically, equally susceptible to the hardships of the environment. All humans are born into the same plight. At this time, the question of political equality took the form of something very simple, the right to individual self-preservation which later was developed into the right of the sovereign to protect his nation/people at all costs. Peace, for Hobbes, overrode equality as the ultimate good. Locke, though very similar to Hobbes in a number of respects, had a more sophisticated view of rights and argued that the community must always retain the power to overthrow government if "legislators ever become so foolish or wicked as to lay and carry designs against their liberties and properties."[97] What counts as "designs" against such "liberties and properties," especially with respect to contemporary accounts of the appropriate places for government intervention, remains undeveloped.

Rousseau, however, changed all that with his optimistic view of man that sees him born in a garden rather than the Hobbesian jungle. As such many of the problems that befall man, both as separate individuals and as a collective, are the fault of society itself. "Man is born free; and everywhere is in chains."[98] Here we see the first rumblings of the change in blame and responsibility—from man to society. With this came a new look at what it means to be "equal" and just who was responsible for such "equality."

The hallmark year 1776 finds the founding fathers, having drafted *The Declaration of Independence,* claiming that "all men are created equal…endowed by their creator with certain inalienable rights…life, liberty and the pursuit of happiness." A few years later this is joined by the Constitution with its aims to establish a "more perfect Union, establish Justice, insure domestic Tranquility, provide for the common Defence, promote the general Welfare, and secure the Blessings of Liberty to ourselves and our Posterity…" With the spirit of elasticity backed up by ambiguous language, equality becomes a notion of *equal under the law of the land*, but the actual role of government in helping individuals achieve their own personal pursuits of happiness, as well as our general pursuits of welfare, are left indeterminate.

Some interpretation of government's role is given in *The Federalist Papers,*[99] though the original Constitution guarantees very few rights. One is our right to national security (both from foreign and domestic enemies), another a concomitant commitment to economic prosperity (in order that one can tax the people to fund such security.) Even a commitment to the education of the masses is not directly addressed since at the time a primarily agrarian society needed nothing more than strong bodies to efficaciously defend the Union.

It wasn't until the advent of the abolition of slavery that a more positive account of *equality under the law* was created which grew into what we now call legal equality[100] (though the language remains negative). The Thirteenth Amendment (1865) makes slavery illegal, the Fourteenth Amendment (1868) outlines due process, and the Fifteenth (1870) ensures that all men have the right to vote. Nonetheless, all of these precepts are couched in a language of "shall nots." The point is simple; all three of these pre-civil rights amendments[101] attempt to ensure that no rights (interpreted as rights already granted elsewhere in the Constitution) are to be *taken away* from any group of men, not that any privilege is *added.*

Nonetheless, something in the zeitgeist of the now developing "American mindset" was set on instituting a more positive account of equality (though one important commentator of American life at the time, Alexis de Tocqueville, is quite hard pressed to discover why). In one chapter of *Democracy in America*—the chapter entitled "Why Democratic Nations Show a More Ardent and Enduring Love of Equality than of Liberty"—de Tocqueville states:

> Freedom has appeared in the world at different times and under various forms; it has not been exclusively bound to any social condition, and it is not confined to democracies. Freedom cannot, therefore, form the distinguishing characteristic of democratic ages. The peculiar and preponderant fact that marks those ages as its own is the equality of condition; the ruling passion of men in those periods is the love of this equality. Do not ask what singular charm the men of democratic ages find in being equal, or what special reasons they may have for clinging so tenaciously to equality rather than to the other advantages that society holds out to them: equality is the distinguishing characteristic of the age they live in; that of itself is enough to explain that they prefer it to all the rest.[102]

Though most of his work is purely descriptive, he does add a warning:

> The evils that freedom sometimes brings with it are immediate; they are apparent to all, and all are more or less affected by them. The evils that extreme equality may produce are slowly disclosed; they creep gradually into the social frame;

> they are seen only at intervals; and at the moment at which they become most violent, habit already causes them to be no longer felt.[103]

Drunk on equality, however, America was not. One major group remained, even legally, unequal. It wasn't until 1920 that the Nineteenth Amendment was passed, which, again in negative language, stated that "the rights of citizens to vote shall not be denied or abridged by the United States or by and State on account of sex."

This is where the story of the changing face of the nature of equality (with respect to feminism) begins, at the start of the twentieth century. But this is by no means where it ends. As feminism stands today, there is clearly a "divide" between theorists who, on the one hand, tend to argue that sex/gender "equality is the key goal for women—men and women should be treated essentially in the same manner by the state,"[104] and those, on the other hand, who argue "that women are essentially different, and this difference needs to be respected."[105] Some have even gone so far as to argue that the only way to achieve true equality is to deconstruct the need for gender distinctions themselves by simply eliminating sexual distinction, i.e., by having everyone turn to androgyny.

> In my mind, gender equality is too limited a goal. Unless women and men are seen as socially interchangeable, gender equality does not challenge the concept of differences that leads to separate spheres in the family and market place division of labour, which in turn results from women's lesser access to control of valued resources and positions of power.... I would question the very concept of gender itself, and ask why, if women and men are social equals in all ways, there need to be two encompassing social statuses at all.[106]

Androgyny, that is, on female terms. In the political climate that is feminism, the above operationalizes into men needing to become more like women, more feminized, not vice versa.

The history of feminism,[107] then, at its heart, is primarily the last hundred years of history concerning women—women's legal rights, women's economic advancement, women's freedoms, women's desires, and women's perceptions, all in relation to the difficult notion of *equality* with men.

SUMMARY

The rest of this text will be the chronicling of feminism's history through the late 1700's up to today via its differing, and often inconsistent, notions of equality.

The next chapter, *Chapter Two: The First Generation*, is the most uncontroversial. Given that everyone agrees on what it means to be a first feminist—be that a first generation or a first wave feminist—there will be little that is not purely historical about the account that will be given. Women's suffrage, the right to vote, and the desire for *equality under the law* are fairly straightforward and, to a great extent, uncontroversial. For first generation feminists there was only one feminism with only one goal: *equality with men*. In addition, equality itself meant only one thing: having the exact same opportunities and privileges as men (which at the time was operationalized into the right to vote). The *U.S. Constitution* needed amending and it was, in fact, amended to give women the right to vote when the Nineteenth Amendment was added in 1920. Feminism, as a first generation movement (what came to be known as the *women's movement*), was clearly defined, clearly beneficial to women, and clearly gaining equality.

Chapter Three: The Second Generation—Its "First Wave," follows a similar tack to the one above, tracing the notion of equality from the 1920s and 1960s. This is what I call the "first wave" of "second generation" feminism. At this time feminism still maintained a commitment to the same ideals of equality held by its first generation sisters. Somewhere between 1950 and 1960, however, much more radical strains of feminism started to influence the mainstream, and by the end of the sixties, feminism had decided to champion a notion of equality that wants to take seriously the fundamental biological differences between men and women.

Chapter Four, The Second Generation—Its "Second Wave" documents a feminism that begins where its first generation sisters left off, but then spawns the "second wave," which includes all of the different factions listed in *Chapter One* above. Through an exploration of how the construct of equality is transformed by this "second wave" this chapter will suggest that many of these new notions of equality are, at best, theoretically ill-conceived, and at worst, wrong-headed to the point of actually harming women more than helping them. Equality came to mean, for feminists of some form or other, anything from equality under the law—rising above gender differences—to the desire to rewrite the *U.S. Constitution* such that gender differences are acknowledged;[108] from radical egalitarianism, to downright sexism against men. The history of "second wave" feminism, as well as the practical and legal consequences of its theorizing—from the 60s to the present—testifies to the fact that there is a seriously turbulent relationship between feminism(s) and contemporary notions of equality.

Chapter Five: The Third Generation—Looking "Back to the Future" offers some of the most pressing criticisms of contemporary feminism—from Camille Paglia, Christina Hoff-Sommers, and E.R. Klein—which focus on challenging the feminist commitment to exposing constructs of equality that are theoretically problematic, if not downright inimical to women. Paglia outlines a broad social criticism of feminism, while Sommers focuses on the ways in which feminist politics have harmed education—from colleges and universities all the way down to grade schools. Klein, following in their footsteps, shows how feminist theories and ideologies, especially concerning the invention of the "date rape" construct, bare out in a harmful way to today's women. All three women espouse a return to first generation or at least first wave second generation ideas of equality so that women will see themselves as fully participant—fully privileged and fully responsible—members of society. In addition, the second wave account of equality will be viewed through today's men, specifically those who have gone on to form a "men's movement"[109] or "masculism,"[110] as well feminism's responses to all of the above. Although this chapter will be seen as polemical, little will be viewed by contemporary feminists as surprising.

The Next Generation, the sixth chapter, may be the most controversial of all of the chapters since everyone in academia, as well as the feminist body politic, is trying to reach out to the "next" and newest generation of young people. This chapter will document the most recent trends in feminism represented by a chronological series of responses to the critical voices of women and men. The first response, that from the old gals of the second wave, will be to scream "backlash" and/or respond by advocating—both in theory and in practice—"separatism," even in the public sphere. From the X-generation, there is an array of responses. As they are identified in feminist writings that advocate these outlooks, "sluts," "girlies," "bitches," and "cunts" are representative of hyper-responses, each with its own bone to pick with feminism, men, or both. I will argue that none of these recent attempts to attract today's young people to the feminist party have yet to become (and, I predict, never will become) interesting and important enough to attract enough members to revitalize the movement.

Interestingly, what is attracting converts are two independent movements, both of which grew out of feminism, but neither of which is actually compatible with any of the above accounts. On the one hand, there is the move to reinvent feminism qua political action committee (PAC), which attempts to offer activism specifically focused on women without the bother of any particularly unified feminist theory. The rhetoric proclaiming the desire for equality with men is simply and straightforwardly abandoned. On the other hand, there is the recent trend to unify all of feminist thought world-wide. This well meaning, broad-stroke egalitarianism, however, results in a very un-feminist, and maybe even anti-feminist commitment to gender neutral egalitarianism. While both positions may be attractive to the next generation, neither is consistent with any account of contemporary feminism.

Chapter Seven brings the discussion full circle by asking: *Is feminism dead?* I begin by rehashing what I have been arguing all along: that feminism, to have been viable, needed to sustain some common sense notion of equality. Since this was not the case, and in fact its proponents actually forced the construct into absurdity—making 'equality' mean 'difference'—feminism actually caused its own demise. Nonetheless, there does seem to be a form of the contemporary women's movement that, though not well represented, is worthy of consideration. This is the movement of "warrior" women. Although "warriors" are often subsumed under the feminist umbrella, their commitment to unadulterated equality with men, as well as their distaste for any gender distinctions with respect to the path to human excellence, sets them seriously apart and worthy of consideration for the newest generation.

I would also like to suggest that feminism has actually been, at least indirectly, responsible for the overall sense of insecurity and powerlessness that existed in our culture prior to, but was made painfully prominent by, the September 11, 2001 attacks. The prevailing zeitgeist of our culture is one of insecurity in the fundamental beliefs that have made our culture such a positive force in the world—constructs such as equality, justice, autonomy and excellence. It has made our culture one that is powerless to judge, let alone respond and punish, given our society's belief in relativism—that every belief, idea, action is valuable from some perspective. The overall lack of respect in academia for such classical notions began with, and has remained at the heart of, feminism. The perpetuation of the logically inconsistent and pragmatically misguided commitment to relativism has always been feminism's theoretical life's blood. In the final analysis, I urge everyone to see this text as a justification for why feminism should not be wanted—dead or alive.

CHAPTER TWO

THE FIRST GENERATION

In 1777, John Adam's wife Abigail warned her husband in a letter that while he and the other "founding fathers" were drawing up the American Constitution, if they did not pay "care and attention" to the "ladies" a rebellion would foment. The writing was on the proverbial wall, and the first rumblings of feminism began in the latter part of the eighteenth century with what was later to be called the "women's movement." By the beginning of the nineteenth century, the political focus of the women's movement would center on *suffrage*—the political right or act of voting, and those who advocated such rights for women *suffragists* or *suffragettes.*

During this beginning era of feminism, it is clear that equality means one and only one thing: *sameness.* That is, *being* viewed as essentially the same as men; *having* the same rights, opportunities and privileges as men.

IN THE BEGINNING

Feminism, even in its nascense, had so many faces that many scholars claimed that "there is no point looking for the moment of origin."[1] Nonetheless, most scholars claim that contemporary (American) feminism had its start with Mary Wollstonecraft (1759-1797) and her work *A Vindication of the Rights of Woman* (1792). At a time in history when countries all over Europe debated the rights of kings over the rights of men *qua* human beings, an analogous Enlightenment argument concerning the rights of men *qua* males over the rights of females seemed only natural. In France, for example, Olympe de Gouges (1748-1793) published her seventeen articles of the *Declaration of the Rights of Women*

(1791) in which she called for equal rights under the law—equal participation in government and equal education.

> Women awake! The tocsin of reason is being heard throughout the whole universe; discover your rights! The powerful empire of nature is no longer surrounded by prejudice, fanaticism, superstition and lies. Courageously oppose the force of reason to the empty pretensions of superiority, unite yourselves. Oh women, deploy all the energy of your character and you will soon see these haughty men. Not groveling at your feet as servile adorers but proud to share the treasures of the Supreme Being![2]

Hypocritically, women were at the time held responsible for crimes and punishment like men (e.g., they were put to the guillotine) but were given none of the rights and privileges of men (e.g., political voice). DeGouges proudly and bravely proclaimed in "Article Ten" that "woman has the right to mount the scaffold. She must also have the right to mount the podium." She was beheaded soon after.

Wollstonecraft, however, being English, did not suffer the same fate and her work has lasted and become seminal in historical feminism.

> *A Vindication of the Rights of Man* as a response to Edmund Burke's *Reflections of the Revolution in France*, in which Burke had argued against the concepts that grounded the great political revolutions of the eighteenth century; universal human rights, liberty, equality, and fraternity. Burke believed that talk of equality can only bring unhappiness to those 'destined to travel in the obscure walk of laborious life.' And regarding women, he seems to have had decidedly negative views: 'A woman is but an animal, and an animal not of the highest order.'
>
> Wollstonecraft's reply to Burke, published in 1790, is a spirited and closely reasoned defense of natural rights, followed in 1792 with *A Vindication of the Rights of Woman*, designed to address both the misogyny apparent in Burke's tract and the inconsistency in much of the natural-rights

> moral philosophy of the day. According to many philosophers, possession of full moral and political rights is based on the possession of reason; but the possession of reason is denied to women, therefore women do not possess full moral and political rights.
>
> Wollstonecraft argued that the most significant gender differences in intellectual skills, temperament, and ethical values were products of socialization and education, rather than natural or biological facts.[3]

Equality, in its most obvious, simple and fundamental form, was key. Women, according to Wollstonecraft, were essentially the same as men, i.e., just as "naturally" rational as men, or at least there was no evidence to suggest that there was any kind of *fundamental difference* between the two sexes.

Actually, Wollstonecraft's argument was less direct but more scientifically damning than merely assuming "sameness." Her argument began with the assumption that the two sexes were essentially the same (i.e., inherently rational) but added that in the absence of any actual empirical disconfirming data—women who were raised with the same opportunities and privileges as men and yet *did not* exhibit the same rational behaviors and growth as men—Burke's claim was nothing but an unscientific bias. Ironically, it was Burke's thesis (which was the accepted view of the time), not the women he cited, that was in fact irrational: "Only when women are ruled by reason [not men] will they be able to share in the equality of opportunities in society."[4]

Wollstonecraft, realizing the strength of the above challenge, made a leap and offered a concomitant normative prescription. Given that there is no reason to believe in a fundamental *difference* between men and women with respect to the most essential attribute—rationality—a truly just society has little choice but to assume *sameness* and therefore to, at the very least, offer women an opportunity to prove their rationality. It is not that Wollstonecraft did not see that women behaved superficially and immaturely with respect to society—always caring more for their beauty treatments than politics—but she truly believed that this was a "natural consequence of their education and station in society."[5] "Men had power because they were educated and economically independent."[6] Therefore, if society wants women to behave like true citizens, then it should "strengthen the female mind by enlarging it, and there will be an end to blind obedience,"[7] it must "teach them in the public schools the elements of anatomy and medicine"[8] and it must ensure that "for man and woman truth must be the same."[9] In other words, society has a duty to treat—first to educate both and then to demand civic duty from both—men and women equally.[10]

Interestingly, women were not the only people writing on this subject at the time. For example, Theodor Gottlieb von Hippel (a friend of the famous philosopher Immanuel Kant) produced a book which caused quite a stir in Germany called *On the Civil Improvement of Women* (1794). Essentially he makes the same argument proferred two years earlier (in England) by Wollstonecraft.

> Hippel argued that women's abilities were the same as men's but 'they are simply neglected, they are deliberately suppressed'. Women were coddled into laziness and educated to be ignorant: "'Reason' is a gift which Nature has vouchsafed to all human beings to the same extent. The most basic principles of Natural Law, in the implementation of which compulsion may be used without fear of contradiction, is the law 'oppose anything that endangers the full development of all human beings'. This principle resides in the highest material law of morality, 'develop every human being to the fulfillment of its potential'."[11]

This common sense notion of equality, propounded by both men and women of this era from all over Europe, will be the centerpiece of feminism for the next hundred years of the "women's movement" in the United States.[12] During this time, then, the first generation of philosophers and writers of feminism (on both sides of the "pond") were concerned solely with a notion of equality for women that was equivalent to being treated the same as men.

But it was not until the nineteenth century that feminism really began to take hold as a social and political movement.

> Women have always protested against their oppression in some way, and individual writers and thinkers throughout the ages have often devoted their attention to women's plight; but it was only in the nineteenth century that women began themselves to combine in organisations expressly created in order to fight for the emancipation of the female sex as a whole.[13]

On the English side the push from the movement can be seen in the work of J.S. Mill, who wrote *The Subjection of Women*[14] as a "joint project"[15] (although it was actually written after the death of his wife Harriet Taylor in1869).

Mill's reputation had already been established as a great philosopher and political theorist, and the writing of *Subjection* was just one example of how feminism and feminist ideas were beginning to take hold in mainstream intellectual thought. The first paragraph of the book states:

> That the principle which regulates the existing social relations between the two sexes—the legal subordination of one sex to the other—is wrong in itself and now one of the chief hindrances to human improvement; and that it ought to be replaced by a principle of perfect equality, admitting no power or privilege on the one side or disability on the other.[16]

And although the first part of the conjunction is essentially philosophical and normative, it is (unfortunately) not actually defended directly throughout the text.

The second part, argued via numerous examples, is defended but does not lead to the meatier claim that one ought not subordinate women, only that in present society the subordination of women leads to an unjustified fifty percent narrowing of the pool of human beings from which true excellence can arise. Moreover, as Mill emphasizes again and again, if it were true that women were naturally "disabled" in such a way that they *could not* perform tasks outside the home, it seems silly to *continually pass laws preventing them from doing what they, supposedly, cannot do*. Therefore, despite the fact that Mill never directly tackles the issue of the intrinsic value of women, *Subjection* becomes one of the most important and influential feminist texts of the first generation.

> Mill defined female emancipation in terms of the 'removal' of women's disabilities—their recognition as the equals of men in all that belongs to citizenship, the opening to them of all honourable employments and of the training and education which qualifies for those employments, and the removal of excessive authority which the law gave to husbands over their wives.[17]

The spirit of the prescription from *The Subjection of Women* is what lives on in the history of the women's movement and it is a spirit identical to that presented by de Gouges, Hippel, and, of course, Wollstonecraft before them: women and men must be treated equally in terms of education and opportunity. "Women's freedom of choice must replace the arbitrary rule of men."[18] And that "equality of opportunity for women requires their full citizenship."[19]

"Never were women talked about so much as in the nineteenth century,"[20] and on the American side of the Atlantic, things were no different.

> Elizabeth Cady Stanton (1815-1902) continues the feminist struggle started by Wollstonecraft, John Stuart Mill, and Harriet Taylor, but as part of an American women's movement. Along with Lucretia Mott, Stanton called for the first Seneca Falls women's rights convention in 1848. In 1853, Susan B. Anthony left the ranks of temperance and abolitionism to help her begin building an independent women's movement.[21]

Stanton and Anthony, then, became the new carriers of the first generation torch, their main objective being to secure the right to vote.

On July 19, 1848, one hundred women (and men) packed into the little Wesleyan chapel at Seneca Falls to hear the reading of the *Seneca Falls Declaration of Sentiments*:

> We hold these truths to be self-evident: that all men and women are created equal.... The history of mankind is a history of repeated injuries and usurpations of the part of man toward woman, having in direct object the establishment of an absolute

> tyranny over her.... He has never permitted her to exercise her inalienable right to the effective franchise.... He has made her, if married, in the eyes of the law, civilly dead...[22]

The motion to accept the declaration was passed and campaigners to help with the right to vote began pouring in (including Susan B. Anthony, 1820-1906); Elizabeth Cady Stanton (1815-1902) became America's newest feminist.

Though this torch shown brightly for the rights of women, it did so in a way that was not without tarnish. "Many in the white feminist movement in the USA, casting themselves as they did, used their role in the private sphere to denounce vehemently the right of black women or men gaining the vote before they did."[23] Elizabeth Cady Stanton and fellow white suffragist Susan B. Anthony openly opposed the Fifteenth Amendment which would, in 1870, give *only black men* the right to vote, claiming that they should not defer to the "negro's hour."

> You say, "this is the negro's hour." I will not insist that there are women of that race, but ask, Is there not danger that he, once entrenched in all his inalienable rights, may be an added power to hold us at bay? Why should the African prove more just and generous than his Saxon compeers? Again, if the two millions of Southern black women are not to be secured in their rights of person, property, wages, and children, then their emancipation is but another form of slavery.[24]

For Stanton and Anthony, there was no sense in fighting for the right of black people to vote if one half of that population, i.e., women, were to stay disenfranchised.

> This is declared to be a government "of the people." All power, it is said, centers in the people. Our state constitution also opens with the words "we the People." Does any one pretend to say that men alone constitute races and people? When we say parents, do we not mean mothers as well as fathers? When we say children, do we not mean girls as well as boys? When we say people, do we not mean women as well as men?[25]

Stanton and Anthony and other women of this first generation wanted nothing more than equality—individual freedom, autonomy, equal educational and professional opportunities, and any other privileges that men have as full citizens of the United States. "Women's exclusion from citizenship contradicted the universal promise of equality of opportunity."[26] Operationally, this meant they must first get the right to vote. To this end the *First National Women's Rights Convention* was held in 1850 and by the mid-1850s "state legislatures began showing sympathy towards women's property rights."[27]

Women's personal lives also took a change toward equality. Due to the availability of vulcanized rubber in 1859 condoms became accessible to the average woman. As such, women began to control their personal lives in a way they never could before. In this last half of the nineteenth century women would raise two or three children as opposed to the usual five to seven. The birth rate in the United States dropped, and women's desire for equal opportunity in the public sphere grew in direct relation.

THE CIVIL WAR (1860-1865)

The Civil War seemed also to have a serious impact on feminism in two ways. The first was the fact that many women, especially in the South, found themselves alone and totally in control of their own homes, farms, and businesses. As depicted in *Gone With the Wind*, this had an effect on women which was not surrendered if and when their men returned from the war. The positive effects of the war were that women became in many ways self-reliant and educated in areas of business and politics that were unheard of prior to their being left alone with their family's business. The home, farm, shop, etc. was a training ground of sorts for the near future when women would enter the public sphere in numbers too big to ignore. Women also volunteered to help in the war effort by collecting donations of food, clothing, and valuable metals. One interesting way in which women helped the war effort, especially near the end, was through smuggling. "One woman in Tennessee was stopped while making her way toward Confederate lines in a voluminous skirt; discovered tied to a girdle beneath it were twelve pairs of boots—each stuffed with medicine and whiskey."[28]

On the downside, many women began to show themselves to be just as, if not more, aggressive when it came to the treatment of slaves. Though it has often been reported that women plantation owners befriended their slaves, this was probably not true, at least with respect to the male laborers. Women owners were often as, if not more, harsh and violent to their slaves than their husbands, fathers or brothers had ever been.[29] Although many wealthy Plantation women were sympathetic to slave women at the beginning of the War, by the time the War ended—when Northerners had moved in, their farms had been burned down, supplies short and their money devalued—Southern women's attitude toward slaves changed drastically. With the Reconstruction, Southern women had discovered that the housework they used to delegate to slaves now freed was actually quite unpleasant and difficult[30] and the resentment felt by the Southern mistress toward the newly "free" black women "widened the distance that separated them."[31]

With respect to the North, changes for women also occurred. With the War came an increase in manufacturing technology, and such technology increased the production of, among other things, wool, paper, and, of course, rifle cartridges. The number of women workers employed in all of these industries increased dramatically. In addition, women entered the field of nursing by nursing on the battlefield. Several became heroes in their own right, including Clara Barton, who would seek out Federal soldiers on the battlefield and help them with food and medicine, and Louisa May Alcott (author of *Little Women*), who became the superintendent of the Female Nurses of the Federal Army. One woman, Sarah Emma Edmonds, actually enlisted in the Union Army and went on to write her autobiography *Nurse and Spy in the Union Army*.[32]

Politically, the women in the North were also impacted, for many of these women began to parallel their position with that of slaves. The rhetoric which grew out of the Civil War was to carry feminism through to the ratification of the Nineteenth Amendment.

THE THIRTEENTH, FOURTEENTH AND FIFTEENTH AMENDMENTS

First, however, feminism had to deal with the end of the War and the question of the freed slaves. Although feminists stood behind the *Thirteenth Amendment*, due to the specific language used, this was not the case for the *Fourteenth* and *Fifteenth*. It seems that feminists at the time wanted women to have equality with men, but not at the expense of giving more men (i.e., Black men) more equality.

The *Thirteenth Amendment* (1865) abolished slavery.

> Section 1. Neither slavery nor involuntary servitude, except as punishment for crime whereof the party shall have been duly convicted, shall exist within the United States, or any place subject to their jurisdiction.
>
> Section 2. Congress shall have power to enforce this article by appropriate legislation.

Feminism, for the most part, stood behind this amendment and in many cases placed suffrage on the back burner to help with the effort.

This was not, however, the case with respect to the *Fourteenth Amendment* (1868) and the *Fifteenth Amendment* (1870) because of the introduction of the term 'male' in the former and the lack of the term 'sex' in the latter. The *Fourteenth* offered due process under the law to blacks, but in so doing made specific reference to *males* over the age of 21. The relevant section, Section 2 of the *Fourteenth Amendment*, is cited below:

> Section 2. Representatives shall be apportioned among the several States according to their respective numbers, counting the whole number of persons in each State, excluding Indians not taxed. But when the right to vote of any election for the choice of electors for President and Vice President of the United States, representatives in Congress, the executive and judicial officers of a State, or the members of the legislature

> thereof, is denied to any of the *male* inhabitants of such a State, being twenty-one years of age, and citizens of the United States, or in any way abridged.... [my emphasis]

With respect to the *Fifteenth Amendment*, the problem was what was *not* in the amendment. It is obvious from the amendment cited below that in granting the right to vote to blacks, women, in terms of sex or gender, were being excluded.

> Section 1. The right of the United States to vote shall not be denied or abridged by the United States or by any State on account of race, color, or previous condition of servitude.
>
> Section 2. The Congress shall have power to enforce this article by appropriate legislation.

Male abolitionists working for the rights of blacks almost universally rejected women's claim to suffrage, insisting that this was not the time to stress women's rights. Citing Lincoln's famous claim of 'one war at a time,' both men and women tried to discourage suffragettes from further action. To this Susan B. Anthony was said to have replied, "Do you believe the African race is composed entirely of males?"[33] Anthony insisted that "this is the hour to press women's claims; we have stood with the black man in the Constitution over half a century.... Enfranchise him, and we are left outside with lunatics, idiots and criminals."[34] With all of the above Amendments now ratified, it was time for feminism to get focused and to get serious about suffrage.

TOWARD THE TWENTIETH CENTURY

In 1888, forty years after Seneca Falls, Susan B. Anthony and Elizabeth Cady Stanton reunited to form the *National American Women's Suffrage Association*. That same year, speaking to the *International Council of Women,* Stanton both warned young women of their new burdens and promised a brighter future.

> We who like the children of Israel have been wandering in the wilderness of prejudice and ridicule for forty years feel a

> peculiar tenderness for the young women on whose shoulders we are about to leave our burdens.... The younger women are starting with great advantages over us. They have the results of our experience; they have superior opportunities for education; they will find a more enlightened public sentiment for discussion; they will have more courage to take the rights which belong to them.... Thus far women have been the mere echoes of men. The true woman is as yet a dream of the future.[35]

More of this dream, however, was soon to come true.

> In 1893 English women obtained the right to make wills and in the United States the principles of common law were modified without recourse to equity. A far-reaching New York State law awarded married women full powers over their property and professional earnings. One by one, most states passed similar laws. Women had full rights under the system of separate property.[36]

Legal advances in the name of equality with men were clearly under way.

Women began making advances in the workplace as well. In the years between the Civil War and World War I, "the United States emerged as the leading industrial power in the world."[37] The impact of this certainly had a great effect on women. In 1903 the *Women's Trade Union League* was established, "through which middle-class women struggled along with their laboring sisters to better working conditions."[38]

> The first series of major strikes involving large numbers of women occurred in 1909 among shirtwaist makers in New York, about 20,000 of whom walked out to protest their working conditions. (Some of those participating in the strike were employed by the Triangle Shirtwaist Company, in whose crowded unsafe quarters 146 women lost their lives by fire just two years later). In Chicago, a similar walkout of about 40,000 employees of clothing manufacturing firms took place in 1910. Both the New York and Chicago actions were terminated after three months without clear-cut union

victories. But the organization of the mass of women workers had begun."[39]

A poignant poem beautifully articulates the mood of the time.

As we come marching, marching, in the beauty of the day,
A million darkened kitchens, a thousand mill lofts gray,
Are touched with all the radiance that a sudden sun discloses,
For the people hear us singing, "Bread and Roses, Bread and Roses,"
As we come marching, marching, we battle too for men,
For they are women's children, and we mother them again,
Our lives shall not be sweated from birth until life closes,
Hearts can starve as well as bodies; "Give us Bread and Give us Roses"
As we come marching, marching, un-numbered women dead
Go crying through our singing their ancient song of bread;
Small art and love and beauty their drudging spirits knew—
Yes, it is Bread we fight for, but we fight For Roses, too.
As we come marching, marching, we bring the greater days;
The rising of the women means the rising of the race.
No more the drudge and idler, ten that toil where one reposes,
But a sharing of life's glories, Bread and Roses, Bread and Roses.[40]

"The workplace taught women to appreciate their abilities."[41] And all of this hard work and suffering began to pay off.

It is evident that, on the whole, there has been a certain expansion of woman's sphere—a decrease in the proportion employed in certain traditional occupation, such as "servants and waitresses"...but an increase in the proportion employed in most other industries, many of them not originally considered as within woman's domain.[42]

The women of the nineteenth century argued for, fought for, and protested for, a number of changes aside from legal rights and better working conditions for women. For example, they began to initiate prison reform and to discuss the problems of alcohol abuse (that eventually led to prohibition.)

Finally, "women's widening place in the U.S. labor force demanded that schools deliver more education and vocational training for girls."[43] And it was in the realm of education, eventually and especially with respect to higher education, that the work of women and their desire for equality would have the most impact on feminism.

Academia has always been on the forefront of feminism, even as the century turned from 1800 to 1900 and the prevailing ideology was still in play—men and women are essentially the same. In 1912, Helen Thompson surveyed University of Chicago graduate students, finding "only slight difference in mental abilities" between men and women. In her dissertation, "The Mental Traits of Sex," she concluded "that it was training and social expectation that accounted for the differences that did emerge."[44]

With Freud's theories hitting America for the first time, the questions concerning the individual psyche—the ego, the id and the superego—were on everyone's mind, especially with respect to the sexes and their respective sexual desires. Were men and women the same in this primeval and fundamental way as well? According to Freud himself the answer was no. Through his studies of the sexual behavior of the two, and the supposed psychosis of the female sex drive, Freud concluded that while legal equality was a necessity, moral, intellectual and, most importantly, sexual equality was to be abhorred.

> "I am not speaking of a woman's desire to be treated externally on the same footing as a man but rather of her wish to be like him inwardly, to achieve the same freedom of thought and morality, to take an interest in the same things, to exhibit the same creative force." Therefore an irreducible difference between the sexes must be maintained at all cost...Evil is feminine; it comes from the feminine in woman. The woman is a being without moral capacity:

> "Woman is man's SIN."[45]

Such beliefs allowed men's adulterous activities to be seen as normal and held no legal sanctions, while women's were viewed to be punishable by law. Nonetheless, by the early 1900s, adultery for women had been decriminalized.

In 1916, Jeanette Rankin was elected to the United States Congress and in 1918, supported by Rockefeller funds, Dr. Katherine B. Davis undertook a massive study of the sexual activities of normal women (2,200 respondents) which clearly showed that women were at least as highly sexed as men and concluded that sex was "physically necessary to women as well as to men."[46] And although there were still no women engineers, by this time women were attending medical and law school (and even becoming doctors, lawyers, and judges) in greater and greater numbers. The field of education—primary and secondary—saw a large number of women, a trend that endures today. Women, by the sweat of their brows, even without the vote, had made steps toward being viewed as politically and sexually equal.

WORLD WAR I

With the declaration of war on Germany on April 6, 1917, the political, industrial and social position of the United States drastically altered. Industrialization expanded at an incredible pace and the U.S. emerged as the world leader.

But to be a leader in industry at a time when men were going off to war meant that women would have to be called upon.

> In *Women's Work in War Time*, published several months after the declaration of war, Irving Bullard pointed out that for every man in the trenches, twenty workers were required to provide the supplies for carrying on the war. He therefore insisted that women must immediately be recruited to fill the gaps created by the disappearance of male hands.[47]

In fact, women were very actively and publicly recruited. Ads went out in all the major newspapers and magazines for women to become trained in traditional men's jobs such as conductors for streetcars, laborers in the steel mills, printers, railroad workers, and shingle packers. Auto schools were set up to train women for Red Cross work and government jobs. Unfortunately, however, once women were recruited, their actual contributions to the work force (or the war effort) were "limited by prejudice."[48] Many women ended up doing traditional women's work—sewing, cleaning, and clerical work (only now they were doing this outside the home). "WWI did not only not render 'women's sphere' and the 'old line motherhood occupation' a 'thing of the past' but actually had the opposite effect."[49]

Nonetheless, this was a time of radical change for women, labor and, especially women in labor. Feminism and its "first generation" call for equality with men, particularly in the public sphere, had a huge impact on industry and the country as a whole.

> The most enduring legacy of women's war work and the most effective instrument in continuing to emphasize women's competence and women's problems in the workplace was the *Women's Bureau* in the *Department of Labor* which grew out of the *Women in Industry Service* (WIS) in the Labor Department in 1918.[50]

The mission of the latter was to regulate the conditions of work for all workers—including the eight-hour work day, forty-eight hour maximum work week, and, of course, the "principle of equal pay for equal work."[51] When the WIS turned into the *Women's Bureau*, the legislative charge was much more feminist: to "formulate standards and policies which shall promote the welfare of wage-earning women, improve their working conditions, increase their efficiency and advance their opportunities for profitable employment."[52]

THE NINETEENTH AMENDMENT

Though women in general were on both sides of the political fence with respect to topics such as war and labor, feminism still stayed focused on the notion of equality, especially equality under the law. This operationalized into wanting, simply, the right to vote. Therefore, the years immediately following WWI marked the single most important feminist win to date. In 1920, what was called the "Susan B. Anthony amendment," the Nineteenth Amendment, was finally ratified.[53] With it "the right of citizens of the United States to vote shall not be denied or abridged by the United States or by any state on account of sex."

The first generation, then, is marked by a commitment to what has come to be known by feminists as "liberal feminism"[54] and by social/political theorists as "formal" or "legal" equality.[55] Times, however, change and so will Feminism. And when Feminism begins to lose its taste for the essence of this line of argument—where "equality" means simply having every advantage and opportunity as men—the "second generation" is born.

CHAPTER THREE

THE SECOND GENERATION: ITS "FIRST WAVE"

With respect to what I call the first generation of feminists, then, equality and sameness are linked. The feminist quest was essentially a political one and the politics was essentially to "find equality between men and women by opening up opportunities for women to take on the same roles as men."[1] This goal remained on the forefront for the entire nineteenth and most of the twentieth century, what I call the first wave of second generation feminism.

The first wave of second generation feminist thought is more akin to the first generation than it is to the second wave of its own generation. For, as with its first generation sisters, its ideological and practical goals are "united by a commitment to sameness, equality, universality and scientific understanding."[2] This "wave" begins in the 1920s.

SEX, PROHIBITION, AND THE CHARLESTON

There are only two decades in recent history that have been known primarily for their radical and liberal lifestyles—the sixties and the twenties. Historians have piled up titles for this latter "decadent" decade including: "Roaring twenties, Fords, Flappers, and Fanatics, the Decade of the Dollar, the Period of the Psyche, the Time of Tremendous Trifles, Alcohol and Al Capone, and the Dry Decade."[3]

In some ways the '20s and '60s were quite similar; however, with respect to the women's movement they were quite different. Women had just won the right to vote and already they had decided that being equal in the polling booth was not enough. They wanted equality in the social world as well. Women no longer wanted to be demure asexual homebodies; instead they wanted to be suave and sophisticated adventurers.

> Thus the flapper of the 1920s stepped onto the stage of history, breezy, slangy and informal in manner; slim and boyish in form; covered with silk and fur that clung to her as close as onion skin; with carmined lips, plucked eyebrows and close-fitting helmet of hair; carefree, plucky and confident.... She cared little for approval or disapproval and went about her "act," whether it was a Marathon dancing contest, driving an automobile at seventy miles an hour, a Channel swim, a political campaign or a social-service settlement.[4]

Women were demanding recognition as women first and as wives and mothers second. For these early citizens of the Nineteenth Amendment, being equal to men in all areas of life was the goal. "The true woman would never be the same."[5]

> In 1920, eight women's organizations founded the Women's Joint Congressional Committee (WJCC) to serve as a clearing house for the ratification of the Nineteenth Amendment. In 1921, the agenda set by the WJCC founders featured six Ps: Prohibition, public schools, protection of infants, physical education in the public schools, peace through international arms reduction, and protection of women in industry.... By 1922, the WJCC was described by the *Ladies Home Journal* and *Journal of the American Medical Association* as the most powerful and highly organized lobby in Washington.[6]

While all of the above were important political agendas for the women of the 1920s, and although all of the above were seriously connected, the tension amongst the above goals became its own issue. Having both a job and a family were of importance, and this empirical "fact" held stigmatizing weight for society. Women themselves had ambivalent feelings about women and their "equal" status with men. On the one hand, both society, and even the "modern" woman herself, believed that "having a job (much less a career or a profession) lessened the chances for marriage."[7] Women wanted economic independence and satisfying work, but "if forced to choose might give up the law book for the cookbook."[8] On the other hand, it was argued that marriages failed, not because "of slovenly housekeeping or inept childrearing but because of uninteresting wives;"[9] women who had never worked or traveled outside the home were not of equal education, sophistication or social status to the men they married. Therefore it seemed that for the benefit of the workplace, the women themselves, and, a bit ironically, the family unit, equal education and opportunity were musts.

Professional jobs were also opening to educated women for the first time. A bureaucratic society required literate works, so public schools and public libraries became essential instititutions. Once middle class women could attend college, they sought professional jobs as teachers and librarians. Although men performed these tasks, women cost less and seemed well suited to work with children.[10]

On university and college campuses throughout the country things were no different. College women lobbied for "freedom and equality,"[11] which consisted of not only an equal education—to be given an education that is "full-blooded, and manly" as opposed to "ornamental, dilettantish and feminine"[12]—but also given an equal opportunity to party. As would be the case again in the sixties, the youth of the time had a huge impact on the culture. "Undergraduate men and women were challenging traditional values and forging new rules and new relationships…their clothes, their music, their athletics, and their slang—merged into the consciousness of a decade."[13] Nonetheless, problems with respect to the equality of men and women prevailed, for it was expected that "women graduates would both marry and have a career."[14] The behavior of these women was so unusual that women of the "first generation" were "confused and saddened by the preoccupation with sex."[15] In "A New Generation of Women" (1923), first generation feminist and author Charlotte Perkins Gilman[16] bemoaned the "physical indecencies of our misguided young people."[17]

Though the decade ended with the crashing of the stock market, for feminism things were not fully bleak. Women of this decade gained economic, educational, professional and personal aspirations, and never gave up on their desire to acquire full equality with men. Although such desires were not fully fulfilled, the struggles of the women of the twenties did give contemporary women new options for success and gave feminism its new mantra: Freedom of choice.[18]

DEPRESSION YEARS

Although the thirties began in economic depression they did not take their toll on women in nearly the way they took it on men. "Actually, women's lives were probably less disrupted by the Depression than men's."[19]

> Overall, women at work survived the depression in much better shape than previously suggested…in the midst of the greatest economic crisis this country has ever seen, in the face of strongly hostile public opinion, women actually increased their participation in the work force from 24.3 to 25.4 percent, a numerical gain of more than 2 million women workers.[20]

"Contrary to widely held views, women workers were not devastated by the Depression."[21]

As a matter of fact, "women were often called to carry heavier burdens for weathering such crises than men."[22] But with these burdens came certain blessings, for the Depression itself was one of the reasons that more women, especially married women, entered the job force. "If a husband lost his job, his wife often looked for a position to take up the slack."[23] While jobs in heavy industry were laying men off, women's jobs, such as clerical and sales work, were actually hiring. And with this increase in the number of women in the workforce came increased power for women. "Women workers were to benefit from new federal relief programs and the dramatic growth of unions."[24] During the thirties, the women's movement "mobilized housewives to support workers through consumer boycotts"[25] and "stressed and exalted the importance of jobs for women."[26]

Though women in general faired well (relative to men) during the Depression, feminism itself did not. Traditional women's jobs—nurses and librarians—still maintained low pay and poor benefits, and certain professions such as doctors and lawyers were still out of reach for most women. In addition, educated women still saw college to be simply a "way station before marriage and children, instead of a training ground for feminist ideals."[27] Furthermore, fashion, which is often a barometer of the general zeitgeist of the nation, seems to have regressed during this decade into something less stylish and more matronly. "Women's fashions underwent noticeable changes in the 1930s.... Instead of the boyish, low-waisted, no hipped styles of the 1920s, 1930s fashions emphasized curves and fuller bosoms."[28] Finally, there was an empirical test of male/female role reversal which showed that despite the "roaring" twenties, in the thirties, traditional gender typing was still the norm. Due to the Depression, many American households were forced to reorder: woman as breadwinner and man as housekeeper. Studies done at the time emphasized the fact that this forced role reversal "was desired neither by men nor women."[29] And in 1935 Genevieve Parkhurst claimed that "the woman's movement was crippled by lack of vision and uninspiring leadership" in her *Harper's* article, "Is Feminism Dead?"[30]

Still, there were a few unifying issues that kept feminism kicking, including "restrictions on married women's rights to work and the meaning of equality as embodied in the proposed Equal Rights Amendment."[31] These feminists, usually members of the National Women's Party, wanted men and women to be treated exactly the same. And on this political ideal, the movement maintained a pulse. Thirties feminists argued that:

> Protective legislation had done more harm than good for women workers: restrictions on the hours that women could work, minimum wage standards, and limits on night work impeded rather than improved women's opportunities in the workforce. ERA advocates objected that women were singled out as a group for special treatment: they wanted men and women treated alike in the work force and in all aspects of American life. Protective legislation for women struck them as paternalistic and patronizing.[32]

In the final analysis it seemed that despite all the hardships endured by men through the First World War and the Depression, thirties women wanted nothing more or less than equality.

WORLD WAR II

The forties had just begun when on December 7, 1941, the Japanese bombed Pearl Harbor. Where the Depression had encouraged public criticism of women workers—women, after all, were ostensibly taking away jobs from out-of-work men—the labor shortage of these war years "necessitated appeals by government and employers for women to take jobs."[33] Women's employment grew in every occupational field; women enjoyed higher incomes and better benefits. "During World War II, millions of American women, dubbed Rosie the Riveters, entered the paid workforce, taking jobs formerly open only to men—usually at higher wages than they could earn doing traditional women's work."[34] In the early part of the decade, The War Production Board, the War Manpower Commission, and the National War Labor Board all joined forces to ensure that there was equal pay for women doing men's work with respect to government contracts, which induced most corporations, even those not involved in military production, to follow suit. Eventually, the sheer numbers of women involved in heavy labor brought them under the protection of the big labor unions.[35]

Though these financial gains helped millions of individual women and their families, from the perspective of feminism they were superficial, limited, and temporary.

> The public discourse on women's new wartime roles established three conditions which set limits on social change. The first was that women were replacing men in the world outside the home "for the duration." Particularly during the later stages of the war, employers and public officials asserted that women workers were proud of their contributions to the war effort, but were eager to return to the home and would gladly relinquish their jobs to returning soldiers. The second condition was that women would retain their "femininity" even as they performed masculine duties. Photographs of

> women war workers emphasized glamour, and advertising copy assured readers that beneath the overalls and grease stains there remained a true woman, feminine in appearance and behavior. Finally, the media emphasized the eternal feminine motivations behind women's willingness to step out of customary roles. Patriotic motives were not ignored; but also highlighted was women's determination to serve their families albeit in novel ways.[36]

Although women's educational patterns and even their job opportunities in the service of the military itself, where the most novel opportunities were to be had, seemed to be improving, the actual day-to-day activities of most women were "traditional." Educationally, women trained to be nurses or clerical workers so their military work usually revolved around such occupations as well, if not the more mundane tasks of cleaning and cooking. In other words, though women were in college and/or the military, their training or jobs were quite "feminine" and ill-prepared them for a public life post World War II.

When the war did end, women, despite their overalls and fatigues, were still simply women, and they experienced a diminution in their newfound "equality." "With the end of the war, many women were laid off, and overall the number of working women declined sharply for several years."[37] Certainly this was true in the military as well, but their military loss came with a victory since women veterans were allowed many of the rights and privileges of male veterans including access to the GI Bill, which paid for their college or university education. And although women were only allowed limited access to the Veterans of Foreign Wars (as part of the ladies auxiliary), "servicewomen could join the American Legion as full-fledged members."[38]

In addition, the 1,074 Women's Airforce Service Pilots (WASP), who from 1942 to 1944 flew military planes throughout the United States and Canada for the Army Air Forces (AAF), were given an opportunity to enter the highly visible and well paying jobs of commercial airflight as pilots, copilots and navigators. "The fledgling aviation industry's need to promote public acceptance of air travel led to utilizing women, because if a mere woman could pilot a plane, then flying must be safe."[39]

Overall, despite unequal treatment, for most forties women, professional and military work was very rewarding and worthwhile. Individual women not only earned economic wealth, they also gained a good deal of self-esteem.[40] Feminist goals were on the upswing, although, ironically, feminism itself—as a political and social movement—was barely breathing.

Feminism had been put on the back burner for obvious reasons during the war; post war it seemed that women in general were not as excited about equal rights as they were just after the ratification of the Nineteenth Amendment. Nonetheless, the old-fashioned issue of equality was on the minds of most of feminism's supporters, and in 1943, the ERA (1923 version[41]) actually gained support from numerous special interest groups. "Over thirty women's organizations supported it, arguing that the Supreme Court repeatedly held that existing constitutional amendments, especially the Fourteenth, failed to assure women's rights and permitted pernicious inequalities in federal, state, and local laws."[42] There was also an election of several new women to the House of Representatives and the Senate which aided in its support. The question of true equal rights for women became, in the latter part of the forties, one of the most important political and social topics of the time.

But the popularity of social and political issues was short lived for the typical American, and the feminist rhetoric surrounding the ERA did not seem to be giving women, let alone Americans, what they wanted.

> In the midst of the postwar debate over equal rights, a Supreme Court decision illustrated the power of prevailing judicial doctrine to restrict women's opportunities. In 1948, the Court upheld Michigan's law prohibiting women from employment as bartenders. Enacted in 1945, the stature prevented women from obtaining licenses unless they were wives or daughters of male tavern owners. The plaintiffs, two women who owned bars and their daughters whom they employed, argued that the law violated the 14th Amendment. Twenty-four other women who owned or tended bars swore

> affidavits describing the economic hardship they suffered under the law and demonstrating that they had fixed drinks without detriment to themselves or their customers. Despite these claims and the failure of the defendants to show any deleterious effects of women tending bar, both the district court and the Supreme Court assumed that female bartenders might give rise to "social and moral problems"...The *Goesaert* case, though extreme in nature, demonstrates the extent to which women could be victims of protection...[and ironically] failed to help supporters of the ERA.[43]

It seemed that despite the desires of feminism, and despite all of the rhetoric surrounding the need for equality for women in the public sphere, this venue was not as important as hearth and home to most Americans. It was the traditional roles of wife and mother that still held claim to most American women, and their commitment to feminism waned almost as quickly as it had waxed. Even today, "feminists have difficulty explaining the fact that so many women appear to support not just marriage but the traditional division of sex roles within it...even independent women are not prepared to countenance a reversal of sex roles."[44]

By the end of the forties, although millions of American women had prospered individually from WWII and the work of feminism via, e.g., the National Women's Party and the League of Women Voters, the desire for postwar normalcy had kept feminism itself from making any serious headway. The problem was not that feminism had changed its tune (although it had somewhat); its fundamental spirit remained. The problem was instead that the tune itself—*the call for equal education, opportunity, and equal pay for equal work*—just did not have the same ring as before. Sure, while women were in the public sphere they needed equality, but what's the point of such policies in the home?

And the home is where the typical American woman returned. "The continuing attachment to the prewar social order and values was nowhere more apparent than in the area of sex roles and women's status."[45] The wartime climate was tough on families as a whole and even tougher on women as individuals who often had to scrimp and save while nonetheless holding down a job and performing the usual household chores. As such, not only did women want[46] to return to their old roles and customary divisions of labor, the popular press made this decision easier. Women were told by everyone, from fashion magazines to psychiatrists and psychologists, that their men and children needed them more than ever. The typical American woman was also warned that feminists were "neurotic or worse."[47] Women's "biological destiny," as well as their patriotism, requested that in order to preserve the American way of life, it was best that they simply go home.

HAPPY DAYS

Though one could blame the American propaganda machine for having, in just over ten years, coerced women both into the workforce and then back into the home, there is some reason to believe that this phenomenon was really a matter of women's choice.

First, the typical American family no longer needed women to work. Given that the number one reason women worked was financial,[48] when their men came home to good paying post war jobs, their economic situation was no longer an issue. In addition, women, even today, let alone in the 1950s, "found themselves very reluctant to yield their prime role in the caring of children to men."[49] Finally, connected to all of this was the fact that the home itself—with all of its new gadgets such as washing machines, refrigerators, and televisions—had drastically changed. Not only could most people afford all kinds of appliances (not to mention automobiles), but these new items made the home a virtual museum of modernity. The 1950s home was, for millions of American women, just the way it is portrayed on the sitcoms now in rerun on *Nick at Night*, and it seems that many women, far from being victims of their traditional role, actually luxuriated in it.

Such happy days, however, did not offer feminism a very ripe environment in order to foment support for equality with men. Worse, feminism was viewed more and more as some kind of disruptive force, maybe even a communist plot. After all, the family was the core of the American way of life, and women were the core of the family. To disturb their traditional role as wife and mother would be downright un-American. With respect to this text, it is no wonder that the 1950s are most notable not for bobby socks and pep rallies, but as a decade which lacked any kind of "organized" feminism.[50]

Even for women who were in college or university, the desire for the American dream—the white picket fence, the dog and the 2.3 kids—loomed large in the background.

> Although there were, indeed, large numbers of women going to college in the 1950s, only 37 percent of those who entered stayed to graduate, and the percentage of women who went on for higher degrees was lower in the 1950s than in the 1920s or 1930s. Most women had put their values before the pursuit of their careers...[51]

This fact was problematic, especially for feminist organizations such as the *National Federation of Business and Professional Women* who claimed that "unless we get more women equal education, we can't get them equal pay and opportunity."[52] Women went to college more for their MRS degree than for any other reason. Women chose to marry doctors or lawyers, not become them. It's not that feminism wasn't interested in equality, it was that women were not interested in feminism.

Despite the above, the fifties saw a rise in recognition of women both as *feminine* in the eyes of the typical American male and as *feminists* qua serious voting block in the eyes of politicians and pollsters. The first issue of *Playboy* magazine was sold in 1953 and by 1956 both the Democratic and Republican parties stood behind the ERA and its basic mantra of the time: *equal pay for equal work*. "In 1956, in his State of the Union speech, Eisenhower declared that the principle of equal pay for equal work without discrimination 'because of sex' was a matter of 'simple justice.'"[53]

But the fifties were more a time of talk than action, and this decade offered "almost no institutional encouragement"[54] to women as workers, let alone as individuals. Feminism, therefore, as a means to a better life, held little personal interest for most women.

THE SIXTIES

The sixties, however, were another story. This infamous decade of sex, drugs, and rock n' roll was also the decade in which women achieved "consciousness raising."

> Consciousness Raising (CR) groups developed all over the nation in the late sixties to politicize individual women through informal, confessional discussions with friends about experiences of discrimination in their personal lives. The *Redstockings*[55] organized some of the first cell group "bitch sessions," and each meeting attempted to spawn another group."[56]

Within these groups the "connection between sexuality and politics was first made.... These groups met regularly to discuss the effects of male supremacy upon women's public and private lives, and they resulted in a great outpouring of emotion against the way women were used sexually."[57] That is, this is the decade where, for the first time, women started to seriously and openly struggle with their social/family role and the numerous ways in which it conflicted with their individual needs, deepest desires and personal development.

The tension between the public and the private spheres of the lives of eight million American women was so intense that it actually became a source of national concern.

> In November 1960, the *Women's Bureau, Children's Bureau, Social Security Administration*, and *Department of Health, Education, and Welfare* jointly sponsored the *National Conference on Day Care*, pointing to a 'serious problem' generated by eight million mothers working outside the home—one of every four mothers with children under 18—400,000 with children under 12.[58]

Feminism's concern at this time,[59] however, was not for children. Women were unhappy; actually, they had always been unhappy in their roles as housewives and mothers, but, in the sixties, due to feminist "consciousness" they had finally realized it. More importantly, as the decade progressed, more and more women gained the "consciousness" to recognize and speak out for themselves. Feminism began to grow, both in terms of ideology and sheer number of supports, that it was eventually unable to contain itself.

First there was the recognition that sex was not bad. The "hippie free love" generation's ideas of sexuality were taking hold in the minds of mainstream women. As a matter of fact, in 1962, Helen Gurley Brown wrote *Sex and the Single Girl,* arguing that they should reconsider the fact that sex without marriage is dirty. In addition, and an oft cited historical starting point for such "consciousness" can be demarcated with the groundbreaking book *The Feminine Mystique*, in 1963, by Betty Friedan. *Mystique* turned public attention to the discontented housewives all over America who wanted to "find themselves" and, therefore, "find fulfillment" in the public sphere. She had, in the words of one scholar, "let the genie out of the bottle."[60]

> The problem lay buried, unspoken, for many years in the minds of American women. It was a strange stirring, a sense of dissatisfaction, a yearning that women suffered in the middle of the twentieth century in the United States. Each suburban wife struggled with it alone. As she made the beds, shopped for groceries, matched slipcover material, ate peanut butter sandwiches with her children, chauffeured Cub Scouts and Brownies, lay beside her husband at night—she was afraid to ask even of herself the silent question—"Is this all?"[61]

This book "reawakened millions of women to their lot as women…it was a compelling and transformative experience."[62]

The problem that has no name—which is simply the fact that American women are kept from growing to their full human capacities—is taking a far greater toll on the physical and mental health of our country than any known disease…. These problems cannot be solved by medicine, or even by psychotherapy. We need a drastic reshaping of the cultural image of femininity that will permit women to reach maturity, identity, completeness of self, without conflict with sexual fulfillment.[63]

However, many women felt victimized, not liberated by their new-found self. "Consciousness-raising" groups encouraged and enabled women to at least question, if not defy, the "male supremacy" that affected even their sex lives. It seemed as if it was not only "patriarchy" outside the home, but in the bedroom, that was victimizing women.

> Women were expected not only to perform the usual women's work—typing, mailing, coffee making, and the like…—but also to sleep with the radical men they worked for without making any demands in return. "Their own feelings, their needs for affection, recognition, consideration, or commitment did not count."[64]

Personal fulfillment, however, was only the beginning of the feminist lament; professional and political fulfillment were soon to follow.

> Women's workforce participation rose gradually and steadily through the fifties. By 1960, 24 million or 35 percent of American women 14 to 65 were in the labor force, an increase of 19 percent over the fifties. By 1970, women's participation increased to 44 percent of all women, surpassing the WWII rate, when 16 million had worked full time. The percentage of women in the total work force rose from 33 to 38 percent through the sixties.[65]

And, "throughout the sixties, two-thirds of new employees were women, courted to fill new job categories rather than serving simply as a reserve labor force as before."[66]

With an army of new unfulfilled women, feminism marched into its most politically productive time since the twenties.

> The 1960s saw the first major legislative advances for American women since the suffrage amendment. President Kennedy set the process in motion by establishing the *Commission on the Status of Women*, and in 1962, issuing a directive prohibiting federal agencies from discrimination

> against female employees in appointments or promotions. The following year Congress enacted the *Equal Pay Act*, authored by Representative Edith Green, Democrat of Oregon—a severely limited but precedent-setting measure requiring employers to offer equal pay for equal work, without regard to sex.[67]

By 1963, an executive order was delivered, recognizing that "[p]rejudices and outmoded customs act as barriers to the full realization of women's basic rights."[68]

"But far and away the most important step forward for women came unexpectedly from *Title VII* of the landmark *1964 Civil Rights Act*,"[69] which seriously strengthened the already existing *Equal Protection Clause of the Fourteenth Amendment*. The latter, which had been in place since 1868, guarantees that no state shall "deny to any person within its jurisdiction the equal protection of the laws." "Under the *Equal Protection Clause*, which protects individuals from sex discrimination by the government, similarities and differences are measured in relation to a 'legitimate state purpose.'"[70] The main purpose of this amendment, then, was simply equal protection under the law.

The former *Title VII* of the *Civil Rights Act of 1964*, as amended (in relevant part), states that:

> a) It shall be an unlawful employment practice for an employer—
>
> 1) to fail or refuse to hire or to discharge any individual, or otherwise to discriminate against any individual with respect to his compensation, terms, conditions, or privileges of employment because of such individual's...sex...; or
>
> 2) to limit, segregate, or classify his employees or applicants for employment in any way which would deprive or tend to deprive any individual of employment opportunities or otherwise adversely affect his status as an employee, because of such individual's...sex.

Title VII, then, "protects individuals from discrimination in employment, where the similarities and differences are measured in relationship to the job."[71] Its main purpose was to strengthen and focus the *Fourteenth Amendment* for problems of discrimination, specifically in the job market.

> The *Civil Rights Act*, a response by the Johnson administration to the black freedom movement, was intended primarily to alleviate injustices suffered on account of race. Women came into it by the back door, more or less uninvited. What happened was that during congressional debate on the proposed legislation, Representative Howard W. Smith, Democrat of Virginia, an old-line southern conservative who vehemently opposed it, submitted a surprise amendment. To *Title VII* of the bill—which barred discrimination in employment on the basis of race, color, religion, or national origin—Smith proposed as additional basis: sex. By saddling the cause of black civil rights with the unpopular cause of women's rights, he hoped to deter legislators from passing the entire bill.... However, Representative Smith's cynical maneuver backfired.... In July 1964 Congress enacted the *Civil Rights Act*—with *sex* still firmly embedded in *Title VII*.... The new law provided for the establishment of a federal agency, the *Equal Employment Opportunity Commission* (EEOC), to hear complaints of bias in the workplace.[72]

However, the above legislation and watchdog commission were still not enough for feminists.

In 1966, under the auspices of Betty Friedan, the newly formed *National Organization of Women* (NOW) breathed new life into feminism. The purpose of NOW was clear, and *clearly interested in equality with men.*

> The purpose of NOW is to take action to bring women into full participation in the mainstream of American society now, exercising all the privileges and responsibilities thereof in truly equal partnership with men.... WE REJECT the current assumptions that a man must carry the sole burden of supporting himself, his wife, and family, and that a woman is automatically entitled to lifelong support by a man upon her marriage, or that marriage, home and family are primarily women's world and responsibility—hers, to dominate—his

> to support.... WE BELIEVE THAT women will do much to create a new image of woman by acting now, and by speaking out in behalf of their own equality, freedom, and human dignity—not in pleas for special privilege, nor in enmity toward men, who are also victims of the current, half-equality between the sexes—but in an active, self-respecting partnership with men...[73]

And NOW and feminism wasted no time focusing on their true agenda: Attempting to ratify the *Equal Rights Amendment* (ERA).

> An Equal Rights Amendment (ERA) to the U.S. Constitution was proposed in 1923 by members of the National Women's Party, originally a militant suffrage organization. It was first introduced in Congress that year, and the seemingly indefatigable ex-suffragists caused the amendment to be reintroduced every succeeding year—through the twenties, thirties, forties, fifties, and sixties—without success. Even in 1963 the report of the President's Commission on the Status of Women did not back the ERA, because organized labor considered the measure a threat to various state laws meant to protect the health and safety of women workers. Shortly after the founding of NOW (1966), Betty Friedan proposed that the fledgling organization endorse the ERA. But when she broached the issue at NOW's national convention in 1967, some of those present warned that supporting the ERA might cost NOW the aid of labor unions, which it could ill afford to lose. However Friedan stood firm. She was convinced that in backing the ERA, NOW would forge "the crucial generational links between the century-long battle of women's rights that was our past and the young women who were the future." The NOW convention voted to take a pro-ERA stand, and the director of the *Women's Department of the United Auto Workers*, Caroline Davis, promptly resigned as secretary-treasurer of NOW.[74]

The ERA, as the name suggests, was understood to be simply a further articulation of what women since the time of suffrage had always wanted: Equality. This move by NOW proved to be successful and feminism qua "women's liberation," that is, as a social and political movement to bring about *equality with men*—politically, educationally, professionally, and personally—began to become part of the mainstream.[75]

"The inability or unwillingness of NOW to escape the mainstream contributed to its relative success, as well as to its internal divisions."[76] That is, this insurgence of new blood into NOW proved to be good for feminism at the time, but bad for it in the long run. For it was during the latter part of the sixties that feminism started to take a radical turn. Everything imaginable came under debate, and in 1967 and 1968, even the term "women's liberation" was challenged by members who "preferred simply to call themselves 'radical women.'"[77] Though feminists were tasting real political power for the first time since they won the vote, feminism itself was being splintered into unfocused factions.

> During 1967 and 1968 leftist women in several cities around the country banded together in small, independent groups to discuss gender discrimination and how to combat it.... What was probably the first of these discussion groups—which evolved into the *Chicago Westside Group*—was founded in the fall of 1967 by Jo Freeman, Naomi Weisstein, Shulamith Firestone, Heather Booth, Amy Kesselman, Fran Rominski, and Laya Firestone. As described by Weisstein decades later, their motivation was unfocused—composed of anger, inchoate need, confusion, and frustruation—and their purpose was equally unclear.[78]

That same year, Shulamith Firestone left the *Westside Group* and moved to New York City where she started, in chronological order, the:

> *New York Radical Women*, *Redstockings*, and *New York Radical Feminists*—each new group representing a shift in ideology and tactics. About half of the New York Radical Women's lively twenty-eight page mimeographed journal, *Notes From the First Year* ("$.50 to Women, $1.00 to Men") consisted of articles by Firestone. In 1968, she helped stage a mock burial of "traditional womanhood" at *Arlington National Cemetery*, conducted in the midst of a woman's anti-Vietnam War peace march, and she took part in the *Miss America Pageant* Protest.[79]

The "protest" was one of the most radical and memorable events of the decade.

> In fall 1968, some 200 demonstrators suddenly appeared at the annual *Miss America Beauty Pageant* in Atlantic City, New Jersey. The demonstrators—young women carrying picket signs with such messages as "Women are people, not livestock" and "Can makeup cover the wounds of our oppression?"—had come to Atlantic City to denounce beauty contests as harmful to women's self-image. They set up a "freedom trash can," into which women were invited to toss "objects of female torture," like hair curlers, girdles, bras and high heels.... The protestors were inaccurately branded "bra-burners," an epithet that afterward was widely applied to feminists...[80]

"The ideal was to live the revolution by examining personal difficulties, developing alternative institutions, such as communes or collectives, and carrying out an individual act of revolution, no matter how irrelevant it seemed to the mainstream political system."[81] In other words, feminism became more interested in individual "life-styles" than in grand social/political change.

Not surprisingly, all of this "individuality" led to chaos. And although the Beauty Pageant event was a collective of liberation groups including members of the *New York Radical Women*, "as political differences gradually developed among its members, they split up and joined a number of new groups," including the *Redstockings*, WITCH (Women Inspired to Commit Herstory),[82] *The Feminists*, and the *New York Radical Feminists*,"[83] each with its own poems, songs, ideology, and homespun zines. The *Redstockings* even had their own seven-part "manifesto."

> *The Redstocking Manifesto* (excerpts)
>
> I. After centuries of individual and preliminary political struggle, women are uniting to achieve their final liberation from male supremacy. *Redstockings* is dedicated to building this unity and winning our freedom.
>
> II. Women are an oppressed class. Our oppression is total, affecting every facet of our lives.

> **III.** We identify the agents of our oppression as men.... *All men* receive economic, sexual, and psychological benefits from male supremacy. *All men* have oppressed women. Men have controlled all political, economic and cultural institutions and backed up this control with physical force. They have used their power to keep women in an inferior position.
>
> **IV.** Attempts have been made to shift the burden of responsibility from men to institutions or to women themselves...we reject the idea that women consent to or are to blame for their own oppression.
>
> **V.** We regard our personal experience, and our feelings about that experience, as the basis for an analysis of our common situation. We cannot rely on existing ideologies as they are all products of male supremacist culture. We question every generalization and accept none that are not confirmed by our experience.
>
> **VI.** We identify with all women.
>
> **VII.** We call on all our sisters to unite with us in struggle. We call on all men to give up their male privileges and support women's liberation in the interest of our humanity and their own. In fighting for our liberation we will always take the side of women against their oppressors. We will not ask what is "revolutionary" or "reformist," only what is good for women. The time for individual skirmishes has passed. This time we are going all the way.[84]

But despite the call to organize all women under one cause, no real unifying cause was developed. The early momentum of sixties feminism had "quickly fallen victim to the splintering effects of internal dissention, as groups labeled each other and themselves according to political coloration, issues, and style."[85] To this day, the sixties image of "bra burning" is remembered far more than any of the numerous feminist factions.

Worse yet, one of the most notorious events of the decade also involved feminism, leaving both those inside and outside the movement aware that fanaticism can sometimes go terribly awry. Feminism for the first time showed not merely its radical face, but a side of itself that could be openly hateful and violent toward men.

> In June 1968, the aggrieved writer, Valerie Solanas, tried to assassinate Andy Warhol with a .32 caliber gun. In 1967 Solanas had issued the manifesto for her *Society for Cutting Up Men* (SCUM). "There remains to civic-minded, responsible, thrill-seeking females only to overthrow the government, eliminate the money system, institute complete automation, and destroy the male sex.... It is now technically possible to reproduce without the aid of males and to produce only females. We must begin immediately to do so. The male is a biological accident...an incomplete female, a walking abortion, aborted at the gene state.[86]

Of course such overt man hating was not the norm. Nonetheless, this kind of radical behavior must have struck a cord for some women, and feminist "consciousness" scattered into numerous versions of feminist "consciousness*es*," each with an entirely different mindset about women, men, the relationship between the two (especially sexual relationships), and, most important for this text, the nature of "equality."

For most sixties' feminists, feminism operationalized into supporting NOW. Supporting NOW meant, primarily, supporting the ERA. And supporting the ERA was understood in its most obvious and simple form as being about equality. Therefore, by the transitive property, being a feminist meant wanting simple equality. After the sixties, this syllogism would no longer remain true. Sometime in the next decade, and until the present, feminism, regardless of faction, would make a drastic change in both its form and content. The desire for equality, understood thus far to mean the desire to be *equal with men*—under the law, in the voting booth, in the job market, in the political arena, in short, in all areas of public life—would no longer be feminism's goal.

The second wave of feminism's second generation was beginning to swell and in its wake was the traditional American family unit. With the works of Wollstonecraft, this part of a woman's life remained in some sense sacred, i.e., outside the scope of any political commentary. Although her book *Vindication of the Rights of Woman* radically asked for equal education and opportunity in the public sphere, none of those rights was intended to interfere with domestic life. As a matter of fact, Wollstonecraft believed that the educated and worldly woman was the woman who made the best housewife and mother.[87]

This was true of all first generation feminists and even the first wave feminists of the "second generation." Equality was a social and political notion and these notions were a part of the public, not the private sphere. This will no longer be the case as the second wave comes to shore.

The change in feminism's relationship with the concept of equality did not come all at once with the second generation movement. But by the late 1960s it was clear that feminism had changed its political agenda dramatically. No longer were feminists interested in *equality as sameness*. The new goal was to carve out a notion of *equality qua difference*. The "second wave" of "second generation" feminism was out to show that all of Western thought and practice was "gender biased." By the latter part of the twentieth century, the "war" between the sexes had really begun.

> From its beginning in the 1960s, the modern women's movement was riddled by contradictions and competing agendas. Were women the same as men, and therefore entitled to demand that they should be treated in exactly the same way? Or were they quite different from, and superior to them? [88]

With this question, what I call the second wave of this second generation feminism surfaced. It is this intriguing, albeit radical, change in political ideals—from equality as sameness to equality as difference—that will be chronologically discussed and analyzed in the next chapter.

CHAPTER FOUR

THE SECOND GENERATION: ITS "SECOND WAVE"

The seventies were not as easygoing as depicted on *That 70s Show* and disco was not the decade's only problem. Discontent with all aspects of American life—the lack of honesty in government (i.e., Nixon and Watergate), the problems in Vietnam, the growing concerns about drugs, and racial riots—made this era one of the most troublesome for people in general and women specifically.

The "American Dream" seemed to be more of a fairytale, if not a nightmare, for most women, with the ideal of the perfect suburban family quickly disintegrating with more and more divorce, and increasing numbers of teens "dropping out" of society. With all of this, the typical American woman seems to have decided that her duty to herself was more important than even her duty to her own family, let alone society as a whole. With this in mind, she too, metaphorically, if not literally, "ran away" from home.

Unfortunately, the public sphere proved almost as unsatisfying. "In 1970, after five decades of the *Women's Bureau*, after three decades of a steadily increasing proportion of women in the labor market, and mounting pressure for women's economic rights, women remained occupationally disadvantaged."[1] And so feminism started to mean something again, albeit something different. Women's liberation combined with more radical sixties feminist ideals, such that the mainstream feminist movement had changed to include both the older notion of women's rights and more radical ideals of "consciousness." During this era, the first generation phrase "women's liberation movement" was readopted as "women's lib" in an attempt to reunite and focus the numerous feminist factions that formed in the last decade. What it meant to be a feminist, however, was still not as easy to determine.

At first it seemed that "if the 1970s women wanted men's power, prestige, and status, they would have to prove that women are the same as men...it made sense to minimize men's and women's biological difference and insist on the strong role socialization plays in the construction of masculine and feminine behavior."[2] But this was not at all the case. Underground rumblings in the late '60s to create a new "wave" of feminism had started to swell, and by 1970 there was no going back.

What I call the second wave of second generation feminism is sometimes termed the later second wave. This form of feminism "begins by questioning basic "traditional" premises such as sameness, equality, universality and scientific understanding, yielding instead ideas like difference, particularity, embodiment, multiplicity, contradictions and identity."[3]

> Later second wave feminists, have argued, in response to these early second wave feminists, that rather than striving for equality and sameness between men and women, feminists should recognize and value the differences between men and women. This has come to be known as the difference versus equality debate. For difference theorists, the problem with western thought and practice is not that it distinguished between men and women on the basis of biological differences, but that it gave more value to masculine over feminine roles.[4]

What demarcates the first wave from the second wave is, most fundamentally, the feminist view of equality.

> This new wave of feminism(s) has posed a fundamental challenge to western dualism in particular...beginning with "women's" points of views, this new wave embraces the diversity and differences in perspectives among 'women' ultimately straddling both the "one" and the "other"....These new feminisms begin with concepts of difference rather than sameness, identity and particularity rather than universality,

> celebrating the status of other or outsider rather than wanting inside, embodiment rather than binary approach. At the core of this approach is an attempt to base the analysis of politics on the experience and perspective of women rather than men.[5]

SEX, POLITICS, AND SEXUAL POLITICS

This second wave continues to swell today with the heart of the distinction between a "man's perspective" and a "woman's perspective," between being *equal with men* and having *feminist equality*, being, of course, sex—sexuality, reproductive rights, and pregnancy. The first thing on the second wave agenda is to challenge the power and legitimacy of the traditional family, where these notions had force. Both first generation and even first wave second generation feminists dealt only with challenging and changing women's roles within the public realm, something which had, by this time, become part of mainstream culture.[6] It was, however, a radical and new turn for feminism to blatantly attack the personal sphere itself—that is, home and hearth. Three books published in 1970 hallmark this radical move for feminism: *The Female Eunuch*, which argued for women to transform themselves; *The Dialectic of Sex*, which argued for women to transform their relationships within the overall family structure; and *Sexual Politics*, which argued that women, to be truly free, must recognize the oppressive nature of sex with men.

> Germaine Greer announced in the opening sentence of *The Female Eunuch*, "This book is a part of the second feminist wave."...If her book was thoroughly outrageous—and it was—that was exactly her intention. Her barbed comments were aimed even at other feminists. She ridiculed Betty Friedan for seeking "admissions to the world of the ulcer and the coronary" for women. As for the socialist feminists she thought they left women stranded, waiting in the wings for world revolution. In fact, Greer seemed to regard herself as a committee of one, the only feminist with a feasible program for the liberation of her sex. What that program amounted

> to was a kind of bootstrap feminism: an insistence that it is up to the individual woman to transform herself.[7]

In Shulamith Firestone's book, *The Dialectic of Sex,* "the genesis of the family—which she saw as the key institution of oppression of both women and children—lay in the female's need for food and protection during pregnancy and when nursing her young."[8] Kate Millet's book, *Sexual Politics*, applied a feminist perspective to thinking about sexual relations between men and women. The main thesis was that "sex has a frequently neglected political aspect." That is, in the patriarchal state—and all modern states are patriarchal—men dominate women in sex, as they do in other aspects of life."[9]

Feminism had moved itself from defense to offense. No longer was it attempting to achieve *only* equality with men, it was actually counterattacking with claims of "male domination," which ostensibly infected all arenas of life, even the creating of law and the construct of equality. If such arguments held any weight, the logical next step for feminism was to "drop out" of male society completely. With respect to one's sexuality, it meant embracing *lesbianism.*[10]

> As the *Second Congress to Unite Women* convened in New York City in May 1970, an unscheduled event interrupted the first evening's program. As some 400 feminist activists listened to the final moments of a presentation by the drama group Burning City, the auditorium suddenly went dark. When the lights came up again, twenty women wearing T-shirts imprinted "Lavender Menace" stood at the front of the room...Lavender Menace was a recently formed collective of lesbian feminists.... The Lavender Menace, arrayed at the front of the auditorium, spoke to those attending the congress about discrimination against lesbians in the women's movement.... The next day, conference participants crowded into impromptu workshops on lesbianism conducted by the Menaces.... The issue of gays in the women's movement had emerged into the light.[11]

As "NOW became increasingly open to consciousness-raising and the connection between the personal and the political, active gay women found it difficult to conceal their sexual preferences."[12]

To be, or not to be, a supporter of lesbianism, that was the big question for NOW, the now uncontested leader of feminism.

> The question of NOW's political and cultural identity remained to be resolved. As a social movement organization, it continues to struggle with the dilemma posed by two contradictory goals—credibility versus revolutionary change—a dilemma that has always characterized social movements in a pluralistic society. And the issue of women's political legitimacy, whether that is perceived as acceptance into the mainstream of a revolutionary revision of patriarchal values still remains in doubt."[13]

On August 26, 1970, at the *Fiftieth Anniversary of the Nineteenth "Suffrage" Amendment* the *Strike for Equality* was held.

> The *Strike for Equality*, held on 26 August 1970 to commemorate the fiftieth anniversary of the passage of the *Nineteenth Amendment*, was the largest demonstration ever held for women's rights. Friedan estimated the crowd at Central Park at about thirty-five thousand, but the action was nationwide, involving women (and men) of all ages, social classes and occupations. According to one scholar, this event marked the beginnings of the women's movement as a mass movement. Friedan saw it as an opportunity for NOW to take the lead in organizing a permanent ongoing political coalition of women reflecting the diversity that was represented in the strike. The exhilarating effect of 26 August certainly made the public aware of women's potential political power, but it also created a false sense of unity. The women's movement was already deeply divided, and NOW was both a part of and victim of these divisions.[14]

Nonetheless, "at its 1971 convention, NOW passes a resolution to support lesbians 'legally and morally,' heading Kate Millet's plea that the organization acknowledge 'the oppression of lesbians as a legitimate concern for feminism.'"[15]

Although most feminists claimed that the move to lesbianism was not merely a sexual preference, but "a personal and political choice in which the individual announced to herself and her peers in the movement the degree and the intensity of her commitment to other women,"[16] this move, nonetheless, had the automatic impact of forcing many mainstream women into an anti-feminist backlash. Most American women by this time, of course, wanted equal pay for equal jobs, fewer wanted to completely give up traditional family life to have careers, and fewer yet wanted to abandon their lives with men altogether. Due to the influx of these radical ideas into the mainstream, feminism in general, but NOW specifically, again, suffered from a serious lack of popularity.[17]

However, in response to the political scene, lesbianism was soon forced to take a back seat in the NOW agenda. For abortion rights issues, especially the case of *Roe v. Wade,* came to the fore of the American political scene.[18] "The abortion issue provided feminists with an activist arena at two levels—that of a political pressure group trying to influence public policy and that of abortion referral services for women. Much of the activity at the second level, at least before *Roe v. Wade,*[19] was illegal."[20] Abortions, it seems, could be done "at home," and many women began to serve as "abortionists," strengthening women's bonds amongst themselves as well as offering concrete examples of their non-hierarchical, non-patriarchal, i.e., feminist ideology. "But, in point of fact, not all abortion advocates were interested in assisting with abortions, and even fewer wanted the responsibility of doing them."[21]

Of course the need for illegal abortions became moot when:

> On January 22, 1973, the high courts by a vote of 7 to 2 struck down all state laws that restricted a woman's right to an abortion during the first trimester of pregnancy, and granted to the states only very limited regulatory rights in the second trimester. The decision was based on the right of privacy founded in the *Fourteenth Amendment's* concept of personal freedom.[22]

The ideals generated during the underground abortion times, however, did not become obsolete. As a matter of fact, feminists claim that this was when the activities—e.g., the breaking down of the patient/provider role, and organizations—e.g., *Feminist Wom-*

en's Health Center (Los Angeles), characterized by the "women's health movement," first got their start.[23] Such activities became the cornerstone for the next feminist catchphrase: *Sisterhood.*

THE ERA ERA

"Sisterhood" was made popular by ex-*Playboy Playmate* Gloria Steinem who, to this day, is seen as something of a cult leader for the feminist movement. "On August 16, 1971, Gloria was featured on the cover of *Newsweek*, proclaimed by the magazine as the personification of women's liberation."[24] Due to her New York chic, "single by choice," glamorous lifestyle, she gave feminism a new look and a new identity, which she used to weave her own political agenda.

"The idea of sisterhood is a key element of Steinem's feminism.... Propelled by the wish to unite women around common needs, in 1972 Steinem became a cofounder of *Ms. Magazine*—the first mass-market periodical addressed to the new feminist women."[25] But "sisterhood," the bringing together of all women under one feminist banner, was not as easy to muster under the NOW agenda of abortion as many would have thought. Though most American women were seriously interested in their own reproductive rights, many were less ready to take the drastic position of supporting abortions. Religious women from all sects believed, their feminist sensibilities aside, that the taking of the life of a fetus was morally objectionable.

Given that "the thrust of the women's movement was to overcome this individualistic tendency and to encourage women to recognize their commonality and act within a collective support system,"[26] feminism, once again, was forced to focus on attempts to ratify the ERA. "ERA proponents tried to deny any connection between the amendment and the abortion issue."[27] Although the ERA was first introduced to Congress in 1923, it wasn't until 1972 (when it was rewritten) that it started to have an impact on the changing nature of feminism. The 1972 version of the ERA in its entirety:

> Section 1. Equality of Rights under the law shall not be denied or abridged by the United States or by any state on account of sex.
>
> Sections 2. The Congress shall have the power to enforce by appropriate legislation, the provisions of this article.
>
> Section 3. This amendment shall take effect two years after the date of ratification.

Interestingly, it may be the ERA that best bridges the gap between the first wave and the second wave of second generation feminism. This is because although the *language* of the ERA is consistent with basic "traditional" notions of equality, certainly readings can change its fundamental spirit. At first blush it certain seems as if the ERA does nothing more than restate what are already taken to be basic notions of equality under the *Fourteenth Amendment* and *Title VII* of the *Civil Rights Act* of 1964. But if this is so, then opponents are correct in claiming that it is, at best, superfluous.

For second wave feminists, however, although the *letter* of the law is superfluous, its *spirit* is new, radical, and absolutely necessary for equality. That is, the ERA is only an unnecessary law if one presupposes that the legal system itself, under the democratic capitalism of the United States, is interested in equality for women and that women, individual women, are the kinds of beings that can, in principle, find justice under that law. If, in fact, as more and more feminists are beginning to claim, the entire political and legal system is *inherently* patriarchal and oppressive to women, and the reason for this oppression is that women are not being taken seriously as an oppressed class, then the ERA, far from being superfluous, is an absolutely necessary first step to equality.

> The spirit of the proposed amendment, however, is much more radical. After all, what seems at first blush to be simply a call for a fuller equality under the law, is actually an attempt to make womanness, itself, privileged. Specific cases of discrimination could just as easily be argued under the *Fourteenth Amendment*, but not if being a woman was some-

> how privileged. The reason the ERA is needed in the eyes of feminists is because the "equal protection laws" guaranteed by the *Fifth* and *Fourteenth Amendments* to the Constitution have not been sufficient in ending discrimination against women as a sexual class, within the law. Women are not recognized as individuals; rather they are discriminated against as a sexual class. The law recognizes women as a sexual class, but does not recognize that women are discriminated against as such.[28]

This point, according to feminism, can be seen by looking at the following cases in which the Supreme Court did not recognize the "reality of sex discrimination."[29]

In 1974's *Geduldig v. Aiello*, Geduldig got pregnant and applied to her employer for pregnancy disability under their current insurance policy. When she was denied, she sued under *Title VII*, claiming that the policy discriminated against her on the grounds of sex. The Supreme Court, however, ruled in favor of the defendant, claiming that the policy does not discriminate against women, per se, but only against pregnant persons. Pregnancy, it seems, was being defined as sex/gender neutral. This finding was reconfirmed in 1976 in the similar case of *General Electric Co. v. Martha Gilbert, et.al.*, where, in appeal, the Supreme Court reversed the Eastern District of Virginia Court's and the Fourth Circuit's prior decision to find in favor of Gilbert and her colleagues seeing pregnancy as a "disability." The finding of the Supreme Court case No. 74-1589, 1976 reads as follows:

> It was held that the exclusion of pregnancy-related disabilities from the plan did not constitute sex discrimination in violation of Title VII since (a) the exclusion of pregnancy was not in itself a gender-based discrimination, but instead merely removed one physical condition from coverage, (b) there was no showing that the exclusion was a mere pretext designed to effect invidious discrimination against women, pregnancy, although confined to women, being significantly different in other ways from the typical covered disease or disability, and (c) there was no showing of gender-based discriminatory effects resulting from the exclusion of preg-

> nancy-related disabilities, the plan being nothing more than an insurance package covering some risks, excluding others, and covering the same categories of risk as to both men and women, and there being no proof that the package was in fact worth more to men than to women.[30]

In other words, if feminists want the advantages of *Title VII*, they must see equality to imply being treated as equal to, not more special than, men.

For feminism this was not enough. The feminist argument for why the ERA is a "must" amendment is seen below:

> Must pregnancy be covered because it disables women or may it be excluded because it cannot disable men? In choosing the latter, discrimination law chooses to prevent only differential treatment seen as arbitrarily, sometimes termed "invidiously" based on sex. It chooses not to equalize social outcomes in the face of biological differences."[31]

In other words, feminism is claiming not that the law is not treating women qua individual women as *equals* with individual men, for it is (after all, at least women can, just like men, *be non-pregnant*[32]) but that the law is ignoring the special biological factors that make women fundamentally different from men, such as being able to *be pregnant*. In so doing, according to feminism, the law is *discriminating against women as a class*.

> Under the inequality approach, variables as to which women and men are not comparable, such as pregnancy or sexuality, would be among the first to trigger suspicion and scrutiny, rather than the last; they would not be exceptions to the rule. From the inequality perspective the question on the Gilbert facts would be: is not the structure of the job market, which accommodates the physical needs, life cycle, and family expectations of men but not of women, integral to women's inferior employment status? What can then justify a policy that makes pregnancy, a condition unique and common to women as a gender, into a disadvantage in employment? The affirmative form of the argument is that the health needs of women workers should be accommodated equally with those of men.[33]

Although one could come up with numerous and obvious ways in which pregnancy could easily "disable" an individual (keeping them from performing their job at all, let alone as well as they did prior to pregnancy), the real issue surrounds *Title VII* itself.

Title VII of the Civil Rights Act of 1964, as stated above, makes it illegal to discriminate against anyone because of sex; it does not claim that one ought to be, in addition, privileged on those same grounds. One need only imagine the case of a man who is "disabled" in such a way that he is unable to find a woman who will have his child; let us say he has what is known in the medical profession as a "micro-penis." And let us say that due to some anomalous coincidence it turns out that all of the men employed by a particular company have this same "disability." Can they justifiably insist that their employer include penis-enlarging surgery on their health plan on the grounds that not doing so violated Title VII?[34] Maybe they should all be given the opportunity to have children without women, via an artificial womb transplant? If all women are entitled to childbearing benefits, why should not all men? If one appeals to the argument that it is only "natural" for women to become pregnant, then what of the "natural" desires for men to impregnate someone? Should companies be forced to provide for their "needs" as well?

Furthermore, in what sense is pregnancy really a "disability," given that disabilities are at least undesirable if not simply impossible to prevent? Neither is the case with respect to pregnancy. Pregnancy, unlike, e.g., all kinds of incurable cancers, is usually desirable and eminently preventable.

Of course the above is meant to be outrageous, but it also brings to the fore the point that if feminism is serious about equality it will have a difficult time making this case while focusing on that part of one's humanity that seems to be most fundamentally different.

Feminism, however, does precisely this. Not only did it continue to champion the ERA, it actually began to reread the spirit of the ERA as something that not only valorizes difference as opposed to equality, but actually has the additional goal of taking down the "system."

> I think the ERA should be understood as a first step in building consciousness about the necessity of the destruction of male supremacy and capitalism as systems of power. The ERA as a demand for equality can be used to uncover the built-in inequality of the patriarchal system we live in.[35]

Feminism, it seems, wants "women to be equal and different too,"[36] even if the cost is the destruction of the social and legal system that has underpinned our common sense notions of equality since the Nation's inception.

The promotion of the ERA as the central platform was working, and in 1977, in Houston, Texas, *The First National Women's Conference* was held, an event that "marked the high point in the women's movement of the 1970s."[37] Even First Lady Rosalynn Carter "took a forthright stand on the ERA and played an active part in the conference."[38]

But by the end of the decade things had again gone sour. The 1979 *Feeney v. The State of Massachusetts* case illustrated feminism's new spirit of supporting *difference,* not *equality*, and prompted women to realize that the ERA may not be giving them what they really wanted. *Feeney* argued in appeal that Massachusetts did not have the right to give civil service job preference to veterans as opposed to non-veterans on the grounds that this was a violation of *Title VII.* The Supreme Court, however, thought differently. Although most veterans of war were men, this was by no means a case of sexual discrimination. Women had already been veterans of WWII, and, more recently, the events of the Gulf War bring home the case that while such a law may discriminate against non-veterans, it certainly does not discriminate against women.

"From the beginning, "equal rights" meant, for most women, "ending special benefits"[39] for men. In feminism's hands, however, the ERA was starting to look as if it meant *providing special benefits for women.* In the final analysis, it may have been, ironically, that feminism itself got in the way of the ratification of the ERA, although some scholars believe that the ERA really had no political teeth to begin with.

> The ERA would have had much less substantive effect than either proponents or opponents claimed. Because the ERA

> applied only to the government and not to private businesses and corporation, it would have had no noticeable effect on the gap between men's and women's wages. Furthermore, during the 1970s the Supreme Court began to use the 14th Amendment to the Constitution to declare unconstitutional almost all the laws and practices that Congress had intended to make unconstitutional when it passed ERA in 1972. Thus by the late 1970s it was hard to show that the ERA would have made any of the substantive changes that most Americans favored.[40]

On June 30, 1982, the deadline for ratifying the amendment passed with only thirty-five of the required thirty-eight states having ratified it and all discussion of the ERA came to a screeching halt.

Worse yet for feminism, "its defeat was a major setback for equality between men and women,"[41] and many savvy successful women—those who had "come a long way baby!"[42] and were now "dressed-for-success"[43] "superwomen,"[44] whose feminism should have been most proud to claim their own, were now calling themselves *postfeminists*.[45]

THE PERSONAL IS THE POLITICAL

This overall skepticism about feminism may have shaken its branches, but it did nothing to hurt its new roots. During the seventies and eighties, feminism had entrenched itself deeply into the halls of the academy where "feminist consciousness was nurtured by the thousands of women's centers and women's studies courses that sprang up on nearly every [college and university] campus across the country."[46] The goal: to produce a feminist collection "that encompasses at least all of the core subject areas commonly taught in anglophone undergraduate philosophy courses."[47]

In addition, the number of women students in academia increased, making the conditions favorable for the continuing development of Contemporary Academic Feminism. It was now the *American Association of University Women* (AAUW) that became the leading proponent of the most powerful form of feminism yet, a form that still holds great power in academia (and related disciplines) today.

> Feminism became a mainstream academic discipline as the universities in Britain and the US set about rewriting the culture to a different gender script.... Women's peripheral achievements were talked up as fast as men's significant achievements were talked down, with quilting, for example, put on par with the Sistine Chapel.... Courses in gender studies abounded. Within twenty years feminism had become the dominant voice in public policy, carried from the universities into the burgeoning public sector.[48]

The second wave had peaked with the mantra: *The personal is the political!*

This call to arms, feminism aside, seems to be true at some level. When one looks at the life and death of Socrates, for example, one realizes that if Plato had not been so upset with the actions of the Athenian government, if he had not "taken it personally" so to speak, the *Apology* of Plato and the other dialogues so important to Western thought would never have been written. The same could be said about the life of Mohandas Gandhi, who, it is believed, was inspired to become the religious and spiritual leader of Indian emancipation by a very personal experience of discrimination in South Africa. And look at the life of Rosa Parks, whose fateful day on an Alabama bus changed the course of history for African Americans. But this sense of "the personal is the political" is not what feminism has in mind. Feminism's point is not simply that sometimes very personal events can inspire or motivate individuals or groups to make changes in their lives that will have a huge effect on society, if not the world at large. Feminism's point is that even the most mundane or ordinary events of one's life—housework or sex—should be reexamined in the light of feminism, that is, as expressions of *sexist male oppression*.

"The assumption that the personal is political is deeply entrenched in the gender debates."[49] The most blatant example of second wave feminism's having taken the political perhaps a bit too personally shows itself in their critique of American democratic/

capitalistic society at large. Feminists argue that this system, being inherently "sexist" and "male biased," has ensured that there is what they call a "gendered division of labor with serious and direct impact on the opportunities of girls and women..."[50]

> The right of the individual to the pursuit of liberty and progress is acted out, in liberal theory, against an assumed background of certain kinds of labouring and ownership relations. These relations are, implicitly and historically, relations between men. These relations between men are made possible by, and sustained by, the political and economic subjection of women. In other words, the free-enterprise 'equality' between men necessarily excludes the participation of women *on an equal footing...*
>
> This notion of free-enterprise 'equality' is an ideal that is based on the 'freedom and equality' of men in market relations that in turn presupposes the unpaid labour of women. As such one can attempt to bring women 'up to' the stage of labour market relations to ensure their equality with men without questioning the domestic basis of these relations but then this will have the consequence of either doubling women's workload or obscuring the political and economic functions of the domestic sphere. There is a third 'option', which is for women to 'become men,' that is for women to function in the public sphere 'as if' they are men. However, even this option disadvantages women, both individually and as a group. It disadvantages women individually in that they do not have the benefit, as do their competitors, of an unpaid domestic worker. It disadvantages women as a group in that if they do not reproduce they are not able to consolidate and accumulate wealth through inheritance.[51]

That is, according to feminism, the capitalistic market in the United States is biased against women, i.e., inherently unequal and fundamentally sexist because it does not incorporate what goes on in the private sphere, i.e., the home, as if it had value in the public sphere (e.g., it is not part of the Gross Domestic Product (GDP) and it is not on the stock exchange). Therefore, for there to be true equality for women, women's in-home work should be treated exactly like men's out-of-home work. Insisting that women go into the public sphere to seek equality with men is asking them *to be men*, and this, according to feminism, is inherently unequal. "The goal of a society should not be that every woman work, but that every person be given broader opportunities to choose...that advancement be equally possible for all."[52]

This, however, seems to be nothing more than misguided feminist bravado, with the ultimate effect of making their position(s) more and more inaccessible and/or undesirable, if not downright harmful, to most women. First, because it is still not clear that most women really want men to take over 50/50 with domestic chores, especially those involving their babies.

> In the 1994 book *Peer Marriage*, sociologist Pepper Schwartz reports that many women committed to equal parenting in theory start "hogging" the baby when they become mothers, and often settle into traditional roles unless they make an effort to curb their possessiveness. Yet only a few of the feminist writers who advocate a more equal sharing of child care responsibilities have started to acknowledge the dirty little secret of maternal chauvinism...[53]

In addition, a true emphasis on free-market housework would lead to a *The Man Show*[54] scenario of competition from which I do not believe women could possibly benefit. Housework and childrearing would have to be looked at solely as forms of labor and production whose only goal is the accumulation of capital. Women would compete for the "job" of being someone's wife—housewife and/or mother, or, if she wishes to remain single, of proving that the children she produces will somehow be worth some stranger's capital investment. Now, although this may produce better wives and mothers, I doubt it is what feminists have in mind when they flippantly claim that non-market activities such as housework and childcare should be added into the GDP figures in order to "lend some dignity to the position of housewives."[55]

Nor do I believe most women are ready to accept the grand social upheaval that would be caused by forcing men to share in this new "home market." When feminists claim that for true equality not only must women make up 50 percent of the public sphere, but men must reintroduce themselves 50/50 to the work at home[56], they may not really want for what they wish. As foreseen by an English woman with respect to Britain, such a change would, at the very least, radically uproot the present economy.

> If women are to share domestic labour equally with men, then men will have to increase their time spent on unpaid work. If women are to increase the level of their earnings to the point where they match men's then men's earnings will inevitably decline. If women are to occupy skilled, higher-paid jobs in equal numbers with men, there are bound to be fewer of these jobs available to men. In other words, women had to be economically emancipated from men, a move that would depress the wages of men and drive them out of work.[57]

Unless women are secretly trying to simply *replace* men in the workplace, forcing them to stay at home in precisely the form they believe is oppressive and installing a truly *reverse sexism*, such drastic advice, given the above consequences, seems questionable if not inconsistent with the spirit of feminism—i.e., the empowerment of women.

The personal—women's bodies, women's sex, women's private lives at home—has, as the mantra of the second wave will attest, become the political. What started, then, as an attempt by first generation feminists to deny an essential bodily difference—in order to set themselves up as being equal to men, deserving of all the rights and privileges afforded to men, being, i.e., *essentially the same*—has ended in the second wave claim that what is truly important to feminism is *not equality as sameness, but equality and "equity as difference."*[58] "The roots of embracing difference are found in second wave feminism's celebration of that which makes her different; that is, women *as* 'the other'."[59]

"To some extent, feminism has always politicized the personal, inasmuch as it sought to change the relations between women and men"[60] but it was the feminist denial that there is any way to draw a line between the personal and the political that leaves the "second wave" with no checks and balances.

> Feminism has shifted dramatically from its early programme of equality between women and men. Driven by the belief that men are incorrigibly violent and antisocial, it seeks now to destroy not merely the traditional relationships between men and women but something more fundamental.[61]

What was considered throughout Western culture to be a natural barrier—one that, for example, allows for the separation of church and state articulated in the First Amendment, and the maintaining of the search and seizure laws stated in the Fourth Amendment—has been completely repudiated by feminism and the second wave will begin to crash down on American society with its new ideology of *equality as difference.*

EQUALITY AS DIFFERENCE

Why is it that feminism has to take everything "personally"? The feminist response, oddly, is because of "women's bodies." Why is this odd? Because for nearly the last two hundred years women have been fighting for equality under the claim that their biological differences are not essential to their womanhood. Women, equally with men, have as their essence not their bodies but their minds. And their minds are just as rational as any man's. How odd that feminism has now changed its tune 180 degrees.

The new tune is sung by, for example, Carole Pateman, who claims that when women seek "nothing more than equality in the sense of women attaining the same status as individuals, workers, or citizens, as men, it is difficult to find a convincing defense against the long-standing anti-feminist charge that such theorists want to turn women into men."[62] And, until notions of equality recognize the "political significance of women's bodies, to press for the inclusion of 'women as women' rather than as equals to men,"[63] true feminist ideals of "equality" cannot be achieved. Why? Why is it that equality itself is even being viewed as male, as opposed to sex/gender neutral?

There seem to be three possible responses. The first is that unless feminism desires a *different kind of equality*, one that values women's differences with respect to men, then they will have to actually compete with men and, in many cases, may lose. For example, with respect to military service requirements, although "male marines must complete a fifteen-mile march carrying a forty-pound pack with weapons in five hours, women must march ten miles with twenty-five pounds and no weapons in three and a half hours."[64] In all areas of military service, "if women and men are held to equal standards in combat training, then either the standards will have to be lowered or, conversely, the standards kept the same and about 80 percent of women won't be able to hack it."[65]

> 'Gender norming' which was required to permit men and women equal opportunity for equal work, even though some traditional physical requirements of military life, such as upper-body strength in climbing and carrying packs, are differently distributed among men and women.[66]

Civilian life would be no different. One has to wonder why, when men and women compete—as the best painters, philosophers, athletes, physicists, musicians, etc. in the world—men nearly always win. Unless there's "gender norming," that is, *women's* track and field or the National Museum of *Women's* Art, even today, despite birth control and legal equality in all venues of public life, the best of the best continue to be primarily men. If a woman wants to be truly *globally excellent* she will have to equally compete with, equally fight like, work equally hard, and ultimately beat out, some man. Feminism, however, does not seem to want a fair fight.

> We want good doctors, certainly, but at the same time we want to encourage people to think of women as doctors. *If, as a matter of fact*, we think that the best way to achieve this is to have a good many successful women doctors, we may consider making rules which allow women to become a doctor with slightly lower medical qualifications than a man.[67]

In connection with the above, feminists have also realized that if equality means "equal to a man," women, obviously, will be seen as *fundamentally similar* to men, and this may have even more dire consequences than simply losing the global excellence game. If women are equal then they can not be more physically valuable than men, for example during a wartime draft. And this has posed a serious dilemma for both feminism and the women they claim to represent.

On the one hand it is obvious that feminists desire acquiring *equal privileges and benefits* for women in the military (e.g., loans, health care, pensions, etc.). With this in mind, "the argument made in favor of women being in combat was that only individuals who have served as effective warriors at the core of their service can scale the carefully controlled military hierarchy. Real combat produced real senior officers."[68] However, there are two interconnected problems with this line of reasoning.

The first is that if women were to share in the equal benefits of combat, they would also have to share in the risks. This would require that women not only expose themselves to equal harm and the heightened chance of death, but they would have to be prepared to be drafted, just as men are. To this day 99 percent of all people killed in wars are men. Equality, with respect to war, seems to be so much lip service. For it is obvious that there was a "sharp gap between feminists who reflect their ideology and political goals, and women in the military itself."[69] Although,

> there have been exceptional female warriors and unusual historical cases, and certainly women have claimed their right to military careers and rewards. However, in general, they have not clamored to join in warfare. They have not made as strong appeals to fight as they have to vote or enjoy equity in employment.[70]

The Supreme Court, however, had reached its "cultural limits"[71] and decided to reject a mandatory draft for women.

> Combat positions in the armed services are now divided into dangerous versus less-dangerous combat positions. In wartime, *only men* can be *forced* into the dangerous combat positions. Restricting women from even volunteering for the most dangerous combat positions is clearly discrimination

> against women. But it also discriminates against the men who must fill these dangerous positions.[72]

What seemed to be the perfect opportunity for feminism to flex its anti-sexist muscles ended up being much ado about nothing, for there was no outpouring of feminist protest. It seems that although feminism sees itself as having a "duty to make sure that women have access to every echelon of military service,"[73] there is no correlative duty within its theorizing to ensure that women are part of a mandatory sign-up to be drafted and possibly killed at eighteen.

Although feminism has called the United States government "inherently sexist and oppressive," this particular governmental decision remains unchallenged. It seems that when equality means sharing equal risk of serious injury or death, feminists and their arguments for true equality are nowhere to be found. It is difference, not equality, which ultimately seems to be valued.

And this brings us to the second problem with the feminist speak. When one takes a close look at those women who, despite feminist protectionism, really did want to accept equal risks, feminist theorizing turns out to be a hindrance, not a help.

> By treating gender differences as entirely socially constructed, activists have failed to equip military women with the tools to understand physical difference or to challenge arguments based on that difference. By focusing on women as victims of sexual harassment, activists have failed to recognize and pass along the strategies of women who have confronted and managed gender conflict despite the hostile environment.... They alienate women who simply do not find their male coworkers to be 'the enemy'.[74]

This feminist schizophrenic commitment to difference can also be seen in civilian life. If women really push for equality they lose the chance to be seen as more valuable in the workplace than men, for example, when they need leave from work while they are pregnant, nursing or otherwise caring for children. With respect to, for example, the *Family and Medical Leave Act* of 1993 (FMLA)[75]—which grants "a family temporary medical leave under certain circumstances"—proponents fought for the enactment of the law in order to ostensibly allow both women and men the chance to avoid workplace discrimination when caring for a newborn child, a handicapped family member or an elderly parent. Although the argument for protection was not clear under the *Equal Protection Clause of the Fourteenth Amendment*, the argument for the protection to be viewed as "gender neutral" was. Interestingly, however, is the fact that in one of the FMLA findings Congress lists as evidence for why it must support the Act "due to the nature of roles of men and women in our society, the primary responsibility for family care taking often falls on women, and such responsibility affects the working lives of women more than it affects the working lives of men."[76]

> equal access to health care, regardless of income, which includes coverage equivalent to men's, though keeping in mind that women use the system more often than men do because of our reproductive capacity…while safeguarding a woman's rights to bear (or not to bear) a child, regardless of circumstances, including women who are younger that eighteen or impoverished…[77]

Therefore, the FMLA was put on the books not in a spirit of equality but, on the contrary, primarily in order to protect the "other" sex. This is true for numerous social problems and their concomitant benefits. Though 94 percent of all people killed in the workplace are men, and 90 percent of all homeless people are men, and the fact that men die seven to eight years sooner than women (regardless of the type of death),[78] feminism does not seem to be interested in any of these inequalities. One can only conclude that despite the posturings by feminists for equality, it is difference that really works for women.

Additionally, if women are viewed as equal they lose the chance to be seen as more morally valuable than men, i.e., more innocent when there is responsibility to be taken for any kind of physical abuse or even non-abusive sexual activity. For example, "expert testimony on the battered women syndrome is now admissible in all fifty states,"[79] even though "Feminists can no longer assume that domestic violence only occurs in heterosexual relationships and that lesbian relationships are immune."[80] Actually, statistics now show that women often batter themselves (e.g., in lesbian relationships) as much or more than men batter them.[81] Furthermore, in over half of all domestic violence cases, it turns out that it is the woman, not the man, who did the initial or only battering in the event in question.[82]

Most problematic, however, is the fact that the definition of battering does not even require physical assault. "A battered women is a woman who is repeatedly subject to any forceful physical or psychological behavior by a man in order to coerce her to do something."[83] It seems that the feminist concern with the "war" on domestic violence "was meant to be a war against men."[84]

It is the rape bias in feminism that offers another obvious case of the desire for difference from, not equality with, men. Despite convoluted stories, and even confessions by women about why they lied, most feminists are "offended by the very idea that women could lie about abuse to gain advantage."[85] Despite such protestations, however, we do know that there are such cases given the few men who are eventually exonerated. "Feminist-initiated reforms have made it easier to bring credibility-contest rape cases to trial *and* more difficult to raise legitimate questions about the credibility of the accuser."[86] As such, not only will society be forever unable to actually determine how often men are sent to prison on the basis of false allegations of rape,[87] there seems to be no way to prevent such abuse even with DNA forensics since what is at issue is not the sex act per se, but whether it was consensual. When women are always seen as the victim, then even when they lie—causing severe harm to the accused as well as upsetting a community while wasting its resources—they are not punished.

In one case the following is reported to have occurred:

> He 'put the screwdriver in my vagina, the handle, and then he put the other one in my rectum' and then he 'moved the screwdrivers at the same time while they were inside of me'. He said 'Just lay there like a good little girl' as he 'took the screwdrivers out of my vagina and rectum' and eventually 'pushed his penis in my vagina....' This statement

> to the police launched a manhunt for a violent rapist who had abducted the woman at gunpoint, and taken her to an underground garage where he raped and sodomized her.... When he was arrested, the shocked young man said that he had met the woman at a bar and had invited her back to his small apartment where they had consensual sex. He pointed out that they were not alone in the house and, in fact, when his landlady had intruded on them at one point, the young woman made no effort to protest or seek help.... After his arrest and statement, the woman changed her story, saying that she had been picked up in the bar and gone home with this man, when they had, what he was quite likely to perceive as, consensual sex. With this and other information gathered by the police, it became clear that no attack had taken place. The woman had lied about the event. Having expended over $300,000 on an investigation the police charged her with Public Mischief, to which she responded: "How can you charge me, you can't prove I consented to the sex." Meanwhile she continued to receive counseling at a sexual assault center where she was seen by a social worker and psychiatrist. At the trial, the psychiatrist testified that, regardless of the facts, the woman was suffering from Post Traumatic Stress Disorder due to the trauma of the rape.[88]

To summarize the above example, although feminists claim to be interested in being treated equally under the law, when the issue is women's bodies—at war, at work, or at play—difference rules. The obvious lack of commitment to true equality can be seen in yet another political event surrounding the notion of the statutory rape laws argued in the courts in the 1980s. Feminists never did insist that the law (which made sex with a female underage partner illegal) be broadened so as to include sex with an underage male partner.[89] Instead they have spent the last two decades attempting to reconstruct the entire definition of rape so as to broaden it to include marital rape, date rape, and for some, every act of sex between a man and a woman.

Although the "rape" question in feminism, especially the construct of "date rape," will be discussed in some detail below, one interesting event offers a case in point of some of the outrageous consequences of feminist theorizing.

> In Wisconsin, 1990, Mark Peterson is found guilty of sexually assaulting a woman who, doctors say, has forty-six personalities.[90] She claimed that one of her personalities, a girl the age of 6, informed her afterward that she had been having sex. She then accused Mark Peterson of having sexually assaulted her. Six of the woman's different personalities were summoned to the witness stand; four were individually sworn in. She acknowledged that the personality that had sex—the "fun loving" personality—did not object. To add insult to injury, Mark made the national press as a criminal. He will always be known in his community as a man convicted of rape.[91]

Men and women are, in the eyes of feminism, different. More importantly, men and women vary in value. Men are more expendable and therefore less valuable in a time of war. Because men do not usually become pregnant and care for children, women deserve more benefits of value in the workplace. Men are usually more aggressive and therefore less innocent when it comes to any physical, especially sexual, encounter with women.

Finally, second wave feminism values difference more than equality because, it is argued, *everything* in Western culture—our law, our democratic ideals, our capitalism, and even our deeply rooted philosophical ideals *such as equality itself*—is inherently male. As such, it would follow trivially that the notion of equality was male. This position is so philosophically intricate and convoluted that it has become a haven for feminist theorizing.

Evidence of feminists adopting this kind of response can be found, for example, in the work of Catherine MacKinnon.

> Virtually every quality that distinguished men from women is already affirmatively compensated in this society. Men's physiology defines most sports, their needs define auto and health coverage, their socially designed biographies define workplace expectations and successful career patterns, their perspectives and concerns define quality in scholarship, their experiences and obsessions define merit, their objectification of life defines art, their military service defines citizenship, their presence defines family, their inability to get along with

> each other—their wars and rulerships—define history, their image defines god, and their genitals define sex. For each of their differences from women, what amounts to an affirmative action plan is in effect, otherwise known as the structure and values of American society.[92]

MacKinnon claims that looking at the notion of equality as the foundation for feminism would not be truly equal; for women cannot be equal citizens until there is a radical rethinking of philosophical commitments which separate the public and domestic sphere of life. For MacKinnon, every relationship with a man—from private sex to public office—is so infused with male bias that there would be no way to even understand the construct of equality under such patriarchy. "In short, women are the sexually objectified, men the objectifiers."[93] For feminism to succeed, the United States must "abandon its pose of [sex/gender] neutrality, which [she claims] in reality is only a guise for more male dominance."[94]

MacKinnon is not alone. Other feminists are on board about redefining 'equality' to mean difference. Elizabeth Grosz has, on several occasions, reappropriated the term 'equality' to mean something that is all about 'difference', warning women to stay away from first generation or even first wave second generation forms of equality. "Even if it remains desirable for women to struggle towards equality with men, it is simply not possible to include women in those theories (and daily tasks) from which they have been excluded.[95]

> Try as it may, a feminism of equality is unable to theorize sexual and reproductive equality adequately...a feminism based on the acknowledgment of women's specificities and oriented to the attainment of autonomy for women has emerged over the last ten years or more.... Only sameness or identity can ensure equality. In the case of feminists of difference, however, difference is not seen as difference *from* a pre-given norm, but as *pure difference*, difference in itself, difference with no identity.... For feminists, to claim women's difference from men is to reject existing definitions and categories, redefining oneself and the world according

> to women's own perspectives.... The right to equality entails the right to be the same as men; while struggles around the right to autonomy imply the right to either consider oneself equal to another or the right to reject the terms by which equality is measured and define oneself in different terms. It entails the right to be and to act differently.[96]

For many feminists then, "'equality' on male terms is not enough."[97]

> The dual system of values described as the traditional value system has operated to legitimate sexist institutional arrangements in the family, education, the occupational world, and the political sphere. People have tended to accept a double standard of values wherein women were expected to be acquiescent, passive, supportive, dependent, and cooperative in response to men's active, aggressive, independent, competitive behavior. As a result, women have been defined as being unsuited for the rigors of the competitive occupational and political worlds, have been channeled into certain areas of education, and have been expected to be naturally suited to the nurturing homemaker role. This dual system of values has been internalized by most persons in American society, simply because we are socialized to believe in these values and accept them. [98]

This theoretical position has the obvious attraction that any time a woman fails at anything, or is harmed at anything, it is always the fault of the system, never her own. The reasonableness of this position is simply unassailable from the feminist perspective. "If women never seem to attain the kinds of positions in society that men attain, it is sensible to assume that some of the reasons are built into the structure of society."[99]

Therefore, given that all three of the above "reasons" are intimately intertwined, feminists will insist on decrying "patriarchy" at some level or other. Neither first generation nor even first wave second generation notions of equality, with respect to the feminist desires for difference, are constructs most women can afford.

THE PATRIARCHY INHERENT IN WESTERN CULTURE

Feminism of the second wave comes to a head, then, with a critique of everything—the government, the workplace, the home, even the self. Everything is interconnected, both the personal and political, and being infected with "masculist" bias is suspect and in need of deconstruction if not complete destruction. "If one's going to go deeper politically and criticize the presuppositions of liberal political theory, then one must coordinately go deeper conceptually and criticize the presuppositions of the epistemology and metaphysics that underwrite the politics."[100] Therefore, nothing is sacred, not even the most deeply ingrained constructs which have been the cornerstone of contemporary politics, philosophy, science, and religion—e.g., that persons are selves that are distinct from their bodies, that science is based on objective evidence, and that such beliefs can be universally true. "By starting from the idea that human subjects are socially concrete and socially diverse beings, feminists encourage suspicion of any given universal claim."[101] A new worldview, a new "philosophy in the feminine," would be the only acceptable social construction of basic values for feminism.

> When the gender-ideological aspects of a piece of philosophical theory are unveiled, the theory is exposed as masculist...It may be charged with masculism when its generalizations are taken to exclude the *symbolically* feminist...the task of feminism is to find a surrogate for philosophy—philosophy in the feminine.[102]

With this in mind, feminists attempted to denounce as male and sexist every major philosophical notion—e.g., the conceptual (if not metaphysical) distinction between mind and body, the notion of objective evidence, and the belief in moral absolutes. Although the history of philosophy has been wrought with challenges to such ideals and values, the heart and soul of the feminist criticism is not to simply replace one philosophical ideology with another, but rather to disavow the methods and principles which allow one to even assess the claims themselves. The feminist critique of deep philosophical constructs is not that they are *actually wrong*, but rather that, given their male history and male bias, they can not possibly be *right for women*.[103]

With respect to the notion of objectivity itself, feminists claim that it is a male political construction designed to oppress and subjugate women, especially through science and medicine. While most people take a well-grounded and empirically verifiable "fact" to be something that anyone—man or woman—would come up with given specific evidence, feminism takes umbrage with the very idea of such a construct. Given that nothing is exempt from political motivation, and assuming that men always have as their ultimate motivation the oppression of women, the "facts" they develop are, at best, *objective for them*. "Objectivity is the epistemological stance of which objectification is the social process, of which male dominance is the politics, the acted out social practice. That is, to look at the world objectively is to objectify it."[104]

> Feminists see the sciences as an important locus of gender inequality and as a key source of legitimation for this inequality; feminists both within and outside the sciences have developed close critical analyses of the androcentrism they find inherent in the institutions, practices and content of science. Both kinds of feminist questions about ideals of objectivity, the status of evidence and the role of orienting (often unacknowledged) contextual values.[105]

The evidence of this inherent bias in science and its products such as technology and modern medicine, is, of course, social/political sexism.

> First, overtly sexist philosophers have in the past claimed that women are by nature less capable reasoners than men and are more prone to ground their judgments on their emotional responses. Secondly, feminists have explored ways in which gendered oppositions are at work even in the writings of philosophers who do not explicitly differentiate the mental capacities of men and women or connect women with the bodily work of reproduction and domestic labour.... They indicate that the terms associated with the feminine are persistently marginalized by comparison with those associated

> with masculinity, as when the rational powers of human beings are habitually regarded as more valuable than their emotional skills.[106]

The same holds true, according to feminism, with the very structures of analysis themselves, such as "objectivity."

> Assumed Objectivity has bad consequences for women... Guided by Assumed Objectivity, objectifiers believe falsely that women possess by *nature* the properties they acquire through objectification. For example, they believe falsely that women are submissive by nature.... Guided by Assumed Objectivity, objectifiers believe that their true beliefs have come to fit the world, when in fact it is the world that has come to fit their beliefs. For example, while they believe truly that women are submissive, their belief about that belief is false. They believe they believe it because women are submissive. Wrong: they do not believe it because women are submissive; women are submissive because they believe it. Believing so, with the aid of structures and practices of power, has made it so.... Assumed Objectivity has led them away from the truth—the truth about women, and the truth about their own beliefs.[107]

So what is feminism to do?

One would think that women would be best served by reworking the notion of objectivity so that it was no longer merely *assumed*, but actually *justified by strict methodological procedures and a serious commitment to evidence*. In addition, one would believe that the way to ensure a lack of bias would be to appeal to notions of justifiability and evidence that *did not take gender into consideration at all.* That is, it would seem that one would, pre-feminism, attempt to strengthen one's commitment to objectivity itself if one wanted to root out claims that were based in political bias and not on actual evidence. However, feminism argues for exactly the opposite. Feminists are "concerned to understand how the gendered dimensions of background beliefs, institutional structure, social relations and identity shape scientific practice for better and for worse.... A commitment to ensure that gender is taken into account..."[108] Oddly, as science is somehow made more justifiable in the eyes of feminism, *the less objective it becomes.*[109]

How is this so? Because, again, the second wave is more interested in accentuating difference than ensuring equality. Women, feminism argues, are in a fundamentally different position with respect to evidence than men, due to their oppressed state. Instead of calling for an end to sexist oppression via bad science or shoddy reasoning—the equality of the first generation as well as that of the first wave of the second generation—feminism calls for a reversal of privilege. Women, the second wave claims, are inherently under-privileged, which makes their *epistemic view*—their view of the evidence, their truth—a more objective one.

> Although women often lack epistemic authority, in fact they may occupy a privileged epistemic standpoint when it comes to recognizing the partiality of a dominant androcentric or sexist world view and to grasping the underlying realities of life that this world view obscures. Where scientific inquiry is concerned, standpoint theory suggests that androcentric bias of various kinds is to be expected.... The insight central to feminist standpoint theory as it emerges in these accounts is that those who are marginal to established structures of privilege for any number of socioeconomic, political, or cultural reasons, including their gender, may prove to be better positioned to understand a given subject domain (natural or social) than those who are comparatively privileged. What counts as compromising baggage on standard objectivist accounts may confer crucial advantage in maximizing standard epistemic virtues.[110]

Feminism in this second wave, then, must be viewed as having evolved into something fundamentally different from its predecessors.

First, feminists of the second wave want all of the advantages of equal rights—laws and rules that provide, at a minimum, "equal freedom to pursue their goals without violence, equal possession of the necessities of life, equal opportunity to develop and utilize their talents to the fullest possible extent, equality of political and civil rights, and so forth,"—but they want all of this without a so-called "male" definition of equality. Second, in so desiring, second wave feminists have simply refused to desire equality defined as "equal to men." Finally, they have doubled back on the construct of equality itself, the historical basis and philosophical foundations of which are grounded in traditional Western culture and classical Western philosophy, respectively. That is, feminists "have 'decentered' this seemingly 'universal' perspective by insisting on seeing the world from women's point(s) of view."[111] Equality, in the final analysis, cannot be equal for both men and women, and feminism "moved away from the doctrines of individual equality towards an acceptance of sex-role divisions in society."[112]

For some women, however, *equality qua difference* seemed an oxymoron. They refused to buy into the feminist doublespeak and wanted to reinstate "equal" meaning equal. Heeding the warning by Nietzsche made many years ago:

> All women are subtle in exaggerating their weaknesses in order to appear as utterly fragile ornaments who are hurt even by a speck of dust. Their existence is supposed to make men feel clumsy, and guilty on that score. Thus they defend themselves against the strong and 'the law of the jungle.'[113]

Instead of fighting head on, difference feminism simply became more and more ideologically defensive. Even women could not argue against the tiniest aspect of feminism without being labeled a sexist. Resistance seemed futile.

Nonetheless, not every woman was assimilated, and some academics found themselves fighting back against feminism.

CHAPTER FIVE

THE THIRD GENERATION: LOOKING "BACK TO THE FUTURE"

Feminism had changed drastically with the "second wave" of the "second generation." It craved equality whenever it wanted to have a piece of the pie that was men's, but was not willing to share equally in the responsibility of such privileges.

> A having-it-both-ways philosophy is characteristic of much of modern feminism: women are the same as men or different, whichever suits them; sex stereotypes are endorsed if they're positive (e.g., that women are more nurturing than men) and denounced if they're negative (e.g., that women are less intelligent than men).... Feminists acutely sensitive to bias against women show little or no concern for bias against men, whether it's the informal leniency accorded female defendants in court or overtly discriminatory draft registration.[1]

That is, feminism was no longer interested in any notion of equality that was recognizable. Feminists had abandoned their first generation and first wave second generation position of asserting the absence of any innate differences between men and women. Feminism had retreated to a position in which innate differences were "not only accepted but were also made the basis for feminist demands."[2] Given the presupposed moral superiority of their feminine voice (inborn due to their mothering tendencies and then finely tuned from years of oppression), the new feminist demand was that "men should improve their behavior."[3] Men did not simply have to match women's actual behavior (which it turns out is not morally superior), but instead to portray the idealized behavior touted in their utopian ideology. In the final analysis, the acceptance of the existence of innate differences, specifically epistemological and ethical, became absolutely crucial for feminism.

Unfortunately, the reality did not fit the ideal and the world ended up with not just men, but women, behaving badly. Many women resisted feminism the old fashioned way, by simply ignoring it and getting on with their lives. But some fought theoretical fire with fire.

The theoretical accounts that offer resistance to feminism are sometimes also called "feminism" in the same way philosophical schools that argue against the very idea of philosophy are called philosophy. Recently on *Politically Incorrect* with Bill Moyer,[4] Christina Hoff-Sommers called herself and Camille Paglia "dissident" feminists. I, myself, used to enjoy being called an "ultra" feminist. But a rose by any other name is still a rose and Paglia, Sommers, and I are all, with respect to feminism (as it has been defined, described and chronicled above), severe critics. Although Paglia, Sommers, and Klein focus their specific critiques on different areas of feminism, all three come together on one central and, at least at first blush, ironic claim: Feminism, at least what it has become in the hands of the second wave, is harmful to women. The prescription is to go "back to the future;" that is, to again embrace the social and political goals of the first generation and first wave second generation feminists.

These women, however, are not the only critics of Feminism. Men, despite, and maybe because of, fears of being fired or sued, or simply being called sexist, harassers, and even rapists, have started to fight back. On the one hand are the men who are supportive of women. They claim simply that there needs to be more "male" in the world as well. On the other hand, much more aggressively, there are men who claim that there ought to be less "female" (albeit in the name of what they now see as the need to emancipate men from feminist oppression.)

Both sexes' critiques of feminism, however, have one major theme in common: Feminism has gone too far. Feminism not only has misguidedly reworked its first generation and first wave second generation notions of equality to mean something fundamentally different and inherently contradictory, but in so doing has caused serious social and political harm to the American people as a whole—men, women, boys and girls.

WOMEN AS VICTIMS

Most critics of feminism, at some point or other in their critique, mention the feminist desire to view all women as victims. Feminists claim that "not all discriminatory laws are overtly oppressive, but where laws discriminate arbitrarily on the basis of sex, there is oppression;"[5] when the oppression is caused by their own theorizing, however, they are wont to make compromise. Regardless of any consequences caused by their collective or individual theories or actions, feminists often see themselves above any charge of sexism. For they are, always, simply victims.

> When the U.S. Supreme Court ruled in 1996 that the Virginia Military Institute was violating the *Fourteenth Amendment* by excluding women, it dealt an almost fatal blow to same-sex education *for boys*...the Court retained full protection for any female-only programs that could be said to compensate for the disabilities women suffer...to "promote equal opportunity."...In the light of this ruling, all-girls programs could still be seen as compensatory, all-boys programs, on the other hand, are regarded as discriminatory."[6]

It seems that even when feminists act in ways inconsistent with the Fourteenth Amendment, allowing themselves special privileges not allotted to men, this too is justified due to their "victimhood."

> When some feminists circumvent due process they are acting out of despair. But their impatience comes from under-

> standing correctly that "the system" is corrupt. Many radical thinkers have made an important critique of liberalism by pointing out that women and other oppressed people are differently situated than white men and, therefore, often cannot take possession of their basic rights.[7]

Nonetheless, women, feminism tells, are not only victims in the social sphere—where they are still being denied equal opportunity and equal pay—but in the private sphere as well—where they are forced by society to marry men, have families, take care of children and do the housework. Every aspect of a woman's life, at work, at home, and even the workings of her own head are controlled by the oppressive patriarchal system that is contemporary American society. Women, according to feminism, are even victims of their own psyches.

> Thus to oppress is to tyrannize or wield unjust power over, while being oppressed suggests an attitude or permanent hopelessness or psychological distress because of the burden of this tyranny.... Frustration of their positions can engender in women certain "defensive traits" including self-pity, timidity, silliness, and self-consciousness. If a woman accepts her traditional role she may have vague feelings of worthlessness, may lack self-confidence, and may be dissatisfied with herself and her life. Often she takes this as her own failure, attributable to some inner fault or lack.... Psychological oppression in women is perpetuated in mythology and the definition of women as the Other through history, and is maintained today through present social institutions and reinforced by the mass media.[8]

And this brings us to the essence of feminism. At the heart of the second wave, what keeps it pulsing toward the shore are the feminist glasses which view all women as victims in the hands of predatory men—men as individuals in bed, men collectively in the workplace, and men in grand conspiracy within the governmental institutions that make up the civic order of this country. Male domination, and therefore, sexism, is insatiable, and women are simply its helpless prey.

> While feminism was having trouble getting its message out, some of the problem had to do with the message itself. Over the last twenty years, the old belief in a tolerant assertiveness, a claim to human participation and human rights—power feminism—was embattled by the rise of a set of beliefs that cast women as beleaguered, fragile, intuitive angels: victim feminism."[9]

There seem to be at least two immediate criticisms of this form of feminist myopia. The first is the empirical fact that not every man is a predator and the concomitant fact that not every woman is innocent.

> The certainty that men are violent and women are not, so that men are always victimisers and women and children always their victims, is now so deeply ingrained in people's consciousness that to question it is to invite disbelief and derision. In Britain, America and Europe, women's aid is now a multi-million pound concern, a whole industry of refugees and activists and researchers all pumping out the message that men are violent to women.... In fact the research shows nothing of the kind. There are now dozens of studies which show that women are as violent towards their partners, if not more so, than men.[10]

As a matter of fact, men may be much less mercurial and violent relative to their size and strength. "Given the greater strength of men, it is particularly noteworthy that so many women dare to initiate violence against them. The fact is that men actually hold back.... Far from assuming that men are violent, women take men's *non-aggression* for granted, even when provoked."[11]

Another myth needing to be dispelled is that women suffer more violence overall than men. This is simply not true. On the contrary, men themselves are more often the victims of male violence than women.

> No one would dispute that while women are capable of horrific crimes, men commit such crimes more often. What is truly bizarre about the feminist concept of "violence against women"

> is the implication that women are the primary victims.... In fact, men are much more likely than women to be victims of every violent crime except rape.... Gay men are at least as likely to be raped by their dates as heterosexual women.[12]

In addition, women wearing feminist specs seem to go out of their way to see harassment in anything men do.

> In 1992, female students in Berkeley, California, forcibly clothed a nude man in the name of feminism. A twenty-two-year-old student who calls himself the Naked Guy had taken to walking around the University of California campus wearing nothing but a sun hat and sandals.... His clothing-free existence was a statement: antimaterialist, anticonventional, pronature, and profreedom. Several women students tried, unsuccessfully, to get him to cover up. Finally, they told the administration that he made them feel "sexually harassed" by his nudity. The administration acted, and the Naked Guy sorrowfully wrapped up his genitals in a sporty red bandanna."[13]

Such an example raises some interesting ironies. First, Naked Guy was protesting the very same kinds of oppressions that many feminists protest. Why was he not seen as an ally? Has not feminism made it clear that the "establishment" is itself sexist, and is not Naked Guy making an antiestablishment statement? Did not feminism insist in the "bra burning" days that one's body is not something to be hidden or molded by societal ideas of dress, but flaunted and loved as it is? Certainly Naked Guy is on board with this ideology as well. So what did Naked Guy do wrong? Was it merely Naked Guy's penis that was the culprit?

More hypocritically, it seems that had a group of men "forcibly" done anything to a woman, let alone touched her and dressed her, she would have immediately sued the institution for harassment, if not assault. She would have been the victim. Why was Naked Guy the culprit? If feminists really believed in relieving oppression, they should certainly take pains not to "set the scales straight" by becoming oppressors themselves.

> 'Victim' feminism is a composite...victim feminism has developed an elaborate mythology to support its way of seeing the world and seeking power. It harks back to a myth of origin, to a harmonious, nonviolent, egalitarian past that predated recorded history, in which women were worshipped, "female" values predominated, and war was unknown. This mythology...was literalized into a supremacist myth as chauvinist as any other.[14]

And, interestingly, feminism's chauvinism is aimed at the very people who legitimize their ideologies and victimization mentality.

Feminism has complained about Western medicine and its hierarchical and invasive ways for decades. The most common complaints concern birth control techniques, e.g., that there is no male "pill," and heart disease research, which feminists claim has completely ignored women. There are other disparaging comments as well.

> The case against what feminist wits call "medical mal(e)-practice" includes other offenses, from patronizing treatment to unnecessary surgery. It is claimed that "20 to 90 percent" of hysterectomies performed in this country are "medically unjustified." Yet as the vagueness of this estimate indicates, there is considerable debate on the issue. (Ironically but perhaps predictably, efforts by managed care health plans to curb hysterectomies have also been denounced as antifemale.)[15]

The new book by Dr. Sally Satel, *P.C. MDs: How Political Correctness is Destroying Medicine,*[16] documents the now fashionable way in which P.C. attitudes toward doctors and other health care experts, especially in the mental health field (such as psychiatrists and psychologists), may actually be getting in the way of good medicine.

Interestingly, however, is the fact that "victim" feminism on the one hand uses the traditional medical institutions to legitimize its beliefs, attitudes, actions and status, while on the other hand claims to be a victim even in its hands. One researcher has pointed out that:

> When so many "cry victim" it becomes almost impossible to know what is true and what is false.... As well, Fabricated Victims, especially those who accuse others of crimes and evil acts, run the increasing risk of eventually experiencing guilt and shame, and possible humiliation and blame. While initially supported in their beliefs, many Synthetic Victims will at some time in the future begin to realize the destructive effects that their accusations have had on others and feel personal responsibility and profound embarrassment.[17]

It seems that those whom feminism has made into victims—e.g., the women who just would not look away from, or simply walk away from, Naked Guy—have, ironically, made themselves susceptible to the victimhood of their own feminist theorizing.

Betty Friedan, long time feminist, stirred up controversy when she attacked the victim persona of women touted by the feminists when she wrote "obsession with rape, even offering Band-Aids to its victims, is a kind of wallowing in the victim state..." In the final analysis, "proclaiming victimhood doesn't help to project strength."[18]

And strength, the need for a woman to, shall I dare say it, act like a man, is at the heart of the "dissident" critique of feminism from both women and men. The "dissidents" are tired of "equal" meaning "more for women" and they are ready to stand up against feminism and the P.C. world it has created.

PAGLIA: BROAD SOCIAL CRITICISM

Paglia's critique of feminism is broadly based while being loosely focused on the social and political consequences of feminism for contemporary American society as a whole, and for women in particular. Paglia is completely unsympathetic to feminism and the dual party line it feeds women: Women are victims; men are bad.

> I categorically reject current feminist cant that insists that the power differential of boss/worker or teacher/student makes the lesser party helpless to resist the hand on the knee, the bear hug, the sloppy kiss, or the off-color joke. Servility to authority to win favor is an old story; it was probably busi-

> ness-as-usual in Babylon. Objective research would likely show that the incidences of sycophancy by subordinates far exceed that of coercion by bosses. That a woman, whether or not she has dependent children, has no choice but to submit without protest to a degrading situation is absurd. Women, as much as men, have the obligation to maintain their human dignity.[19]

Women must behave like men if they want to compete with men for the best stuff. If they want to be the best doctor, they'd better forsake partying and maybe even having a family; if they want to be the best swimmer in the world, they may have to forsake long hair and chocolate. If they want to be the top dog at anything, they will have to do more than show that men can bare their teeth and bite; they will have to "bare their own fangs."[20]

If feminists concentrated on acting more like men, rather than raging at them, there would be more equal representation in the kinds of jobs that require one to show human courage and dignity. Paglia calls for an end of the "jabber" about victimization—by fashion, medicine, pop music, glass ceilings, and even nude paintings. The message feminism is sending is that in the rough play of the arena of life, women are simply too weak to take seriously. The best argument for women in combat, claims Paglia, is simply the very existence of "combative women."[21] Victim feminism is not helping anyone, especially women.

Christina Hoff Sommers writes:

> It is very rare these days to hear anyone praising masculinity. The dissident feminist writer Camille Paglia is a refreshing exception. Her observations are effective antidotes to the surfeit of disparagements. For Paglia, male aggressiveness and competetiveness are animating principles of creativity: "Masculinity is aggressive, unstable, combustible. It is also the most creative cultural force in history." Speaking of the "fashionable disdain for 'patriarchal society' to which nothing good is ever attributed," she writes, "But it is patriarchal society that had freed me as a woman. It is capitalism that has given me the leisure to sit at this desk writing this book. Let us stop being small-minded about men and freely

> acknowledge what treasures their obsessiveness has poured into culture." "Men," writes Paglia, "created the world we live in and luxuries we enjoy." "When I cross the George Washington Bridge or any of America's great bridges, I think—*men* have done this. Construction is a sublime male property."[22]

Paglia's prescription for today's women: "Study football."[23] Certainly a far cry from the victimization mentality of feminism.

SOMMERS: DEBUNKING EDUCATION

While Paglia offers a broad based, articulate, and humorous critique of feminism, Sommers focuses her attack on education. Her first book, *Who Stole Feminism*?[24] gives a well evidenced and intensely systematic account of how feminism, especially in the form of Women's Studies programs, has infiltrated American college and university campuses to the detriment of everyone, especially women. More horrifyingly, in her latest book Sommers convincingly argues that this feminist party line has trickled down into primary and secondary education where it may actually do even more drastic and long-term harm to the nation.

When feminism, NOW and the ERA were on everyone's minds in the sixties, J.F.K. established the *Commission of Education* and one of the main issues under investigation was the status of girls and women throughout the educational process. "In 1963, when the *Commission of Education* turned into the *Kennedy Commission on the Status of Women*...educators could see how women of every class were segregated unfairly or denied access to male activities from kindergarten on."[25]

> As Chair of the Education Committee of the New York City chapter of NOW, Kate Millet authored the pamphlet *Token Learning* (1967), challenging the validity of college and university curricula for women and the shunting of young women into nursing, teaching, and home economics. Millet traced female deprivation of ambition to deep cultural roots and decried the socialization that squelched the ambitions of young women to enter traditionally male professions.[26]

Feminism, it seemed, had its first government sanctioned political platform focused on the education of women. And the myth that women always have been, as so therefore always will be, systematically discriminated against had begun.

> In 1971, Dr. Bernice Sandler of the *Women's Equity Action League* testified to a Judiciary Subcommittee of the House of Representatives that discrimination against young women permeated all of higher education: 'Girls need far higher grades for admission to many institutions. Numerous studies have shown that between 75 and 95 percent of the well-qualified students that do not go on to college are women. And discrimination is one of the major reasons why.[27]

The possibility that women simply did not want to go to college was never even an issue; the belief that discrimination at all levels of the educational experience was, for feminism, the only possible reason.[28] The feminist history of oppression was writing itself; for the only reason for any statistic was that there was a huge male conspiracy against women. From the feminist perspective:

> Opportunities for women academe eroded into and through the '60s…the whole academic establishment, especially graduate literature departments, were indicted for systematically excluding women from admission and making professional teaching, creation, and criticism of literature a male domain…. The problem recurred in all disciplines. Alice Rossi's survey of 188 major sociology departments revealed that women comprised 30 percent of doctoral candidates, 14 percent of assistant professors, nine percent at the associate rank, only 4 percent at full, and less than 1 percent as department chairs. In art history women made up 30 percent of the doctorates in the sixties and 48 percent by 1970/71; but as late as 1978, only 17 percent of tenured faculty in departments were female.[29]

The only possible reason: Sexism.

> Discrimination begins in early grades, continues and is reinforced throughout the educational experience, and eventually

> is taken, not as oppression of women, but as the social reality of their inabilities in intellectual skills.... Early education could be changed to improve the societal image of all women, regardless of their eventual educational attainment, and to break down some of the early stereotypes about the possibilities all children have for the future.... College and graduate schools could change to reflect greater female input, through courses in women's studies, greater numbers of women as faculty members, and general raising of consciousness about women's issues.[30]

Sommers' work makes it so that one cannot help but challenge this kind of response. Even if one grants, for the sake of argument, that the above feminist laments are true, and that college and university campuses discriminate against their women students, their women faculty, and a feminist course curriculum, how does one explain that at most college and university campuses there are more women than men? (And when one looks at the recent graduates of the schools of education and nursing, the percentage is approximately 10 to 1 against men.) More interestingly, if the faculty and curriculum of most colleges and universities is antifemale, how does one make sense of the fact that institutions throughout the country are inundated with feminism—courses offered by women, solely for women, and strictly about women? Worse, why are so many courses being taught "feministly" with an eye toward developing "women safe"—noncompetitive, nonaggressive, and nonheirarchical—atmosphere?

> The feminist classroom is the place to use what we know as women to appropriate and transform, totally, a domain which has been men's.... Let us welcome the intrusion/infusion of emotionality—love, rage, anxiety, eroticism—into intellect as a step toward healing the fragmentation capitalism and patriarchy have demanded from us.[31]

And, finally, most disastrously, why is it that so many academics who do not tow the party line are punished and/or fired? For example, the case of *Silva v. the University of New Hampshire*—the writing professor who was fired for having used sexual metaphors as examples in class.[32] Or, in the 1998 the case of *Sakren v. Arizona State University*, a professor was fired for maintaining an emphasis on teaching the dead white male "classics," e.g., Shakespeare, despite recent PC trends.[33] Both professors and students learn quite quickly that "open criticism of the feminists' classroom will not win them support from teachers who privately agree with them."[34]

One recent example of how the feminist desire for their own political gains shows itself in the use and abuse of *Title IX* legislation.[35] Feminist social activists[36] have, in the name of equity, forced many college sports programs to fold. Debates concerning the value of such teams aside, in order to comply with federal *Title IX* regulations concerning gender equity in college sports, feminists nonetheless whine that despite the market factors—high cost, low turnout—women's sports deserve the same financial support as men's. Because of the law, in order to comply and yet stay solvent, "colleges and universities are increasingly dropping men's athletic teams rather than support women's teams."[37] It's not clear how this kind of feminist activity is in the interest of anyone, especially women.

Although higher education was the original breeding ground for this most recent and awesomely powerful version of feminism, the range of influence has not been contained. Now feminism has infected primary and secondary education as well.

In Sommers' *The War Against Boys*,[38] she carefully documents the faulty reasoning behind the feminist belief that girls are being harmed in the K-12 classroom. On the contrary, Sommers argues that exactly the opposite is true and that boys, not girls, are the ones being systematically harmed. The perpetrator, feminism (and its misguided beliefs, specifically those centering on the supposed moral superiority of girls and women versus boys and men).

This myth, like much of feminist apostasy, began with the "second wave"[39] but became part of mainstream feminism with Carol Gilligan and her book *In a Different Voice*.[40] Gilligan claimed to have empirically demonstrated the descriptive point that girls think about moral issues in a fundamentally different way than boys do. Girls, claim Gilligan, are more likely to think contextually (as opposed to universally) and privilege emotions (over reason).

But instead of seeing this as evidence of girls' moral immaturity (for Gilligan's evidence showed that girls are more likely to make moral decisions in the heat of the moment, thinking only of their own particular circumstance), instead of seeing girls as unable to reason to correct moral behavior via general and universal laws of logic used by boys that same age, Gilligan made the very feminist leap of saying that such behavior is, in fact, actually morally superior. Morally mature behavior, and ethics itself, was turned on its head.[41]

> Ethics, or moral philosophy, as a field of intellectual inquiry developed in the west for well over two thousand years with minimal input from women.... The absence of female voices has meant that the moral concerns of men have preoccupied traditional western ethics, the moral perspectives of men have shaped its methods and concepts, and male biases against women have gone virtually unchallenged within...feminist ethics shares the general goal of eliminating the subordination and oppression of women and enhancing societal respect for women's viewpoints and capacities...[including] a search for alternatives to Kantian and utilitarian ethics, legitimation of the personal point of view, defense of the role of emotion in moral judgment and development of a relationally oriented moral psychology...to expose and to challenge male-oriented biases in traditional contemporary mainstream work, especially attitudes that would justify or excuse the subordination of women.[42]

How does all of this affect the education of America's children?

> Gilligan's ideas had special resonance in women's groups already comitted to the proposition that our society is unsympathetic to women. Such organizations were naturally receptive to bad news about girls.... In 1991, the American Association of University Women (AAUW) announced the disturbing results; "Most girls emerge from adolescence with a poor self-image"...At the time the AAUW's self-esteem results were making headline, a little-known journal called *Science News* quoted leading adolescent psychologists who questioned the validity of the self-esteem poll...The

> AAUW quickly commissioned a second study, "How Schools Shortchange Girls" carried out by Wellesley College. "The implications are clear," said the AAUW, "the system must change"...Six years after the release of "How"...*The New York Times* ran a story that, for the first time, questioned the validity of the report. By then, of course, most of the damage to the truth about boys and girls was irreparable...boys are resented, being seen both as the unfairly privileged gender and as obstacles on the path to gender justice for girls. There is an understandable dialectic: the more girls are portrayed as diminished, the more boys are regarded as needing to be taken down a notch and reduced in importance.[43]
>
> Gilligan's views are attractive to many who believe that boys could well profit by being more sensitive and empathetic. But before anyone enlists Gilligan's project of getting boys in touch with their inner nurturer, he or she would do well to note that Gilligan's central thesis—that boys are being imprisoned by their conventional masculinity—is not a scientific hypothesis. It is an extravagant piece of speculative psychology.[44]
>
> In the spring of 1998, Judith Kleinfeld, a psychologist at the University of Alaska, published a thorough critique of the schoolgirl research entitled "The Myth That Schools Shortchange Girls: Social Science in the Service of Deception." Kleinfeld exposed a number of errors and concluded that the AAUW/Wellesley Center research on girls was "politics dressed up as science." Kleinfeld's report prompted several newspapers including *The New York Times* and *Education Week*, to take a second look at the earlier claims that girls were in a tragic state. The AAUW did not adequately respond to any of Kleinfeld's substantive objections; instead, its president, Maggie Ford, complained in *The New York Times* letters column that Kleinfeld was "reducing the problems of our children to this petty 'who is worse off, boys or girls?' which gets us nowhere." From the leader of an organization that spent nearly a decade promoting the position that America's girls are being "shortchanged," this comment is rather remarkable.[45]

As has been the case with most feminist myth making[46]—built on false claims, misrepresented data, and obvious political biases—these beliefs, despite debunking, have been very difficult to shake.

> Despite its anti-boy bias and factual errors, the campaign to persuade the public that girls are being diminished personally and academically was a spectacular success...In 1994, the allegedly low state of America's girls moved the U.S. Congress to pass the *Gender Equity in Education Act*, which categorized girls as "under-served population" on par with other discriminated against minorities.[47]

Even where there is no evidence to deny, dispute or misrepresent, feminism is not satisfied. Women and girls always have and always will be discriminated against. Therefore, even when the evidence does not show any lagging on the part of girls, even when girls are actually beating boys, sexism must still be fettered out and destroyed. The bogeyman of patriarchy must exist somewhere, believe feminists, so if it cannot be seen, it must be hidden deep in the psyches of little girls.

> The girl advocates cannot plausibly deny that girls get better grades, that they are more engaged academically, or that they are now the majority sex in higher education. So they point to psychological and sociological difference: self-esteem gaps, "call-out" gaps, confidence gaps. But these, we have seen, do not withstand scrutiny.[48]

Nonetheless, and quite unfortunately, much has been altered in the school systems to counteract this "unseen" and false threat to girls. More unfortunately, none of the changes act to increase the educational excellence of girls, but instead, only to diminish the value of the educational experience for boys.

> Instead of working on raising women that are excellent and self-sufficient, "the gender fairness activists are eager to be in the forefront of effecting that "shocking change" by overhauling the way boys are raised to manhood. To that end, Hanson and her taxpayer-funded organization *Women's Educational Equity Act* (WEEA) are working to make classrooms a place

> for radically changing boys." Changing them via programs such as *Quit It!*[49] because of the bias that their aggressive and competitive behavior is "pathologically dangerous."[50]

Worse, as was the case with feminist myth making affecting academe—where it was impossible to contain and so eventually seeped into the broader political arena, the same is true with respect to K-12. The idea that all boy behaviors are maladjusted and sociopathic has seeped from the classroom into the courtroom. In the *Davis v. Monroe County Board of Education* case a schoolboy was actually charged and found guilty of sexual harassment for doing what all boys and girls do to each other: Teasing.

> The Courts must always be fair. As matters now stand, the courts and the government, in effect, discriminate against boys on a fundamental issue: girls, being default victims of "discrimination," have a mantle of federal protection for their right to attend class that boys don't have. Moreover, with the new decision, boys are worse off than ever before. Schools, fearful of ruinous lawsuits, will treat normal boys as protoharassers."[51]

Sommers warns all Americans that:

> If organizations and institutions such as the AAUWs, the *Wellesley Center for Research on Women*, the *Harvard Project on Women's Psychology*, the *McLean Center for Men*, the *Boys' Project at Tufts University*, and the *U.S. Department of Education's WEEA Equity Resource Center* continue to shape "gender policy" for our schools, the gap that now severely disadvantages boys will become a chasm. And the efforts to "reconstruct" boys—to interest them in dolls, in quilts, in noncompetitive games "where no one is out"—will continue apace.[52]

Via Sommers' work, one cannot help but wonder about the future of our boys and the kinds of men they will become.

KLEIN: THE "DATE RAPE" QUESTION IN FEMINISM

If one accepts, with Paglia, the fact that male energy has been one of the most productive forces on the planet, enabling great strides in science, technology, medicine, philosophy, literature and the arts; and if one accepts with Sommers that the education of boys to men is, at the very least, diminishing this energy, one cannot help but wonder what will happen to our world when all that feminism calls male—e.g., aggressiveness and competitiveness—has been squelched out of existence. Will societies, when "feminized," be truly free of war, starvation, and disease, the bad-making properties of thousands of years of male domination? One need only take a look at how women behave with respect to one another, men and society as a whole to see that this feminist ideal is wildly far fetched.

Klein argues that evidence of the bad-making properties of the feminization of society can be found in how feminists react to one small microcosm of that society, the intimate relationships between men and women in the bedroom. She argues that if women cannot even take responsibility for their one-to-one sexual relationships, it is hard to believe that they can behave any more responsibly in the macrocosm of social life—the classroom, the boardroom or the Oval Office.

In 1975, the feminist perspective on rape was documented by Susan Brownmiller.

> Using fact and theory gleaned from history, classical mythology, psychology, psychoanalysis, sociology, criminology, personal experience, testimony of individual victims, and anything else that came to hand, Susan Brownmiller viciously attacked the societal myths surrounding rape. Her book *Against Our Will: Men, Women, and Rape* is an almost encyclopedic survey of the long-neglected topic, viewed in unwavering feminist perspective.[53]

And in 1979, Susan Griffin in her book *Rape: The Power of Consciousness,* argued that:

> rape was not the act of a madman or of a man suddenly overcome by sexual lust. Rather, it was a political act that

> underwrote the system of male dominance and was beneficial to all classes of men, whether they raped or not. "For rape is a kind of terrorism which severely limits the freedom of women and makes women dependent on men."[54]

Although this socio/political explanation for rape in humans is probably empirically false—given that rape activities have been documented in numerous non-human species and that rape has been viewed by some biologists to be a rational last resort for the completion of an individual animal's inherent need to procreate—the ideology nonetheless spread like wildfire in the feminist community.

The dangers of overdramatically politicizing what is already a felon are minimal; the rhetoric itself, however, was not so benign. For this new "antirape movement aroused women's consciousness on the rape issue, worked actively to change public opinion concerning the causes of rape, and redefined the parameters of what women would tolerate, individually and collectively."[55] The latter point, however, about "redefining parameters," was to become dangerous, not only for men, but, ironically, for women.

Although Catherine MacKinnon had bought into the above party line that "rape is an abuse of physical force, not an expression of male sexuality...rape is an expression of physical force that just happens to be acted out in sex, not an expression of male sexuality acted out a little more forcefully than usual"[56]—it was not until her appearance on *NBC* television in the early eighties that the parameters of rape were dramatically changed. She claimed that "almost half of all women are raped or victims of attempted rape at least once in their lives...[concluding that] under conditions of male dominance, if sex is normally something men do to women, viewing 'yes' as a sign of consent is misguided."[57] Of course "if a woman can be considered raped even if she says 'yes', it is understandable how MacKinnon concluded that half of all women are subject to rape or attempted rape in their lifetime."[58]

The truth is that this number has been shown to be empirically false;[59] nonetheless, it has maintained itself as part of feminist mythology to this day. More heinous, however, is the second part of the above statement—that even a woman's "yes" in contemporary American society, under a feminist interpretation of "male dominance," must be viewed to be somehow coerced.

> To be declared a victim of sexual assault can now mean anything from having been abducted and repeatedly raped at knife point to having an affair with a professor which ended with a grade that wasn't the expected "A," having got drunk one night and gone to bed with a date who looked less appealing in the sober morning light, or even having been whistled at.[60]

The problem of this kind of broadening of the scope of rape can be seen, once again, in the feminist stronghold of academia, where such mythology not only obviously harms men,[61] but, ironically, the women feminism claims to be serving. Recently "date rape" has become a huge issue on college and university campuses, so much so that women such as Katie Koestner, America's "Date Rape" Girl,[62] have been able to turn personal stories of "rape" into their very own six-figure cottage industry.

Katie went to dinner with a male coed, Peter, and then took him to her dorm room. They danced, he pawed at her, and she said "no" (even assume she said "no" a thousand times). He then said "O.K., I'll just go to sleep," after which time he did just that, for approximately six hours.

Koestner claims that the next morning he invited her into the bed and although she did not verbally or physically struggle from his advances, according to Ms. Koestner, he raped her. That is, despite the mace in her room, the crowded dorm in which she could have screamed out, and last but not least, the fact that *she had hours to leave the room while he slept,* we are told by Katie that she was raped.

Feminist supporter or not, Koestner's caricature of the feminine is epic. For example, she claimed she still believed in and wanted a "prince charming;" she claimed she still needed her militarist father to guard the door and tell her when to come home; she claimed she felt powerless and trapped by a *sleeping man*; she claimed she was too afraid even to say anything harsh to this man, let alone scream, flee or fight to get out of an uncomfortable situation. All of this she claims was due to a social desire not to "make a scene" (ironic given the turn of events which put her picture on the cover of *Time* and have her guest speaking at college and university campuses all over the country).

In addition, she claimed she was too afraid to struggle from supposed unwanted physical advances for fear she might tear the buttons off her party dress; she claimed she climbed into bed with a man she said she did not want after six hours of cowering in the corner of her room while he slept; she claimed to have bitten her own lip (not his), while he penetrated her. And when she spoke to her audience she admitted that even now she mourned the loss of her virginity (as if it was the one thing she had of value).

What does this say about the typical American college woman? Is she a child or a full person? If she buys into the feminist account of rape, which is so broad as to include "date rape" scenarios such as the one above, is she even interested in, let alone entitled to, equality?

> While 'rape' used to mean coerced, nonconsensual sex, it now also includes having sex when you'd really rather not but you've been talked into it by a partner who has utilized any of a large number of items in the seducer's classical bag of tricks, e.g., flattery, promises, arguments, appeals to pity, reminders of past promises, threats to break off the relationship, etc. In other words, rape occurs even when consent is given, provided the consent is influenced by external pressure and is not simply the result of internal desire.[63]

Of course feminists, determined to make every man a rapist, and every woman's "yes" a coerced "no," will have to do so at the terribly high price of selling out a woman's autonomy and personhood, let alone her power.

Via the above cases, the problem of selectively viewing only what serves feminist political interests as "coercive" becomes apparent. Koestner, for example, according to the proponents of the date rape construct, freely went to dinner, freely invited Peter to her room, freely asked him to dance, freely told him to stop fondling her, and then, while he slept, freely stayed in the same room for hours. The next morning she freely climbed into bed with him and kissed him; but, she tells us (and feminism supports her claim), when he entered her (without her moving at all or saying anything, let alone "no"), she was no longer free. Oddly, at the moment just before penetration, Koestner lost all her freedom to choose and was, only in this particular act, *coerced* into sex, and, therefore, raped. Feminism's specifically anti-intercourse, and more broadly anti-male, agenda was certainly beginning to show.

Perhaps even more unfortunate than feminism's attempt to show that all men are rapists is the consequence of having turned all women into children, persons incapable of autonomous rational decision making.[64] Under such situations, not only is feminism not accepting that men and women are equal—equally rational, equally autonomous, equally powerful—they are actually suggesting that women are not worthy of equality.

In addition, feminism aids in the overall societal turn to the valorizing of the "victim"—of babying the victim, of even wanting to be the victim. Victimhood, not courage, strength or wisdom, is the essence of today's heroes. This seems terribly misguided given true victims, e.g. the hostages of terrorists:

> the hostages—not one of these people would have chosen to have happen to them what happened.... So, why, when authentic victims would escape if they could, are people today allowing themselves to be categorized as victims?"[65]

Fortunately the bad-making properties of feminist theorizing about rape have yet to make it into law outside academia.[66] This, however, has not been the case with pornography. For feminist Andrea Dworkin, pornography is a prime means by which men assert their power over women. "She argues that, like rape, porn is more about domination and violence than about sex."[67] And in 1983,

> Andrea Dworkin and Catherine MacKinnon—then jointly teaching a course on pornography at the University of Minnesota—were invited by a group of Minneapolis residents to assist their efforts to limit the traffic of pornography in

> their city. Discarding the "community standards" yardstick, the two feminists drafted an antipornography ordinance based instead on the novel argument that porn is harmful to women and violates their civil rights. The Minneapolis City Council passed the ordinance twice, only to have the mayor veto it each time. Similar legislation in Indianapolis was struck down in 1985 by the U.S. Court of Appeals as an infringement of the *First Amendment* right to free speech. But perhaps more significant was the fact that the court seemed to accept the concept that porn harms women. "Depictions of subordination tend to perpetuate subordination," the court's written opinion stated. "The subordinate status of women, in turn, leads to affront and lower pay at work, insult and injury at home, battery and rape on the streets."[68]

The point is that "Men treat women as whom they see women as being."[69] Pornography then "causes" men to harm women. The argument runs as follows:

> (1) If dominance/submission is eroticized, then the submissive participant is both viewed as and treated as an object of the dominant's desire.
>
> (2) Women, qua sex object, exist only for the satisfaction of that desire.

Therefore,

> (3) "The category of women is, in a sense, that group of individuals onto which men project and act out their desire."[70]

The hypothetical nature of the whole proof aside, the cause and effect relationship between pornography—depicting "eroticized" subordination and submission—and actual patronizing, let alone abusive, behavior remains dubious. Furthermore, even if it is harmful, it is not clear that the harm is caused *solely by* men alone and *solely to* women alone. Women produce their own pornography[71] and a great deal of pornography centers around men.[72] "Sex/genderwise, pornography is an equal opportunity enterprise."[73]

Unless one presupposes that men are completely incapable of rational and/or civil behavior—of recognizing the difference between fact and fantasy, acknowledging that erotic relationships are different from other types of relationships with women, respectful of what is civilly and morally appropriate—a huge gap between how one *could* be influenced and how one actually *is* remains.

But such bias against men does seem to be at the heart of the pornography issue in the same way it is at the heart of the "date rape" issue. Men are assumed to be oppressors in the form of "objectifiers." "If the social role of men is the role of sexual objectifier, then taking up the objectivist stance is sufficient for being a man."[74] The question of what is an "objectifier" as well as the metaphysical problems of being "objectified" against one's will aside, there are problems with this belief. For one thing, the statement as it stands has no political teeth. The issue of interest to feminists with respect to pornography seems to be not whether "objectifier" entails being a man, but whether man entails being an "objectifier." Either feminists misunderstand the logical commitments of the claim,[75] or they are simply presupposing the incredibly sexist attitude that only men can be "objectifiers," or both. If the first, then what they want to say is that being a man is sufficient for being an "objectifier," not vice versa. This would, of course, implicate without due process, all men. The latter simply makes women inherently innocent of "objectification." The latter seems to be empirically false, the former blatantly sexist.

Therefore, although I believe that the true spirit of the First Amendment is to protect one's right to criticize government, not to protect pornography, I still believe that the courts did the best thing in overturning what has come to be known as the "MacKinnon/Dworkin" law. The law serves to protect feminism itself more than actual women. Without a great deal more empirical evidence feminists may at best be justified in believing that pornography *depicts harm*, but it is not itself inherently *harmful*.[76]

In addition, as stated with respect to the feminist broadening of rape, women need no more protectionist laws. Feminism fought against such laws in the first generation and in the first wave of the second generation for a very good reason: full rights requires full responsibility. The desire to be viewed as full human beings in the eyes of the law, colleges and universities, and, of course, the workplace, requires that women accept full responsibility for at the very least themselves and their own status in society. Women, prior to this second wave, wanted to show they were smart enough, imaginative enough, strong enough and tough enough to do what it is that men do, have what it is that men have, and be, without qualification, equal. It seems counterproductive to settle for anything less. If contemporary feminism is not on board with the contemporary woman, then maybe the movement, not the people the movement was intended to help, should just step aside.

Feminism, however, even in the face of criticism by women, will not "stand down" from her Janus desire for equality qua difference. Like a spoiled child that refuses to reason, she is still screaming at the top of her lungs until she gets her way (whether it is the right way or not).

MASCULISM

Feminism has behaved in a way that has not only drawn attention by women critics but has forced the American male to see *her* as oppressor, enemy, or both.

> Faced with such a feminised culture, men respond in one of two ways. They either behave in the manner demanded, at the very least keeping their heads down in the hope that the inquisitors of this cultural revolution won't notice their backsliding. Alternatively, driven by fear of losing their male identity, they behave in stereotypical ways that proclaim that identity beyond any shadow of a doubt.[77]

With respect to the first attitude, men such as Robert Bly[78] have themselves whined that the world is desperately in need of more male—more time between father and son, more time with each other doing "boy" things, more time in the woods communing with one's wild side, etc. The second attitude, propounded by popular culture such as the Comedy Channel's *The Man Show*[79] and talk radio's *The Opie & Anthony Show*[80] use parody and humor to suggest that women hate everything men like, they whine about everything, they blame men for all the problems in the world, and they are inherently dangerous. As a matter of fact, women's only saving grace is that their bodies are great for sex. These two positions—man the kinder gentler victim of feminism, and man the proud-to-be-a-pig—make up *Masculism.*

"Soft Masculism" is demarcated by its desire to energize men to accentuate and promote their masculinity, not the masculinity of the beer drinking pornography user, but the "healthy" masculinity espoused in classic myths. Bly uses the Grimm brothers' *Fairy Tales* and Jungian psychology to make his point. His most famous use of mythical imagery comes from the Grimm tale *Iron Hans*[81] that he has renamed *Iron John* (thus the title of his best selling book). The story is a classic hero myth in which a nobody boy (who, unbeknownst to anyone, is of royal blood) breaks away from his mother to run off with the "wild man" to find his destiny—to slay all evils, to marry the beautiful princess and ultimately to bring peace and prosperity to the land. The myth is truly classic, that is, it is so much a part of the Western culture that it appears and reappears in many great works of art and literature throughout recorded time. Three hallmark cases of this myth found in contemporary pop culture are in the films *Excalibur*, *Star Wars* and *Matrix.*

Bly's masculism is simple, and, for the most part, unthreatening. Men need more maleness—"there is not enough father."[82] They need, for example, to be provided rites of passage from other men throughout their lifetime in order to become great people. Such rites of passage require, first, the rejection of the mother—the person who overprotects the boy from the harm of physical and psychic wounds, thereby keeping him from growing into a man who is brave and wise.

> Even the best intentioned women cannot give [boys on their quest for manhood] what is needed.... When a father and a son spend long hours together...we could say that a substance almost like food passes from the older body to the younger.... The younger body learns at what frequency the masculine body vibrates.[83]

Therefore, the boy must "steal the key" to the "wild man's" cell that his mother keeps.[84] If a boy ages without becoming a man he will never be any good to himself, other men, his wife, his children or society as a whole. Bly argues that the reason society is in such a bad state—high divorce rates, alcoholism and drug addiction, school violence, etc.—is that boys grow up without enough "man."

Bly does not disparage women nor argue against feminism. Though his "wild man" is both "fierce" and "hairy," the ideal warrior does not use aggression offensively, only defensively[85]—to defend the boundaries of the just and good kingdom (his country, his family, or simply his own psyche). Nonetheless, feminism has responded nastily. First they angrily claim that the men of the men's movement "present themselves as the tragic victims of maternal domination and paternal neglect"[86] and then, ironically, they proceed to attack the movement.

> If Robert Bly's *Iron John* represents the philosophy of the "men's movement," anyone committed to social and ecological justice has reason to be extremely apprehensive. *Iron John* is steeped in hierarchical/militaristic thinking.... This "men's movement" is not about social change. It is a backlash—men clamoring to reestablish the moral authority of patriarchy.[87]
>
> The "men's movement," as epitomized by Bly's writings, while portending/pretending to be a movement for liberation is actually a manifestation of an authoritarian backlash and joins the political and religious right in reinforcing separatism, hierarchy, contempt for the "other," and invidious distinctions between men and women.[88]

Strangely, feminists find this movement, a movement that resembles feminism itself both in message—we are victims, as well as its style—let's do consciousness raising (though without any of the broad-based political consequences) to also be a danger to feminism. "Soft Masculism" is nothing more than a version of collective psychotherapy, men talking to other men about their need for maleness. "The aim is not to be the Wild Man, but to be in touch with the Wild Man."[89]

"Soft Masculism" offers no critique of feminism, no disparaging remarks about women, and asks for no political favors. Nonetheless, feminists find it deceitful and scary. "The hidden message in the men's movement is, in effect, 'we men will retain our superior power, even increase it'."[90]

Harry Brod,[91] like Bly before him, also advocates all-male consciousness-raising. Unlike Bly, however, Brod sees himself more as a feminist than a Masculist.

> He maintains that "fraternity," by which he means a healthy sort of confessional male bonding, precedes equality and liberty. Brod asks feminists not to dismiss such gatherings of men as yet another version of the "old boys' club." Men are not inherently evil or flawed creatures, insists Brod. Rather they and their masculine traits are the distorted products of the same repressive system of patriarchy that has harmed women. Because men can work to effect the *political* changes in society that feminists propose, men can be feminists even though they lack the *personal* experiences women have.[92]

But not all men have been so understanding and forgiving of feminism's "male-bashing" attitude.

Jack Kramer, for example, claims that "'male' is not a four-letter word" and admonishes feminists for being so cavalier with their statistics about, and attitudes toward, men, especially the attitude that their lives are worth less than women's lives and that the roles of husband and/or father should be completely unappreciated. "Just as women started asking why the 'glass ceiling' is all men, we must start asking why the 'glass cellars' are all men."[93] "Kramer predicts that unless women, and especially feminists, start treating men fairly, they will further worsen male/female relationships. Men will eventually rebel and stand up to women, and the confrontation will be far from pleasant."[94]

Actually, the time for rebellion is here, albeit in varying degrees of aggressiveness. Lionel Tiger, for example, attempts to reach men by focusing on the dangers of feminism, warning, as the title of his book *The Decline of Males* attests, feminism is responsible for a drastic and problematic "decline in males."

> A large and increasing number of men are redundant and peripheral. Marx said about the industrial system that people are profoundly alienated from the means of production—jobs. Political and social radicalism was one response to that. If Darwin were alive today, he might comment that men are profoundly alienated from the means of reproduction—women.[95]

Tiger warns men that feminism may seem to only exist in theory with respect to the lives of most men, but, in fact, all men should beware.

Of special concern is the way the law views men as opposed to women during divorce, and especially child custody and support. "Increasingly, feminists began to champion solo motherhood, as both a matter of women's autonomy and a way to raise children without those nasty men around."[96] Tiger warns of a future where the United States will adopt something like the British plan to "demand common child support payments from all divorced fathers, to be redistributed by the government, or the even more demented suggestion in 1998 that divorced fathers be obligated to pay for the opportunity to visit their children."[97]

As masculism began to get "harder," the messages to men began to get more serious and dramatic. First: Beware of women! "In order for a man to survive in the modern world it is imperative that he understand two things: 1) Women do not want what they say they want; 2) Women do not know what they want."[98] "Women are lost in a psychic swamp, throwing words and ideas and pictures at each other trying to arrange all the furniture in their heads to make sense. Without the presence of a genuine male spirituality somewhere around them, they cannot get out of themselves, they cannot quit serving their own egos—and that will never make them happy."[99]

The second part of the "hard" masculism message: "Respect the cock!"[100] "Women are the reproductive unit of the species but men are the creative unit of the species. The human male has a giant brain and a giant penis; they are both a liability and an asset."[101] "The biological and physiological differences between men and women are vast. Hormonal influence is prodigious. A man is made by hormones."[102]

When the two parts of the message are put together you get a psycho-sexual call for men to gather up their manliness in order to overcome personal oppression by women and political oppression by feminism:

> The War of the Sexes is not a political struggle. It is not about jobs or equal pay. It is a confrontation of ethics and values that is being fought on the vast neural plains of our ancient, animal souls. To the victor goes not the money and power—but inner peace. It is time for American men to realize that it's OK to be a man—to think like a man and stink like a man, to dream like a man and cream like a man. It's OK.[103]

It seems that feminism has handled men exactly wrong and in so doing are not only hindering their own ideological movement but making it more difficult for men and women to work together as equals. Feminism's schizophrenic desire to be viewed as victim while, simultaneously, attacking men—depriving them of even the power to love their own bodies and their own masculinity, let alone have any access to their children—has only served to reinforce beliefs that women are weak, irrational and unfit for global citizenship. Neanderthal feminists simply gloat when they point out that:

> Profound as is Susan Faludi's insight—that men fear feminism because they fear the loss of breadwinner role—that loss is only one of a hail of blows raining down on the Masculine Empire...The astronomer Copernicus caused grief when he said that the cosmos does not revolve around the earth. A shift of similar proportions is taking place around men as they lose the centrality of their gender.[104]

With respect to feminism, "Nothing males have done as a self-conscious gender group is remotely comparable, thorough, or effective. Men in groups do not appear to perceive themselves as men in a group. They do not define themselves as members of an assembly with a collective interest."[105] That aside, men and

Masculism are still seen as the enemy by feminism.

Some feminists appear to have realized the damage they were doing to men, or at least, boys. The famous English feminist Fay Weldon, for example, has said that:

> Too many women are out for vengeance on men "for all past gender wrongs and an automatic affirmation of a woman's right to victimhood," driving men to anti-social behavior. Rosalind Coward's view of the world changed after she slowly realised that feminism had nothing to say about the difficulties faced by the men in her family. She now says she is worried about the pressures on her son's generation, "thrashing around in a new world in which they feel demoralised, the second sex" and that women are being "horrendously ungenerous to men." For making such remarks, both women have aroused the ire of feminists who have accused them of betraying the cause. Polly Yound-Eisendrath and Susie Orbach told Rosalind Coward that she had "failed to acknowledge the continuing subordination of women by men."[106]

Unfortunately, this may all be a bit too little, too late.

Due to the radical change in the agenda of the second wave—a change from seeking equality to insisting on difference, feminism has, to a large extent, hurt its own movement. In the first generation, as well as in the first wave of the second generation, the message of feminism was one that anyone could relate to. This new message, however, is too theoretically obscure, too selfishly motivated, and too fundamentally inconsistent to attract anyone other than those indoctrinated with the party line. Feminism, as stated earlier, is suffering a severe image problem, one it may never recover from. In the words of Naomi Wolf, "we must do a better job of separating hating male violence and sexism from hating men."[107]

CHAPTER SIX

THE NEXT GENERATION

So is there hope for feminism in this new, "now" generation—the generation of women who are in college or university right now, perhaps even reading about feminism for the first time? Of course no one is sure, but there are a few ideas being bandied about.

Feminists have certainly come to realize the problems with respect to the theoretical framework of their own ideology.

> The theoretical frameworks they had been using, built on the foundations of universality, sameness and scientific methodology, were becoming increasingly difficult to reconcile with where feminism had led them: to notions of identity, difference, particularity and embodiment.[1]

The first move, which I believe is being made by some members of the old guard, is to simply bite the bullet with respect to their problematic and inconsistent desires for the simultaneous needs of equality and difference.

> The first way in which feminisms have attempted to deal with identity and differences is by simply living with the contradictions they create; that is, straddling the borders which are supposed to differentiate or exclude women from men, black from white, culture from nature or heterosexual from homosexual. Given a theoretical world of dualities constructed from a political world of multiplicities, many feminists disengage from any theoretical framework other than their own. Rather than engaging in an abstract battle to enter one dualistic sphere and leave the other or to transform the value ascribed to one side of the dualism at the expense

> of the other, or even to attempt to deconstruct the dualisms themselves, feminists are increasingly adopting a position of straddling these dualities as they exist and as they live them in particular contexts.[2]

In other words, one of the most obvious and straightforward responses is to simply admit that there is a serious problem.

Secondly, some of the old guard have come to realize that they cannot wantonly destroy all of Western culture and then have anything left from which to bootstrap their own ideas and practices. They have, therefore, albeit reluctantly, come to accept some of the groundings of Western philosophy, politics, etc. No longer arguing for a massive gutting of the culture, feminism, in the light of the above criticisms, is beginning to finally appreciate that the tools of Western culture—e.g., rationality, objectivity, and evidence—are *not themselves inherently evil.*[3]

> The gender quake should show us that it is *only* the master's tools that can dismantle the master's house; he hardly bothers to notice anyone else's. Now that some women have access to some of his tools, the master has yielded to women the instruments that can rearrange and even open up his stronghold. The question for women now is, "Do we dare to escalate our use of them?"[4]

"Rather than scrapping the master's tools, many feminist philosophers are working to transform them so that we may build a moral household that has no head or master."[5] That is, feminists may still want to achieve many of their original goals, e.g., equality, without first destroying all of Western culture in the process.

BACKLASH AND SEPARATION

Many of the old, guard however, have not been nearly as rational of mind or generous of spirit. Some of these Neanderthals have merely done more of the same; that is, they whine and complain about the unfair treatment they are being given by their critics, what is now called by feminists *backlash.*

"Backlash," from men (or women), according to feminism comes from one or both of two familiar emotions—fear and envy. With respect to the first we have Susan Faludi's *Backlash*;[6] with respect to the second, Marilyn French's *The War Against Women*.[7]

Faludi's claim is quite simple. Women in the '90s were unhappy. The press was telling them that their dream of having it all—proverbially bringing home the bacon, frying it up in the pan and then still looking gorgeous and sexy for her man—was turning into an exhausting nightmare. The "modern" woman found herself working forty hours a week and taking work home. If she was married she was too exhausted to do anything more for her family than microwave a frozen dinner. Sex with her husband, well that was simply out of the question. By the time the kids were in bed she was either too tired to want him or too bedraggled for him to want her. The couple would stare blankly at the Tube and watch the news. Divorce skyrocketed.

Worse yet, if the "modern" woman wasn't married, she was told she never would be. Aside from the hyped "man shortage," men all wanted young women who would stay home and watch the rugrats, not thirtysomethings with careers who were making more money than they were. Between frantically hurrying to the top of her profession and dolling up to hunt for men, a woman would hear her mother nagging her about the fact that her biological clock was ticking. Fear of failure induced a malaise that clouded the mind of the American woman in the '90s and, according to Faludi, she (and the men she was either married to or chasing after) had no one else to blame but feminism.

> A backlash against women's rights succeeds to the degree that it appears not to be political, that it appears not to be a struggle at all. It is most powerful when it goes private, when it lodges inside a woman's mind and turns her vision inward, until she imagines the pressure is all in her head, until she begins to enforce the backlash, too—on herself.[8]

Both women and men were calling for a return to a simpler, more traditional time, a time before feminism. Although the "backlash" "could never mold America into the backward-looking, dad-hail-ing, nuclear family fantasy it promoted, it could implant that image in many women's minds and set up a nagging, even tormenting dissonance."[9]

All of this, according to Faludi, is an "overreaction." Men are overreacting because, well, they "get it;" that is, they too have fears about feminism, namely that it is working too well.

> Male policy makers saw the polls indicating huge and rising majorities of women demanding economic equality, reproductive freedom, a real participation in the political process.... Male evangelical leaders saw the huge numbers of "traditional" wives who were ignoring their teachings or heading for the office. All of these men understood the profound force than an American woman's movement could exert if it got half a chance.[10]

Men "get it." Unfortunately, laments Faludi, women don't. Faludi uses *Backlash* to warn women that if they fall for all of this media hype about their "failure," they will actually lose ground—politically, economically, and spiritually—and become even more unhappy in the long run. She tells them that "whatever new myths invented, penalties levied, opportunities rescinded, or degradations imposed, no one can ever take from the American woman the justness of her cause."[11] No matter how tired or scared, she must show no fear and keep up the feminist fight.

Marilyn French, author of *The Women's Room,*[12] published *The War Against Women* in 1992, arguing that, despite appearances to the contrary, men prey on, and are at war with, women. Men envy women—their power, especially their reproductive power.

> Because men mask their intention by omitting women or granting them superficial inclusion, we have to demystify their aims by looking at effects, not rhetoric. It may be objected that effects may be accidental or incidental, or occur without animus. But it cannot be an accident that everywhere on the globe one sex harms the other so massively that one questions the sanity of those waging the campaign: can a species survive when half of it systematically preys on the other?[13]
>
> Men-as-a-caste—elite *and* working-class men—continue

> to seek ways to defeat feminism, by rescinding or gnawing away at its victories (legal abortion), confining women to lower employment (putting a "glass ceiling" over professional women), or founding movements aimed at returning them to fully subordinate status ("fundamentalism"). As kin-group and community controls erode, men everywhere increasingly fail to support the children they engender, and use violence against females—daughters, wives, lovers, mothers, sisters, and strangers. Men are adapting new technologies to old purposes, for example, using amniocentesis to detect a fetus's sex to abort girls or new fertility techniques to create children they claim as their own ("surrogate" motherhood.) These actions amount to a global war against women.[14]

The message is pointed and clear: Men, bad. Women, good. Men are a part of patriarchy; women a part of the underclass whom men systematically discriminate against. In a word, men subjugate women.

According to French, the reasons for this subjugation are varied—e.g., in the public arena to maintain economic or political power, in the personal arena to gain the physical and psychological upper hand. And according to French men wage these public and personal wars[15] against women because of feelings of inadequacy, because they are "lacking a center,"[16] a center one can only achieve by being pregnant, by giving birth, by raising children; in a word, by being a woman. "It will quickly become apparent that the drive to control female reproduction is a silent agenda in every level of male activity."[17]

> I intend to show in this book that: girls are not silenced or ignored in the classroom, medicine has not neglected women's health, abuse by men is not the leading cause of injury to American women, the courts do not treat violence toward women more leniently than violence toward men, gender disparities in pay and job status are not merely a consequence of sex discrimination, the eighties were not a "backlash decade" but a time of steady progress for women and, generally, of strong support for women's advancement. In other words, the climate of our country is not one of "cultural misogyny."[18]

The upshot of "backlash" is that even today there are feminists who insist that men and women maintain separate spheres, or at least that there are venues where male presence is viewed as, at best, unnecessary; at worst, hazardous to the women involved. I have witnessed for myself feminist conferences where the men in the audience have been asked to leave. Therefore, despite the feminist lip service toward equality and the fact that feminists would make a huge stink if the tables were turned and they were told to leave, separatist mentality is a brute fact of the second wave.

Some feminists even go so far as to argue straighforwardly for separation (at least in certain venues).

> There are good reasons why men should be excluded from working in feminist organizations of diverse kinds.... My argument for feminist separation in such organizations stems from my experience of the reality of gender inequality in dominant regimes of meaning and in women's experiences of sexuality.[19]
>
> First, as a feminist activist I was confronted with the obviously illegitimate reasons men actually gave for wanting to be involved in anti-sexual violence work and in their objecting to their exclusion from certain spheres (such as answering the help-line.) ...They want to "meet women," they want to "teach" women callers that not all men are bad, or they want to "help" women "become more assertive and stop being victims."[20]

Of course the "meeting" of women in such circumstances is illegitimate, but it is not so clear that the "men are not all bad" lesson is out of line. Certainly the advice that women should become "more assertive and stop being victims" is not only *not* irresponsible, it is probably right on the mark.

But the most damning response to the above is simply to point out, again, that if women were told they could not work on a man-help hot-line, they would immediately scream discrimination. And certainly feminists would encourage men to see that they are not "all bad," let alone attempt to convince men that they are responsible for the state of the world in which they are now pleading for help. This distasteful double standard aside, in the long run it is not clear that any kind of job discrimination is in the best interest of feminists or the women they supposedly serve.

SLUTS, WARRIORS, GIRLIE GIRLS, BITCHES AND CUNTS

Similar in spirit to the old gals is the X-generation's version of feminism as a victim of male backlash via the construct of a *slut*. The "slut" is usually a teenage girl who is believed by her peers to be sexually permissive. "Slut" commentary sees the problem of sexism as one of backlash by men but with the new twist of being caused by not having enough sexual equality, i.e., *the same sexual freedom to be promiscuous as men*. "Slut-bashing shows us that sexism is still alive and that as boys and girls grow up, different sexual expectations and identities are applied to them...it is evidence of a sexual double standard that should have been eliminated decades ago..."[21]

The argument is that the construct of "slut" is evidence of continued sexism—patriarchal oppression of women; for it represents a supposed "double standard" that, it is implied, has far reaching and disabling consequences for women. Whether a girl is sexually permissive or not, if she is called a "slut" she is branded for life.

> Teens today are fairly conservative about sex. 53 percent of girls believe that sex before marriage is "always wrong," while 41 percent of boys agree.... Despite the sexual revolution, despite three decades of feminism, despite the Pill, and despite legalized abortion, teenage girls today continue to be defined by their sexuality."[22]

Feminism, of course, is the cure for "the feminist understanding is that no girl deserves to be a slut."[23]

The fact aside that this is one of the weakest claims for the disadvantaging of women, let us examine the above position. First, guys are called "sluts," too. O.K., maybe the term "dogs" or some other term is used more often, but the point is the same. There is a level of promiscuity—where sex becomes the main concern of one's life, and/or when one's sexual activities cause considerable harm to a considerable number of people—where society will begin to shun this activity. To function, society simply cannot sanction such behavior, not in women, and not in men.[24]

More importantly, however, is the fact that by the "slut's" own admission, girls and women, not boys and men, are more sensitive to high levels of promiscuity in others. Even if it were true that "girls today are defined by their sexuality," the labeling seems to be a product primarily of girls and women themselves. Anecdotally, when I was a teenager, it was the girls who did *not* want to have sex who liberally used the label. Thinking about this now, maybe the point of this was an attempt to keep the other girls from "buying" all the boys; that is, to ensure that there were some left sexually chaste, or at least unbonded, for their own "purchase" when they were ready.

Most interestingly, however, is the fact that the cure for "slut" backlash is to view men and women equally. "There is simply no legitimate reason why girls and women should be judged and treated differently than boys and men."[25] Whether this means a revival of the sexual revolutions of the '20s and '60s (more "free" sex for women) or a neo-revolution to a more repressed era (less "free" sex for men) is unclear. What is clear, however, is that this new generation of feminists seems to be, once again, more interested in equality than difference.

In keeping with the new trend of returning to the desire for equality, Gen-X feminists have taken a page from the philosopher Plato. In *The Republic*, Plato talks at length about the fact that human beings—both men and women—have souls that are divided into three parts. This trinity of personhood—the passions, e.g., sexual desire, the spirit, e.g. the need to be courageous and honorable, and finally one's rationality (which guides and balances the other two)—is a recurring theme throughout Western thought. One sees this metaphor for full humanity at work, for example, in the *Wizard of Oz* where the Scarecrow's desire for a brain, the Tin Man's desire for a heart, and the Lion's desire for courage represent the overall human need for personal fulfillment via all three elements.[26] The same theme shows itself in the *Star Trek* series[27] where Spock, Bones and Kirk make up the essence of the crew.

The latest trend with the X-generation is the desire for equality with men that is, in fact, consistent with this metaphor. On the one hand you have women putting their desire for courage and honor above their femininity, being, that is, very manly. Such "warrior women" will be discussed in the final chapter. For now it is important to note that many Gen-X women are wearing very short skirts, lots of pink, and piercing, painting and primping their bodies in every conceivable way. In other words, today's proto-feminist is flaunting her sexuality in a way that, at least traditionally, has been associated with a pre-feminist, non-feminist, and maybe even "dissident" feminist attitude.

These Girlie feminists believe that strength and power come, not from being *like men*, but from being liked *by* men, whether one feels like returning the sentiment or not. The power "girlies" are interested in not the power to fight or rule men in general, but the power to fight and rule specific men: "We love the strength and power over men we derive from our tits."[28]

Girlie seems to have originated with women who still believe that feminism has much to offer women, but that the women representing feminism—the old gals and Neanderthals—are out of touch with the contemporary women. The gap between old and new guard feminism is a combination of confusion about just what feminism is (or should be), as well as a lack of appreciation for the way young women perceive the present culture of their femininity, especially their sexuality and their relationships to men.

> Part of the problem stems from our generation's ignorance or confusion about what feminism is and has been. Some of it stems from the fact that the hubs of feminism—the groups and sub-groups that are active and visible—aren't really connected to one another. For instance, young, culturally driven Girlie feminists share few strategies with the old-school Second Wavers—and vise versa.[29]

These Girlies (who range in age from mid-twenties to mid-forties), although still committed to feminism in spirit, claim they are no longer committed to its letter. They believe that they have grown apart from the second wave and are ready to start their own movement, a movement filled as much with being at dinner parties as in revolutions. "In reality, feminism wants you to be whoever you are—but with a political consciousness. And vice versa: you want to be a feminist because you want to be exactly who you are."[30] For Girlies, the claim is: Anyone who "calls her-or-himself a feminist,"[31] is.

Girlies try to reach a balance between the far right's idea of feminism—"women who encourage other women to leave their husbands, kill their children, practice witchcraft, become lesbians, and destroy capitalism;"[32] and the ideology of the far left—"women who believe that all sex is rape, all men are evil, you have to be a lesbian, you can't wear girlie clothes or makeup, being married is lame, etc."[33] Girlies attempt to combine second wave feminism with popular girl culture—the "embracing of pink things"…"We, and others, call this intersection of culture and feminism 'Girlie.'"[34] Girlie, at least at first blush, seems to be, like Goldilock's porridge, "just right" for today's women.

Much like all daughters, however, when they gain a little power, Girlie uses a no-holds-barred approach to their "rebellious" attack on their mother's generation of feminism. Interestingly, especially prone to such criticism is the feminist icon Gloria Steinem and her *Ms. Magazine* on which many of these prolific Girlies cut their feminist teeth.

> As resilient and unique as *Ms.* was, it could never be all things to all feminists—or even come close…Twenty-five years hasn't helped *Ms.*'s reputation with feminist thinkers much…I try to read *Ms.*, but it drives me crazy. There's something reductive about the way they analyze and frame their politics—it seems committed to really out-dated notions of *power* and *equality*.[35]

"Women's relationship to *Ms.* echoes that of women's relationship to feminism. In freeing themselves from the patriarchy, women became at least a little dependent on "feminism" to take care of them."[36] Now, says Girlie, it's time to "do feminism differently from one's mother."[37]

> The feminist prescription to girls is to say that looks shouldn't matter (but do), to your own unique and miraculous bodies, to nurture your self-esteem and the rest will follow. Let's face the facts: girls do care about their looks, and shouldn't be made to feel guilty about that in the context of a feminist movement.[38]

Unfortunately for feminism, Girlie does not seem to have caught fire with today's women. Young women between the age of 18 and 25 are much more like the student with whose quote I began this text. That is, they are simply uninterested in feminism.

Girlies, however, are not ready to give up the ghost. As with their second wave predecessors, Girlies believe that "stalling" in the movement is due to a "lack of consciousness,"[39] albeit a slightly different, more "girlie" consciousness. I however do not think the problem is with the audience but with the message itself. That is, Girlie may have dressed feminism up in something pink and frilly but, alas, she really has nowhere to go. "Girlie is not a rallying point.... With the old feminists, they had something to work toward, like the ERA with all of its problems.... Without a body of politics, the nail polish is really going to waste."[40]

Girlie states that "in the most basic sense, feminism is exactly what the dictionary says it is: the movement for social, political, and economic equality of men and women,"[41] but in actuality, like their second wave mothers, this is not their true desire. The message of Girlie may be disguised in a rhetoric of returning to the first generation or even the first wave of the second generation, but underneath all that "girlie" makeup, the wrinkles created by the second wave exist with a vengeance.

First and foremost, like all "second wave" feminists, Girlie cannot handle criticism. The book *The Morning After: Sex, Fear, and Feminism on Campus*[42] by Katie Rophie, which criticizes the "Take Back the Night" marches and other political activities organized by feminists ostensibly on behalf of young college women as being driven by an unjustified fear, is treated without the respect and consideration it deserves. Girlies call it "annoying, even insulting—as if the entire feminist movement could be discredited because of one woman's experiences at Harvard or

Princeton."[43] And the problem is not merely one of sensitivity. Rather, it is inherent in the quasi-theoretical, and fully political, commitments of feminism, which Girlie, protestations aside, embraces wholeheartedly.

If one, for example, claims that a certain statistic is false, let us say the infamous MacKinnon claim that "one of every four women will be raped" statistic, no matter what evidence is offered to demonstrate this, it will not be enough. More problematically, the counter evidence will not even be taken seriously. According to feminism, all such evidence is based on a certain form of data collecting that has its origins, at some point, with classical mathematics, science and philosophy; that is, in a word "infected" with patriarchy. As such, the evidence will always be male-biased[44] and therefore can never be fully objective. Finally, even if the collecting of data against some specific feminist belief could be "objective" or "true," neither of these epistemological virtues is valued by the second wave. As shown above, such desires are, albeit at another level of inquiry, just more evidence of sexism. The point is that feminism has made it so that all critique is seen as yet more evidence of oppression, thereby making it un-P.C., and therefore nearly impossible (even for women!), to challenge feminist claims, no matter how false or unfalsifiable. They have, it seems, made feminism into a form of Fundamentalism—that is, inherently immune to any kind of criticism.

Even more like their mothers, Girlies are fundamentally against the political "right," even if its platform is being supported by women such as Christina Hoff-Sommers. However, instead of responding to Sommers head on, Girlies follow their mother's tactics and resort to name calling. Sommers, they claim, is a "conservative-kissing woman"[45] whom, it is implied, only wrote *The War Against Boys* because she received a large amount of "right-wing" grant money and an advance from Simon & Schuster.[46] There is no other way to see this than as a ridiculous and immature way to respond to any scholar. It need not be dignified further.

In the desire to establish "clear political goals"[47] such as the first generation goal of suffrage and first wave goal of ratifying the ERA, Girlies believe they need a declaration of their sentiments: a "manifesta" so to speak. Girlies, unfortunately, again follow almost exactly in their second wave mothers' footsteps. Therefore, despite all of their claims that Girlie is not your mother's feminism, nothing really new is going on. Here are some excerpts:

> 1. To *out* unacknowledged feminists, specifically those who are younger, so that Generation X can become a visible movement and, further, a voting block of eighteen-to-forty-year-olds.
>
> 2. To safeguard a woman's right to bear or not to bear a child, *regardless of circumstances*, including women who are younger than eighteen or impoverished...
>
> 3. To make explicit that the fight for reproductive rights must include *birth control*; the right for poor women and *lesbians* to have children...
>
> 4. To bring down the *double standard* in sex and sexual health, and foster *male responsibility*...
>
> 5. To tap into and *raise awareness* of our revolutionary history...to have women's history taught to men as well as women as a part of *all curricula*.
>
> 6. To support and increase the visibility and power of *lesbians and bisexual women* in the feminist movement...
>
> 7. To practice *activism*...
>
> 8. To have *equal* access to health care, regardless of income, which includes coverage *equivalent to men's* and keeping in mind that *women use the system more often than men do* because of our reproductive capacity.
>
> 9. For women who so desire to participate in all reaches of the military...The largest expenditure of our national budget goes toward maintaining this *welfare system*, and feminists have a duty to make sure *women have access to every echelon*.
>
> 10. To liberate adolescents from *slut-bashing*...
>
> 11. To make the workplace responsive to an individual's wants, needs and talents. This includes *valuing (monetarily) stay-at-home parents*...
>
> 12. To acknowledge that, although feminists may have disparate values, we share the same *goal of equality*...
>
> 13. To pass the *ERA*...[48]

Alas, it seems that when Girlies stop primping and settle into the business of feminism, mother knows best.

Of course, not all Girlies are so conventional. Some are a bit more radical and their claims a bit more interesting. For fringe Girlies the call for liberation is not so much a reworking of feminism, but a reworking of how to respond to men. They answer, selfishly and aggressively, "It's time that we, the grand dames of the New Girlie Order, defy the backlash with a proverbial middle finger…enjoy being the girl with the most cake and ask: 'Can I have some more?'"[49]

Girlie is certainly not for everyone and some Gen-X feminists (even some Girlies) have taken a much more selfish and aggressive approach. One new approach to feminism is to act politically by admiring, valorizing, and ultimately emulating the classic *bitch*—focusing her sexual, political and economic power on being "a difficult dame," especially to men. The other, even more radical approach to feminism is to simply pride oneself on the basic ignoring, if not downright hating, of men—to associate only with women, to use only women's products, and to gain power and money for oneself at all costs, even at the cost of being seen as a *cunt*.

The "bitch" is not fundamentally meanspirited, just difficult; that is, she is difficult toward men, difficult "to handle." "I cheer the bitch because she has broken the chain and made a mess of some poor fellow's life."[50]

However, the "bitch" recognizes that most of the ways in which women think, act, dress, talk, and just generally behave "like a lady" have been conditioned by society (which, for all feminists, is fundamentally male-biased). The first move on the "bitch's" political agenda is a simple reminder: "Let us not deny that this is a form of enslavement meant to please men, not women."[51]

Nonetheless, the "bitch" does not embody feminism by simply behaving in a way that is "unladylike," for any feminist can do this. Instead, one must be unladylike in a way that is ultimately appealing to men, at least from the smoky end of a bar.

> The world simply does not care for the complicated girls, the ones who seem too dark, too deep, too vibrant, too opin-

> ionated, the ones who are so intriguing that new men fall in love with them every day...But most men in the end don't quite have the stomach for that much person.[52]

Unlike old-time feminists she wants to intrigue and attract men, but unlike her Girlie sisters she wants to do this like a woman—in a floor length sequined gown, not a pink party dress. Her model is the sexy and bawdy Mae West, not the "go-go" girl Belinda Carlyle.

The "bitch" feminists, however, can get mean. On one end of the spectrum a "bitch" can merely verbally brutalize a man and wreak havoc with heartstrings; at the other end, she can literally string him up or brutally cut him off.

> The bitch as a role model, as icon and idea, has moments of style and occasions of substance—it at times looks like the latest mask, a game to play, a chance to dress like something out of a Joan Crawford movie, and to act like something out of *Mommie Dearest*; but quite often it reveals itself to be about general anger, disturbance, fear and the kind of fierce resentment and rage the likes of Jean Harris,[53] and Lorenna Bobbit[54]...[55]

Finally, feminist nastiness is best expressed in the book entitled *Cunt*.[56] Although the "cunt" is similar to second wave feminists in a number of ways, there are some important differences. For one thing the "cunt" boldly admits that she values money, something that is usually associated with women who are right-wing "dissidents" such as Paglia and Sommers. That is, a "cunt" feminist does not hold women to the Marxist/socialist standards inherent in much of feminism. The "cunt" can proclaim: "I love money. I love money so much I can hardly contain my passion for it. Money rules."[57] More problematically, the "cunt" can boldly value man haters, even man shooters, and man killers. "I like Valerie Solanas because she represents an extreme hatred of men."[58] "Lady predators are cuntlovin' imaginative women."[59]

And the similarities to the "second wave" outweigh the differences. The familiar feminist refrain that all men are part of oppressive patriarchy is an important part of the "cunt" philosophy.

"Unless stated, throughout this book the words 'gentlemen', 'man' and the like are used to refer to the tightly knit, male social power structure as it is reorganized in American patriarchal society."[60]

In addition, however, much of "cunt" philosophy is soft and fuzzy. Take, for example, "cunt's" desire for sisterhood: "One of *Cunt's* aspirations is to contribute to a language and philosophy specifically designed to empower and unite *all women*."[61] And its agenda is clearly defined and well focused on activism for women, at least other "cuntlovin'" women. "Cunts" and "cuntlovers" qua feminists, then, must behave in certain ways that require one, like a committed vegetarian, to make some serious (and perhaps even difficult and expensive) changes in their lifestyles.

> It sounds *terribly* ideological to say women's power as consumers is a major economic stronghold, but it seems the most promising strategy that does not involve retreat...Cuntlovin' Consumerism is a matter of commitment."[62]

In other words, if the only woman-owned bookstore is twenty-five miles away, one nonetheless, has a duty to do whatever it takes to get there, and only there, when one has books to buy. "Cunts" make demands: "Get CDs and books by women...Go to the theater to see films by women..."[63] To be a "cunt," one cannot merely theorize; one must actively participate in "cuntlovin'."

FEMINISM AS "PAC" AND GLOBALIZATION

The feminist fetishing of difference has factionalized feminism into as many different forms as there are individual women. This has created two entirely different results.

On the one hand, feminism has lost all interest in attempts to coalesce its divergent theoretical standpoints. Instead, feminism, to a large extent, simply focuses on the very specialized needs of very specific groups of women. These feminists "argue that feminist politics must be 'localized'. Feminists must engage at the local rather than the abstract levels, in engaging women from different perspectives in the resistance to different types of power in the specific historical and geographical contexts in which they occur."[64]

This is what I call *political action committee* or "PAC" feminism. There is a sense in which a commitment to some political action or other has been the lifeblood of feminism. First there was suffrage and the *Nineteenth Amendment*, and then NOW and the ERA. Now there really isn't much. The *1998 Declaration of Sentiments of NOW* testifies to the fact that feminism as a movement really has changed, but that it has no real ideas on how to actually bring about change for women. NOW claims that "we still do not have full equality" and envisions a world where "patriarchal culture and male dominance no longer oppress us or our earth." NOW claims to act from "passion, anger, hope, love and perseverance to create a vision of the future," to reaffirm "a commitment to the power of grassroots activism,"[65] but says little about what that future ought to look like for women or how any given feminists ought to bring it about. The letter of the piece gives nothing for women to focus on, and the spirit is clearly not one of *equality with*, but rather *freedom from*, men.

The *Statement of Purpose* proposal which came out of the *NOW National Conference 2000* returns somewhat to its first generation roots, albeit with some second wave terminology.

> NOW's purpose is to take action to bring women into full participation in the mainstream of American society now, exercising all privileges and responsibilities thereof in truly equal partnership with men. This purpose includes, but is not limited to, equal rights and responsibilities in all aspects of citizenship, public service, employment, education, and family life, and it includes freedom from discrimination because of race, ethnic origin, age, marital status, sexual preference/orientation, or parenthood.... The purpose of NOW is to actively and tirelessly pursue the full inclusion of women and girls in all political, social, and economic institutions of society creating a feminist society...[66]

Even if adopted, it is unclear whether it is "equal partnership with men" or the "creating of a feminist society" that is at its core.

This does not mean that there aren't feminists that come

together over one particular movement or other—e.g., abortion rights, worker's rights, ecological goals, specific race rights, etc.—for there are. Reference books[67] and the Internet are filled with sites which allow one access to whatever woman's organization one chooses to support, such as the *Ain't I a Woman? Network/PAC*, the *Latina PAC*, or the *National Abortion and Reproductive Rights Action League (NARAL)*. Although it may be wise to "think and act locally," without one unifying goal, feminism seems to have lost any chance for anything like the sisterhood of the past. Given the fundamental ideological differences betwixt all the different eras and factions of feminism, it seems to have no choice but to break into the very individual PACs it has for decades been trying to avoid if it really wants to get anything actually done.

There does seem to be one exception to this rule: *globalization*. The newest and hottest trend in feminism is to attempt to bring women together on the issue of, well, simply bringing everyone together. There are, however, two major snags with this attempt at a revitalization of feminism.

The first is simply theoretical. Insofar as feminism is interested in some kind of global egalitarianism—where there is complete and total social and economic justice, where all people have the food, housing, clothing, health care and education they need, where all "human beings are born free, equal in dignity and rights, entitling each to all rights and freedoms without distinction of any kind"[68]—it is not clear what about this ideology is particularly feminist. If this is truly for everyone, "without distinction of any kind," in what sense is this feminism? Global egalitarianism, whether one supports it or not, is simply not compatible with feminism. No matter how one defines it, "feminism" must at least have something to do with the empowerment of women. When the focus on women disappears, it is just not clear what is left that is particularly feminist.

The second problem, however, is much more convoluted and difficult. In the same way that feminism began to deconstruct "male" desires for justice, equality, etc., non-white, non-American, non-middle-class women from minority populations at home or in the third world have begun to deconstruct the supposed universal and global desires for *equal* "dignity," "rights," and "freedoms."

Feminism calls such constructs "male;" minority and third world women call them simply *feminist*. Ironically, while women in the United States can often agree on the need to work toward fighting poverty and oppression throughout the world, women from all over the world now fight feminism.

The criticisms of today's feminists come from two camps: minority women from within the United States and oppressed women from developing countries in the Third World. The message from both is complicated. On the one hand, the complaint is that feminism is too theoretical and convoluted. Feminism is perceived simply as the invention of a new hegemony, that of white Western intellectual bourgeoisie who can easily be seen in the second wave's focus on fettering out male bias in the most esoteric and obscure texts.[69] Such activities seem meaningless and distant to women whose immediate needs include survival and political and religious freedom. Until minority and third world women have equal opportunities and equal power with women from the West, feminism is a shameless disguise for still more oppression. Ironically, another complaint is that feminism is not sensitive enough to the many differences of minority and third world women.

Today, in order to be worthy of feminist attention—in the classroom, at conferences, and in print—one must be a "Black Feminist," "Chicana Feminist," or "Hispana Feminist."

Black feminism has roots that go back to the beginnings of feminism. For example, Harriet Tubman escaped from slavery and began the "Underground Railroad" in 1849, and former slave Sojourner Truth delivered her "Ain't I a Woman?" speech which brought to the fore interesting questions about just what it is that makes a woman—both in the eyes of men and in the eyes of other women.

> Well, Children, where there is so much racket there must be something out of kilter. I think that 'twixt the negroes of the South and the women at the North, all talking about rights, the white men will be in a fix pretty soon. But what's all this here talking about?
>
> That man over there says that women need to be helped

> into carriages, and lifted over ditches, and to have the best place everywhere. Nobody ever helps me into carrriages, or over mud-puddles, or gives me any best place! And ain't I a woman? Look at me! Look at my arm! I have ploughed and planted, and gathered into barns, and no man could head me! And ain't I a woman? I could work as much and eat as much as a man—when I could get it—and bear the lash as well! And ain't I a woman? I have borne thirteen children, and seen most all sold off to slavery, and when I cried out with my mother's grief, none but Jesus heard me! And ain't I a woman?[70]

Also making a first generation impact was Harriet Beecher Stowe who published *Uncle Tom's Cabin* in 1852. Dr. Pauli Murray co-authored the *1966 NOW Statement of Purpose*, and helped form the first wave of the second generation. But it was not until the end of the second wave of the second generation of feminism, more than a hundred and fifty years later, that the question about a "particular versus universal definition of 'woman'"[71] is seriously challenged. Such differences, after decades of feminist organizing among black women, made it safe to say "that we have movement of our own."[72]

This however was not entirely true. White middle-class feminists already rooted in the academy, not black feminists or other minority representatives, were the first to recognize this whole new area of oppression ripe for theorizing. This virgin area of research became the next great expansion for the cottage industry that was academic feminism, and no race or oppressed group was ignored. White middle-class women filled the new scholarly void—with conferences, journal articles, books, etc.—at a fever pitch. Resentments flared.

> Feminist theory—of all kinds—is to be based on, or anyway touch base with, the variety of real life stories women provide about themselves. But in fact, because, among other things, of the structural, political, and social and economic inequalities among women, the tail has been wagging the dog: feminist theory has not for the most part arisen out of a medley of women's voices; instead, the theory has arisen out of the

> voices, the experience, of a fairly small handful of women, and if other women's voices do not sing in harmony with their theory, they aren't counted as women's voices—rather, they are the voices of the woman as Hispana, Black, Jew, etc. There is another sense in which the tail is wagging the dog, too: it is presumed to be the case that those who do the theory know more about those who are theorized than vice versa: hence it ought to be the case that if it is white/Anglo women who write for and about all other women, then white/Anglo women must know more about all other women than other women know about them. But in fact just in order to survive, brown and Black women have to know a lot more about white/Anglo women—not through the sustained contemplation theory requires, but through the sharp observation stark exigency demands...the complaint is one of exclusion, of silencing, of being included in a universe we have not chosen.[73]

The multitude of newly found oppressed classes of women wanted the feminist hegemony to know that "we and you do not talk the same language...you are not of our world...[and that] none of the feminist theories developed so far seem to me to help in the articulation of our experience."[74]

Of course, feminists responded. They responded by "inclusion"—e.g., writing joint articles with Black or Hispanic women—and, interestingly, they responded by "exclusion"—e.g., by beginning a talk at a conference prefacing every word with "from my privileged white middle-class position." Whether they were patronizingly apologetic or sickeningly self-deprecating feminists were doing what they do best—generating more and more feminism.

And the minority woman was only the tip of the iceberg. To be truly victimized today, one must be a woman from at least a Communist run country, such as China, if not from one of the very poor or developing nations such as Africa and India. Interestingly, although it is once again the white middle-class women of the American academy that gave birth to the ideology of the Global feminist, the delivery has not been an easy one. Once the minority or third world woman actually gains consciousness—that is, once the theories were actually read and acknowledged by the oppressed women being discussed—she immediately turned around and attempted to devour her feminist mother. For example, some Native American women claim that "Gendered identity standpoints of the dominant culture become for American Indian women a colonial template dictating what our reality is supposed to be; it is stamped on us by both a colonial language and ontology."[75] Feminism, claim such women, is nothing less than racism. Feminism talks a good game *about* minority and underprivileged women but does nothing actually *for* them. Worse, feminism has actually become the oppressor; the epitome of the "Ugly American."[76]

> Initially when feminist leaders in the United States proclaimed the need for gender equality here they did not seek to find out if corresponding movements were taking place among women around the world. Instead they declared themselves liberated and therefore in the position to liberate their less fortunate sisters, especially those in the "third world." This neocolonial paternalism had already been enacted to keep women of color in the background so that only conservative/liberal white women would be the authentic representatives of feminism.[77]

Though women from minority groups and developing countries were screaming for a feminism of their own, much of the second wave rhetoric was again rehashed. "Hegemonic power feminists" replaced "men" as the oppressor, and the overall problem remained "supremacist capitalist patriarchy." More uncanny, while the second wave claimed that it was men who were hiding their sexism behind the construct of equality, minority and third world women were claiming that feminists were pulling the same oppressive stunts.

> In truth their hegemonic takeover of feminist rhetoric about equality has helped mask their allegiance to the ruling classes within white supremacist patriarchy.... While feminists in the United States were right to call attention to the need for global equality for women, problems arose as those individual feminists with class power projected imperialist fantasies

> onto women globally, the major fantasy being that women in the United States have more rights than any group of women globally, are "free" if they want to be, and therefore have the right to lead feminist movements and set feminist agendas for all the other women in the world, particularly women in third world countries. Such thinking merely mirrors the imperialist racism and sexism of ruling groups of Western men.[78]

So what is it that minority and oppressed feminists want? Like their "second wave" (older, richer, whiter) sisters, they seem to want equality and difference simultaneously. They want, for example, power feminists from the United States to help them with their "freedoms," but they want the construct of freedom to be understood "concretely" and "culturally," not from the perspective of the women who are in fact in power. They want power feminists to "reach out and join global struggles to end sexism, sexist exploitation, and oppression,"[79] to "share common oppression and fight equally to end oppression";[80] but not through the development of any universal values.[81] They want to increase their own wealth and power but not by supporting capitalism.[82]

Nonetheless, "a feminist-inspired global commitment to equal rights for women has been gathering force over the past twenty years and some of the strongest instruments of change have been the global women's conventions,"[83] such as the *United Nations Conventions on the Elimination of All Forms of Discrimination Against Women* (CEDAW) 1981, where supporters came up with a sixteen-article *Declaration of Human Rights.*[84] Still problematic, however, is the fact that the articles of the Declaration that are truly feminist (e.g., Article 4 which calls for the adoption of special measures "aimed at accelerating de facto equality between men and women," Article 6 states "Parties shall take all appropriate measures, including legislation, to suppress all forms of traffic in women and exploitation of prostitution of women," and Article 11, number 1, part d which says "to provide special protection to women during pregnancy in types of work proved to be harmful") seem to be fundamentally sexist, while those that are not biased to women have little meat that is particularly feminist (e.g.,

Article 5 which shall in all fields "guarantee women the exercise and enjoyment of human rights and fundamental freedoms on a basis of equality with men.")

It may be that aside from simply attempting to achieve parity with men, feminism can have no other meaningful agenda. Furthermore, once the first generation and first wave second generation goals of equal opportunity, benefits, etc. are achieved, feminism has the choice of either abandoning its political motivation—the empowerment of women—for either a more gender neutral global egalitarianism; or abandoning the desire for equality itself, allowing the purely political goals of *difference from men* and *privilege for women* to show themselves as forthrightly sexist.[85]

Chapter Seven

IS FEMINISM DEAD?

Recently, a colleague gave a talk entitled "Feminism—The Dead Horse Who's Still Alive and Kicking."[1] When I asked why she chose such a title, she pointed to the *Time* magazine question: "Is Feminism Dead?" When I asked her what was still "kicking," she said "feminism as humanitarianism." With respect to the political goal of empowering women, this, as stated above, is inherently problematic. If one is interested in a global humanism, then the needs of men as well as women must be part of the program.

PAC feminism, however, takes the reverse position: it may be committed to specific acts of empowerment, but it is unlikely to form anything like a political coalition that can continue under the rubric of feminism. In other words, neither move is able to maintain a simultaneous commitment to feminism both in theory and practice.

On the other hand, none of the funky Gen-X forms of feminism—"sluts," "girlies," "bitches," "cunts," "globals," etc.—are really that distinct from the "second wave" radicals that have dominated feminism since the seventies. All believe that all men are a part of an oppressive patriarchy and that some form or other of feminism—with its inherent commitment to gender identity—is the answer to solving their problems.

Although "sluts" correctly assume that feminism is infused with notions of gender, they misguidedly believe that it is committed to equality. For the "slut," the problem is a Victorian idea of sex and sexuality that is essentially oppressive. Boys and men, it seems, get to be sexually promiscuous without consequence, while girls and women do not. The upshot for the latter is: the label "Slut!" Feminist "sluts" believe they can save the day by using theoretical and political power to ensure equality between boys and men, girls and women. Whether the goal is to enable women to become more sexually permissive without suffering the slings and arrows of outrageous language, or to disable men (and insist that their promiscuous behavior is also so labeled) is unclear. What is clear is that second wave feminism's desire for difference, not equality, will prove to be unhelpful. The "slut" will have to quench her desire for equality in a return to more "first generation," or first wave second generation, ideals.

"Girlies," "bitches" and "cunts," though, are more interested in power than equality. All three insist that being a woman makes one fundamentally different from a man. Equality, then, is simply not a goal. Of course, there is no need to accept oppression either. Therefore, it seems, the only reasonable goal is power.

Although these women are *committed to difference* more than equality, such women are, nonetheless, not totally in bed with the second wave. There is, in fact, more honesty and forthrightness underlying the feminism of this "next" generation. Feminists have always wanted power; but the second wave, believing they were simply entitled to more than their fair share, asked for power. As such, although their agendas are consistent, the means to their ends is not.

Some old gals even concede their old guard positions to the methods of this "next" generation.

> Whatever feminism is to you, to me it is at heart the logical extension of democracy. Power feminism's use of realpolitik and capitalism for the next stage of women's empowerment is not selfish, not "selling out," not imitating men, not accommodation to a less radical position. "Radical" comes from the Latin word for "root." Nothing is more radical than going to the roots of power.[2]

Of course, while the old gals pretended that they were interested in power for all women (something that was never true[3]), the "next" generation makes no such political nicey-nice with nonfeminists.

Unlike the feminism of old, Gen-X feminists neither whine

to men about their abused state, nor apologize for their one-sided political agendas. They do not pretend they are out for anyone but themselves. They proudly use whatever they have to get whatever they want.

Given, however, the above forms' fundamental commitment to no one but themselves, it is not surprising that what has come to be known as the "next generation" of feminism is not actually attractive to the "next" generation of young women feminism needs to recruit.

WARRIOR WOMEN

Not surprising is the fact that the "warrior" stands alone in her desire to create a generation of women with the kind of dignity and justice that comes from knowing that you competed *equally* for the powers and privileges of life. As such, the "warrior" is most closely aligned to the first generation and first wave second generation feminist. Her desire for equality—the opportunity to (and I say this without apology) work, fight, kill, struggle, and die *like a man*—is theoretically uncomplicated and motivated by neither political ideology nor personal gain. It is simply about being a person, a person struggling with all other persons to be the best she can be; to be the most excellent human being she can. No wonder today's noble and courageous young women, as depicted and exemplified in their combat style of dress, their choice of aggressive and energetic music and their love for women heroes (past and present; mythical and real)—find the "warrior's" message so attractive.

Oddly, feminism has not only ignored the "warrior," she has banished her. Unlike the days of old, today there is little similarity between even the most state-of-the-art feminist theorizing (let alone praxis), and the noble "warrior" woman that started it all.

However, long before the dawn of feminism there were women who behaved, in one way or other, like men. These women whom history provides as examples of behaving like extraordinary men, when men are behaving at their best, become heroes in their own right. Long before feminism there were women who were great poets/philosophers (e.g., Sapho), warriors (e.g., Joan of Arc), saints (e.g., Teresa), patrons of the arts (e.g., Catherine De Medici), rulers (e.g., Elizabeth I), and scientists (e.g., Marie Curie). Such women never thought of themselves as feminists, but rather, simply, as great relative to their respective fields. Nonetheless, such models have been appropriated by feminism as examples of pre-feminist-history feminists. One woman who valorizes the warrior model writes: "This book is dedicated to the old woman with the scar across her face who said: 'Never call me a victim': she made her point."[4]

Warrior women are easy to spot. Like their male counterparts, they are more committed to honor, duty, and dignity than they are to anything else, let alone their femininity or sexuality. As a matter of fact, again like their male counterparts, these women are not focused on "self" at all. Valor and altruism are added to the list of the above big Greek virtues (virtues that are represented over and over again through the ages as essential to excellence in humanity but are gendered "male" by feminists), and are viewed by these women without any consideration of gender whatsoever. As such, the warrior women, having given up commitments to gender, are indeed a different kind of feminist.

Of course this hybrid feminism is highly problematic. Not only have these women opted for a return to a notion of equality, but they have done so under what is considered by feminism to be a "male" ideal of human excellence. However, warrior women are not interested in the feminist-imposed distinction of gender at all, let alone committing themselves to a form of "gender norming" in order to achieve greatness. They are interested in greatness itself. More importantly, such women are not interested in deconstructing or reconstructing the notion of greatness in order to achieve a *different kind of greatness*, i.e., a woman's greatness. Greatness, they believe, means being the best.

The best warrior, for example, would simply be the best—male or female. Joan of Arc was such a warrior, the mythical Xena is such a warrior and Sigourney Weaver's character "Riply" (as well as the character "Vasquez") in *Aliens II* are such warriors. No whining, no crying, no special treatment, no fuss. Their power qua woman is simply an extension of their power qua warrior (in the same way "Maximus'" power as a man is translated into his greatness as a gladiator.) Hand these women a sword or a gun and they will fight...like men.

Real-life warrior women have existed as well. A "gallery of women at arms"[5] includes Queen Boadicea who battled the Roman forces trying to take over the parts of East Anglia now known as Norfolk and Suffolk in 60 A.D.; Agnes Dunbar, the granddaughter of Scottish King Robert the Bruce was left to hold one of the few forts still under Scottish control in 1337; Christina Cavanaugh, who took up arms against the French in Holland in 1693 by disguising herself as a man—a disguise that held up until she was wounded in battle; Charlotte Walpole (the "Scarlet Pimpernel"), who dressed up as a male soldier and risked her life daily trying to rescue Marie Antoinette and her son from the French secret police; Dorothy Lawrence, who disguised herself as a man and set off for the Western Front during WWI to become the first woman war journalist; Josephine Baker, who worked for the French Resistance during WWII; and Nancy Wake, who actually led men into battle during WWII.[6]

In addition, within a sophisticated and civil society such as ours, often the pen really is mightier than the sword. As such, "warriors" can be found, though rarely, in the halls of academe as well. The "dissident" feminists such as Paglia and Sommers are academics arguing *against feminism* and yet are putting these arguments into the intellectual arena in order to *empower women*. They are gladiators skilled with words, and they are not interested in competing for education, opportunities, and success by handicapping the other players (i.e., men), nor by crying for special favors on behalf of the weaknesses supposedly inherent in their sex/gender. These "warriors" understand the spirit of teachings of Sun Tsu: that *everything is war*; but by no means believe that they are ill equipped to compete. For these women, their sex/gender is not even an issue, let alone the burden the second wave has turned it into.

Feminism, therefore, in all of its guises, is struggling to stay alive. The main problem is that the first generation and first wave second generation forms have been so distorted by the second wave's desire for a misguided notion of "separate but equal"[7] that there are few women today who believe that feminism has anything to say to them. Women, plain and simple, seem to want nothing more than what men have—the education and opportunities of men, i.e., the simple message of equal opportunity and, of course, equal pay for equal work. This common sense and universal message has been buried deep beneath the "second wave." If feminism is not interested in equality with men, then it becomes a question just why it is that women should be interested in feminism.

Feminism, it appears, needs to reevaluate its desire for equality as difference. Do women really want a world where there is no more patriarchy, or a world in which there is matriarchy?

> In July of 2001, Nicole Ferry was granted $25,000 in settlement for a sexual harassment suit with the University of South Florida. The lawsuit stemmed from a single incident in a class taught by art instructor Diane Elmeer. In September 1999, Elmeer asked graduate assistant and artist Derek Washington to bring in an example of controversial art for a class discussion. Washington, an African-American, brought in a photograph in which he appears to be having sex with a white woman; you can see his bare back and a woman's hands clutching his buttocks. The photograph is titled *Nigger Lover*. Even though everyone had been warned that the images in that day's class could be offensive and one would not be penalized for skipping out, Ferry and about 250 other students chose to attend. Then she, alone, sued.[8]

Apparently, women get to have the privilege of deciding whether to be educated, but without having to take any of the concomitant responsibilities for the hard-edged and often "offensive" cutting-edge messages inherent in any truly free exchange of ideas and expression. Such examples of ostensive "sexual harassment" are one of the many sad consequences of a hysterical feminism that has overstepped its desire for equality and moved into a desire for privilege.

More generally, feminists need to decide if they want what men have—a liberal education (with its concomitant uncomfortable and problematic ideals), political power (and its often highly public lives), job opportunities (which often entail 80-

hour work weeks), full freedoms of citizenship (and the duty to fight in times of danger to defend such freedoms), etc.—or not. If women do not want equality with men—equal responsibility, equal stress, equal risk, equal pain and equal danger—it is unfair and even villainous to ensure that men get punished for wanting such privileges. If, on the other hand, women do want what men have, then they should just admit that and stop claiming some grand conspiracy. By screaming sexism every time a woman does not succeed, feminism is simply perpetuating a myth.

THE MYTH

In Schopenhauer's Essay "On Women," the German philosopher claims that one cannot expect anything more than childish behavior from women, since the history of the world has shown us that "the most distinguished intellects among the whole sex have never managed to produce a single achievement in the fine arts that is really great, genuine, and original; or given to the world any work of permanent value in any sphere."[9] Although he wrote these words over a hundred years ago, the spirit of the claim may still hold merit. That is, even in this new millennium, despite suffrage, the *National Organization of Women*, sexual discrimination laws, and contemporary feminism, for the most part most women in our culture leave the sphere of the home and family on merely a partial or temporary basis, not to seriously even compete for, let alone achieve, anything like global excellence.

The question which looms large before us, then, is: Why? Why is it that almost every little girl I knew when I was a child wanted to be an astronaut, a doctor or rock star; but is now, in fact, a housewife and mother? Why is it that nearly every woman I attended graduate school with dropped out to get married, or if they successfully completed their Ph.D., never went to work in academia? Or if they did get jobs in colleges or universities, retired from their job within five years—before they had to produce any publications or struggle with the politics of tenure? Why is it that of the over 8,000 students I have taught in my life, nearly all of the women have gone on not to pursue even their most modest college dreams, let alone end up competing globally for the kind of excellence attempted by few[10] and achieved by even fewer (e.g., Plato, Picasso and Einstein)?

Could it be because women really are physically, mentally and emotionally so fundamentally different from men that when they compete with men they are doomed by their nature to fail? Although this is a position that is maintained by some scholars even today,[11] I am with Plato who, 2,500 years ago,[12] denounced this form of essentialism. For even if at one time women's physical size and/or reproductive tendencies kept her out of the public sphere and home with the children, those days are long over. In our time, given our society's technology and resources, claiming that any particular woman is physically condemned to avoid competition seems rather vapid. With modern mechanical and computer technology, the global economic market no longer depends on big bodies. Even contemporary warfare is, in a very meaningful sense, virtual.

More importantly, given access to, and the success of, birth control devices—in all their varied forms—I find it hard to believe that a woman's reproductive physicality is any longer a fundamental barrier to her achieving excellence. The bottom line is that it is no longer reasonable to say that women are chained to the house.

However, a house is not a home, and maybe it is the home—a safe, provided-for, non-competitive atmosphere—that the woman is attached to, not via her body, but via her mind. After all, human beings are a complex intermingling of the mental and physical. Maybe the reason that women do not achieve excellence is because, by their nature, they are simply less *mentally* capable of handling the aggressive and competitive "rat race" that is the public sphere. That is, women may no longer be chained by their children to the home, but they are still tied by their minds to the hearth. Women, being mentally weaker—less aggressive and more emotional than men—are, despite technology and The Pill, nonetheless condemned by their nature, albeit their mental nature, to refrain from competing with the truly world class.

Although I find this modern form of essentialism to be compelling, I am loath to give in to it for two reasons. The first is there have been exceptions to the rule. (Of course, such exceptions have come to the fore usually[13] because they either never had children,[14] had someone else raise their children, or achieved greatness after the end of the reproductive stage of their lives.[15]) More importantly, if it is true that women cannot achieve excellence, then with respect to equal education it seems silly for our society to waste the time, resources and energy attempting to prepare women for such achievements. In addition, with respect to equal opportunity, it seems eminently reasonable to avoid choosing women to be doctors, lawyers, or in any way competitors in the global sphere. In the final analysis, if essentialism—physical or mental—is true, and women are, by their very nature, incapable of excellence, then discrimination in education and opportunity is justified.

Enter feminism and its myth making. Given that the acceptance of women's inferiority is totally inconsistent with its political goals, feminism has invented a series of unjustified conspiracy theories to explain the fact that in most ways most women never achieve global excellence.

The first is that men have purposely perpetuated an overall cultural tradition that ensures social manipulation of the minds of women that begins when we are very young. Little girls are dressed in pink, given dolls to play with, bombarded with Madison Avenue images of beauty, encouraged to get married to a rich man who will take care of them, and then lavished with all kinds of compliments and special privileges when they get pregnant. Women are sugar, spice, and everything nice; precious princesses needing to be coddled and protected.

Their educational experience reflects this. Our elementary schools are filled with women teachers who, feminism tells us, tolerate the presence of members of the "pink team" in the classroom, but encourage the members of the "blue team" to play rough and be competitive. That is, feminism tells us that teachers through grade school supposedly challenge the boys more than the girls to succeed, especially in math and science. Whether such discrimination is intentional or not is irrelevant. According to feminism the societal pressure to cultivate the boy student in one way and the girl in another infects the very fabric of the educational experience itself.

The evidence that girls are discriminated against during their primary and secondary education is now finally being challenged (as shown above) by women like Christina Hoff–Sommers.[16] However, even if it is true, women, ironically, have no one to blame but themselves (after all, there are mostly women in the front of the classes during the formative periods of our primary and secondary educational experiences[17]). Given that the education of children has traditionally been one of the few appropriate public venues for women, those who go into such "careers" are themselves merely products of the sex-biased culture. The cycle of educational mediocrity for women seems unbreakable.[18]

But in fact, it isn't. Again, individuals, even very young ones, can rise above their cultural norms and taboos.[19] There truly are fabulous young female athletes, artists, and scholars. Certainly those girls who have parents who encourage them to excellence will be able to look past the traditional roles to bigger and better things.

However, says feminism, even if our young woman makes it to the varsity sports level, exhibits her art at local galleries or makes a 4.0, once she is in higher education or the job market, it is argued, the societal pressure to behave "like a girl" still abounds. Parental pressure combined with pop culture constantly reminds women that their youth (and therefore their ability to attract, keep and reproduce for a man), is assiduously slipping away. Therefore, even if young potentially excellent women attempt to seriously pursue their global dreams, their culturally ingrained belief that they must (at least some day) have a family will, with each passing year of adulthood until it becomes impossible to ignore, force her into social submission. Potentiality for excellence is, in fact, rarely actualized in men; but in women it is almost imperceptible.

And, for the few women who make it to college, what we often find is that they pursue college degrees that are less demanding than degrees in physics or philosophy, tracking themselves, instead, for bachelors in primary and secondary education[20] or, ultimately, for careers that do not require extended working hours, pursuing ways of life that are not as emotionally, physically or intellectually challenging as, for example, becoming a astronaut, an artist, or a research physician.[21] Those who do pursue such career tracks often quit once such pursuits have paid off by allowing them entry into social circles that allow them to meet, marry, and live off a man's salary. It seems that once a woman is between the ages of 25 and 35,[22] even the most well-educated, sophisticated and seemingly autonomous person will, if she can afford it, opt for a life at home with her children. They realize what society has always said: For a woman, family life is more important than even one's career, let alone one's dreams.

Nevertheless, although the numbers dwindle after each hurdle toward world changing excellence, some women manage to rise above. How? If the stumbling blocks listed—women's nature, both mental and physical; societal discrimination in education and opportunity—are truly real, how is it that any woman, *even just one*, can, even in principle, rise above such constraints? Perhaps because such stumbling blocks are no longer really there? Perhaps feminism is simply perpetuating this myth?

After all, is it not possible that there is another reason women do not achieve global excellence? Is it not possible that it is neither true that women are essentially inferior, nor that they are being systematically discriminated against?

Not according to feminism. Feminism continues to perpetuate the myth that the only possible justification for the state of women in our culture is that there is a grand male conspiracy against them.[23] Oddly, not only do feminists argue that one or more of the above stumbling blocks is real, they actually urge women to add more obstacles to the list.

For one thing, men, according to feminism, purposely deny any evidence of women's excellence. Keeping, for example, excellent medical students and law students from becoming doctors and lawyers respectively; keeping excellent MBAs and other talented entrepreneurs from becoming CEOs; or keeping great painters and violinists from fine galleries and concert halls. Feminism perpetuates the myth that even if women were excellent, men (and our sexist society in general) would refuse to recognize it.

Although most claims of conspiracy are about as realistic and well defended as those presented on *The X-Files*, let us put men and society on trial for this kind of churlishness. First we would need a crime scene, a dead body so to speak. And, for the sake of argument, let's pretend we have one—for example, a woman MBA who competed for a position as the CEO of a major multinational corporation but was not granted the position (it was given to a man). Next, we would need a motive for a legitimate conviction. What could this be? Why would the members of the specific board of trustees (who are, of course, all men) collectively decide to thwart a truly excellent candidate whom they believe will maximize corporate profits simply because of the candidate's sex?

Given that wanting less has never been the driving force of business I find it hard to believe that such a decision would be made on the grounds of sex bias. Isn't it at least possible that there is no conspiracy at all and that the woman in our example just was, in fact, not as committed to excelling in a particular field as the man? Personally, I find it hard to convict anyone, let alone all men in all areas of life, of conspiring against all women without discerning a reasonable motive.

Of course, feminism will not face the hard fact that there may no longer be any real evidence of having a woman who is in fact excellent (by traditional criteria for excellence) and yet is not perceived to be excellent by men because of male blinders.[24] Instead of searching for any other possible cause for the fact that women do not achieve global excellence, feminists ad hoc the above theory by adding a new and deeper level of conspiracy. That is, it is not simply that men have collectively refused to acknowledge excellence when women display it, but that men have actually conspired to develop and maintain criteria for excellence that only they can fit.

After all, we all know that being aggressive, competitive, brave, logical, autonomous, rational, driven, focused, and (to some extent) selfish and egoistic—personality traits that are often the hallmarks of the historically great—are, according to feminism, male characteristics.[25] Women cannot achieve this kind of excellence when the criteria for excellence have been selected by and/or defined by men. Now if only we changed the criteria for excellence to fit "women's natures," such as submissive, emotional, and nurturing, then, claims feminism, we would find that most, even the most mediocre women, are actually excellent.

I hope my readers are horrified by this scenario. First, it destroys both the qualitative and quantitative meanings of excellence. To be excellent means not only that one is far above the statistical average, but far above others with respect to qualitative norms as well. In the words of Jose Ortega y Gasset, "the mass is the average man."[26] That is, when standards for anything are accused of being biased simply to allow for mediocrity, then the conspiracy theory is no longer simply ridiculous, it is dangerous. The criteria for what counts as an excellent soldier, for example, should not be changed so women can meet it, certainly not at the risk of our national security. Though few women may be able to fulfill the criteria without a lowering of the bar, those that do will have done so genuinely and despite feminism.

Interestingly, any critiques of feminism and the above conspiracy theories are met with claims of yet another level of conspiracy. Feminists have argued that any claims which question the legitimacy of the feminist claims of conspiracy simply prove the level, depth and insidiousness of a society steeped in sexist patriarchy. What more evidence does anyone need that there is a male conspiracy to disempower and devalue women than that women themselves have come to realize and admit the simple statistical fact that most women have opted out of the global game to stay home and raise their kids?

I want to suggest, however, that if there is any conspiring going on, it is in the halls of academia, where feminists and their theorizing run amok. Although it is fashionable in our culture to blame anyone but ourselves for our own lives, I will go out on a limb and claim that the above feminist rationalizations are at best weak; and at worst, downright sexist.[27] It seems to me that when all is said and done, despite women's supposed unyielding natures (and their correlative nurtures), and most importantly despite, and maybe even in spite of, feminism, women are free to choose. All persons, as Nietzsche says, can "educate ourselves against our times."[28] As such, the only possible reason why most women do not keep up with men in the race for global excellence, is that they choose not to.

Feminism has invented a false dilemma: Either women are essentially inferior, or when there is a lack of success, men are always to blame. However, given the incredible opportunities for equality in our culture, it seems at least reasonable to suggest that women ought to ignore the whining of feminism and take seriously the fact that they are free to choose the course of their lives.

The above argument is reminiscent of the case made by Simone de Beauvoir in *The Second Sex*[29] albeit with the precisely opposite conclusion. Though in many ways thoroughly "existentialist" in her approach to the woman question, and therefore, at least at some level, committed to the "idea of choice"[30] (chastising women in certain places for not behaving like a truly "free" individual—one who "blames only himself for his failures"[31]), in the final analysis arguments such as the one made above are seen by de Beauvoir to be in "bad faith." Due to the social conditions of her time, woman "in no domain had ever really had a chance."[32] Given that "one is not born, but rather becomes [through social conditioning] a woman,"[33] there is, de facto, no way, according to de Beauvoir, for any woman to escape her oppressed destiny as an "other" in the eyes of a society—which is all societies—where the true self that is always male. In other words, women's lack of global excellence is not her own fault; more specifically, it is the fault of men.

But de Beauvoir had a dream and in that dream there is a chance for equality when women and men "unequivocally affirm their *brotherhood.*"[34] And, only fifty years after the first publishing of *The Second Sex*, it is time to make that dream a reality. But, and this is where I differ from the traditional deBeauvoir reader, I believe that *in order to make equality with men a reality women will have to first abandon feminism*. Operationally, and most simply, women will have to stop blaming men.

When a woman drops out of high school or college to get married and raise children, this is her choice; when she leaves a prestigious career track to get married and raise children, this is her choice. And, in so doing, if she never even seriously competes for, let alone achieves global excellence, this too is her choice. To be blunt, when a woman decides to not even participate in the "struggle for greatness"[35] in order to become a wife and/or mother, it is simply—without resorting to the weak rationalizations for failure of nature, nurture or conspiracy—ultimately, her choice. When women opt out of the global excellence game, with respect to our culture, the inference to the best explanation for why they did so is because they wished to.

This, of course, has the unsettling consequence of having to take seriously the inductive finding that if one is born a woman, one will probably avoid any hard labor, competition, creativity, or scholarship. One will, instead, most likely choose the less taxing route of marrying a man who will provide for one's needs and rear his offspring under their freely chosen belief that nurturing a man, or at least one's offspring, is the pinnacle of womanly excellence.[36] In addition, taking seriously women's choices will have the politically incorrect consequence of having to say that given the traditional criteria for human excellence, not only have women collectively failed,[37] they usually quit trying to succeed before they ever even start down the road to greatness.[38]

Such forthright admittance, however, has a silver lining. If contemporary society truly believes that women are free to choose their own lives, then not only will we be forced to acknowledge women's collective mediocre history, *but we will be free to change the course of the future.* If women deny the feminist myth and take seriously that their choices are truly their own: If women realize that the only dignified and legitimate reason for their failure at this stage in history is that they have freely opted out of the contest for global excellence,[39] they may have to face a sad past, but that is indeed a very small price to pay for a truly open and exciting future.

FEMINISM'S VOICE

The perpetuation of the myth of conspiracy and its correlative rationalization for not taking responsibility is only one of the reasons feminism ought be eliminated from our cultural mindset. The other is the unfortunate fact that feminism's "second wave" voice has offered contemporary society little of value. Feminists have, as described above, argued vociferously for all kinds of political kudos without asking whether such things are even desired by women. Feminism has never kept its mouth shut about anything—slavery, the vote, education, crime, abortion, economics and even past wars. So why now is she silent?

The poignancy of feminism's impotence can be seen, for instance, with respect to the crisis of September 11, 2001. After all, feminism finds herself in the precarious position of being unable to either defend or reject either the Taliban or the policy of the United States. She cannot defend the Taliban for either their aggressive terrorist acts on our country or for the way they treat their women—media images of men beating women for not wearing a veil or for trying to learn how to read are burned in everyone's memory. Feminism must be against such acts. On the other hand, feminism cannot completely stand against such acts, for that would be assuming a culturally hegemonic (and therefore patriarchal) position, something feminist theorizing has always stood against.

Ironically, feminism cannot defend or reject the response of the United States, either, given that their theorizing against patriarchy has always focused on the boutique anti-Americanism so prevalent in today's academic culture. Western civic culture, with its hallmark achievement being the United States, is, according to feminism, essentially sexist. Certainly its very "manly" response of declaring a "war" on anything, let alone terrorism, cannot be something that feminism can consistently stand behind. Of course now, after the terrorist attacks, I find it hard to believe that feminism would risk the freedoms, many of which women *in this country alone* have the luxury of, by not supporting some form of military retaliation. That is, although it has been very fashionable to criticize what feminists have labeled the "maleness" of our culture, it is precisely these "male" attributes—e.g., the belief in the universal notions of justice and freedom, the ability to become courageous and even aggressive when such ideals are threatened and therefore to be willing to fight, die and kill for such concepts and their concomitant political manifestations—which will end up protecting, at least the women in this country, if not those all over the world.

The implicit contradiction between the theorizing of feminism and the needs of actual women is not the only reason for feminism's impotence, however. The other, more problematic reason is that feminism, as I have argued elsewhere,[40] is, in the final analysis, essentially committed to relativism. And although relativism may seem to be tolerant and open-minded on the surface—with its claim that there are no absolute truths—in fact it is dangerously intolerant.

This can be seen concerning the attitude most feminists have with respect to the curriculum on our colleges and universities. While a commitment to relativism may protect the trendy dissident voices of the gays and lesbians, for example, at the same time they work to silence the voices of those fostering more traditional views on the grounds that such views are "intolerant." Feminism, under the umbrella of relativism, and its "anything goes" mentality, has interpreted this to mean that they can foster a culture on campuses that in the name of tolerance has become completely intolerant to any view not toting their party line.

The destructive outcome of this long-term support of relativism by feminism has been documented by numerous scholars in their critique of academia's often misguided notions of "tolerance" and "multiculturalism" which translate into a form of academic fascism.[41] One recent and tragic outcome of such a misguided and inconsistent commitment to relativism is that many students and professors on college campuses across the country believe that, in the name of relativism, one does not have the right to any kind of non-relativized belief, most especially in the light of September 11, any opinion that is not anti-American. One obvious effect on the American people, in the aftermath of the bombings of the World Trade Center, was that our often silent sense of patriotism gained new voice. However, in the name of "tolerance" and "multiculturalism" this voice sounded politically incorrect in the ears of numerous college and university administrators.

For example, Florida Gulf Coast University Dean of Library Sciences Kathleen Hoeth instructed her employees to remove stickers saying "proud to be an American" from their workspace claiming that she did not want to "offend international students."[42] And administrators at Central Michigan University told several students to remove various patriotic posters from their dormitories because such pro-American sentiment was "offensive to people."[43] Finally, and all of this within two months of the attack, at San Diego State University an international student, who rebuked two Saudi students (in Arabic) for delighting in the deaths from the WTC stating: "you should be ashamed of yourselves and not proud," was himself rebuked by the institution and told that any "future incidents...would result in the facing of serious disciplinary sanctions."[44]

In the name of relativism academics urge Americans to distrust all beliefs, especially those that maintain a commitment to the "hegemonic" values underpinning the Constitution of the United States. Oddly, anti-American sentiment, though just as "absolutist" as any pro-American sentiment, is not only allowed, but encouraged. Though I probably do not need to remind the college community that the only reason they have the luxury of voicing such beliefs is precisely because people such as those in the Taliban are not making the rules, I believe it is important to remember that relativism has always been in bed with feminism—that is, as feminism gained power in academia, its relativistic underpinnings came out of the closet. If the fostering of this contemporary anti-American qua relativism attitude toward freedom and justice, and the need to sometimes justifiably fight for such freedoms, is not a *reductio ad absurdum* to the theories and practices of feminism in our culture, then what is?

THE UN-DEAD

In light of the above chapters, then, the response from my student does not seem as flippant as it did at first. Young people may have given up on feminism for any (or all) of the reasons stated above, or simply because it has become too complicated and convoluted to even understand, let alone examine, explore or utilize. Unfortunately, some of the products of feminism—including a strong antagonism toward moral absolutes in general, and most specifically commitments to freedom and justice and, of course, true equality—have, infiltrated their mindset.

It is my hope, therefore, that readers will be able to use the truths exposed by this text to better understand the reasons thatfeminism—its theories, political policies, and overall mentality—no longer should be accepted or sustained. Feminism, if not really dead, is certainly more like the un-dead famous in B movies. That is, her theories need desperately to be ferreted out of our culture and exposed for their misuse and abuse of equality.

NOTES

Chapter One
WHITHER FEMINISM?

1. Naomi Wolf, *Fire With Fire: The New Female Power and How it Will Change the 21st Century*. New York: Random House, 1993, p. 58.

2. *Time/CNN Facts on File*. Cited by Jeremy Fowler, "A Critique of First Wave Feminism: The Hard Case," unpublished manuscript.

3. Melanie Phillips, *The Sex-Change Society: Feminised Britain and the Neutered Male*. London: The Social Market Foundation, 1999; see also *Time/CNN Facts on File* which claims that only 28 percent of women said that "feminism was relevant to them personally."

4. For example *Ms. Magazine's* Gloria Steinem and the *NOW* president Patricia Ireland. This has been noticed by Jennifer Baumgardner and Amy Richards, *Manifesta: Young Women, Feminism, and the Future*. New York: Farrar, Straus and Giroux, 2000, p. 228 and Naomi Wolf, *Fire With Fire: The New Female Power and How it Will Change the 21st Century*. New York: Random House, 1993, p. 88.

5. Coined by Camille Paglia, "No Law in the Arena," in Linda LeMoncheck and James P. Sterba, *Sexual Harassment: Issues and Answers*. New York: Oxford University Press, 2001, pp. 260-264, p. 262.

6. Jennifer Baumgardner and Amy Richards, *Manifesta*. New York: Farrar, Straus and Giroux, 2000. See, especially, pp. 136-139.

7. See, for example, the claims made by Susan Brownmiller, Catherine MacKinnon, and Andrea Dworkin respectively in E.R. Klein, "Date Rape: The Feminist Construct That's Harmful to Women," *Contemporary Philosophy*, vol. 23, 2001.

8. Warren Farrell, *Bringing Children Back to their Fathers*. New York: Jeremy P. Tarcher/Putnam, 2001.

9. See, for example, Warren Farrell, *The Myth of Male Power: Why Men are the Disposable Sex*. New York: Simon & Schuster, 1993, especially chapter five.

10. Cathy Young, *Ceasefire! Why Women and Men Must Join Forces to Achieve True Equality*. New York, The Free Press, 1999, p. 158.

11. Ibid., p. 135.

12. See, for example, Lionel Tiger, *The Decline of Males*. New York: Golden Books, 1999; Warren Farrell, *The Myth of Male Power: Why Men are the Disposable Sex*. New York: Simon & Schuster, 1993.

13. Barbara Arneil, *Politics & Feminism*. Malden, MA.: Blackwell, 1999, p. 3.

14. Wolf, *Fire With Fire: The New Female Power and How it Will Change the 21st Century*, p. 62.

15. Rosalind Delmar, "What is Feminism?," in Anne C. Herrmann and Abigail J. Stewart, ed., *Theorizing Feminism: Parallel Trends in the Humanities and Social Sciences.* Boulder: Westview, 2001, pp. 5-28, p. 6.

16. Rosemarie Tong, *Feminist Thought: A Comprehensive Introduction.* Boulder: Westview Press, 1989.

17. Ibid., p. 2.

18. Janet A. Kourany, James P. Sterba, and Rosemarie Tong, eds., *Feminist Philosophies.* Upper Saddle River: Prentice Hall, 1999.

19. Tong, *Feminist Thought: A Comprehensive Introduction*, p. 39.

20. For a great thorough but compact account of Marx's theories see, Thomas M. Mongar, *The Death of Communism and the Rebirth of Original Marxism.* Lewiston, New York: Edwin Mellen, 1994.

21. Tong, *Feminist Thought: A Comprehensive Introduction*, p. 173.

22. Eve Browning Cole, *Philosophy and Feminist Criticism.* New York: Paragon House, 1993, p. 62, p. 8.

23. Kourany, Sterba, and Tong, eds., *Feminist Philosophies*, p. 415.

24. This label was coined first by Rush Limbaugh and although no true blue feminist would adhere to this name, many did at least give "passive agreement to the charge of 'sexual McCarthyism' during the Clinton sex scandals," Carol Iannone "Either Feminism or Humanity," in *Academic Questions*, Winter 2000-01, Vol.14, No.1, pp. 27-41, p. 29. In addition, the phrase Feminazis has become one of the accepted mainstream classifications of anti-male feminists. Even renowned feminist bell hooks admits that there are "anti-male factions within the feminist movement," *Feminism is for Everybody.* Cambridge, MA.: South End Press, 2000, pp. 67-71.

25. There seems to be a metaphysical bias concerning the notion of 'penetration' vs. 'envelopment'. The former being viewed, misguidedly, as being always the violator, and the latter as always the victim. Empirically, however, this is simply false. Often, for example in nature, the enveloper is the aggressive party. A similar point has been made by Camile Paglia citing an interesting North American Indian myth of the *vagina dentata* (toothed vagina) in *Sexual Personae: Art and Decadence From Nefertiti to Emily Dickinson.* New York: Vintage, 1990, p. 13. Another interesting, albeit South American, Indian myth talks about vaginas containing piranha fish.

26. Reprinted in full in Miriam Schneir, *Feminism in Our Time: The Essential Writings, World War II to the Present.* New York: Vintage Books, 1994, pp. 127-129.

27. Susan Brownmiller, *Against Our Will: Men, Women and Rape.* New York: Simon and Schuster, 1975, see especially p. 16.

28. Catherine MacKinnon, "Sexuality," in *Toward a Feminist Theory of the State.* Cambridge: Harvard University Press, 1989, see especially pp. 126-154 and p. 179.

29. Andrea Dworkin, *Intercourse.* New York: The Free Press, 1987, see especially p. 122.

30. See, for example, "Collected Quotes from Feminist Man-Haters," *www.vix.com/men/bash/quotes.html.*

31. Mary Daly being quoted in Naomi Wolf, *Fire With Fire: The New Female Power and How it Will Change the 21st Century.* New York: Random House, 1993, p. 62. She adds, "In my travels, I have witnessed enough scenes with female audiences in which men were reviled, ridiculed, or attacked for no better reason than the fact of their gender," p. 151.

32. Kourany, Sterba, and Tong, eds., *Feminist Philosophies*, p. 350.

33. See E.R. Klein, *Feminism Under Fire.* Amherst, NY: Prometheus Books, 1996, especially Chapter 4.

34. Sigmund Freud, *An Outline of Psychoanalysis* (trans. James Stachley). New York: W. W. Norton and Company, 1969.

35. Tong, *Feminist Thought: A Comprehensive Introduction*, p. 147.

36. Jean-Paul Sartre, *Being and Nothingness* (trans. Hazel E. Barnes). New York: Philosophical Library, 1956.

37. Simon Beavoir, *The Second Sex* (trans. H. M. Parshley). New York: Vintage Books, 1989.

38. Tong, *Feminist Thought: A Comprehensive Introduction*, p. 211.

39. Cole, *Philosophy and Feminist Criticism*, p. 62.

40. Rosemary Tong, *Feminist Thought: A Comprehensive Introduction.* Boulder: Westview Press, 1989, p. 217.

41. Kourany, Sterba, and Tong, eds., *Feminist Philosophies*, p. 434.

42. While both post-modern and deconstructionist philosophical projects deny that there is any one true interpretation of any author's work, the former rejects any form of rational endeavor, while the latter simply challenges the limits of science and logic. See, e.g. Jacques Derrida's "Plato's Pharmacy" in Peggy Kamuf, ed., *A Derrida Reader: Between the Blinds*, New York: Columbia University Press, 1991.

43. Miranda Fricker, "Feminism in Epistemology: Pluralism Without Postmodernism," in Miranda Fricker and Jennifer Hornsby, ed., *The Cambridge Companion to Feminism in Philosophy.* New York: Cambridge University Press, 2000, pp. 146-165, p. 148.

44. Miranda Fricker and Jennifer Hornsby, "Introduction," in Fricker and Hornsby, ed., *The Cambridge Companion to Feminism in Philosophy*, pp. 1-9.

45. bell hooks, *Feminism is For Everybody: Passionate Politics.* Cambridge, MA: South End Press, 2000, p. 5.

46. Arneil, *Politics & Feminism*, p. 204.

47. Delmar, "What is Feminism?," in *Theorizing Feminism: Parallel Trends in the Humanities and Social Sciences*, pp. 5-28, p. 7.

48. Ibid., pp. 5-28, p. 23.

49. Ibid., pp. 5-28, p. 5.

50. Robert Trevas, et. al. *Philosophy of Sex and Love: A Reader.* Upper Saddle River: Prentic Hall, 1997.

51. See, for example, Christina Hoff-Sommers, *Who Stole Feminism?* New

York: Simon and Schuster, 1994.

52. Even Christina Hoff-Sommers, who calls herself a feminist, does so by defining herself *via negativa* as a non-Gender Feminist.

53. Carol A. Whitehurst, *Women in America: The Oppressed Majority*. Santa Monica, CA: Goodyear Publishing Co., 1977, p. 1.

54. Jennifer Hornsby, "Gender," in Ted Honderich, ed., *The Oxford Companion to Philosophy*. New York: Oxford University Press, 1995, p. 305.

55. This was one of the main reasons for the formulation of *Multicultural or Third World Feminism*.

56. Thus another name for such feminists is *Academic Feminism*. See, for example, E.R. Klein, *Feminism Under Fire*. Amherst, NY: Prometheus Books, 1996.

57. Pauline Reage, *The Story of O*. New York: Ballantine, 1965.

58. This was the perception of my student Jude Wright in his unpublished paper "Sexual Domination, Rape, and Jurisprudence: A Response to Catherine MacKinnon."

59. Andrea Dworkin, *Women Hating*. New York: Penguin, 1974.

60. See, for example, Christina Hoff Sommers, *The War Against Boys: How Misguided Feminism Is Harming Our Young Men*. New York: Simon and Schuster, 2000.

61. See, for example, E.R. Klein, *Feminism Under Fire*. Amherst, NY: Promethetus Books, 1996, especially pages 204-209.

62. Recently one archaeologist has argued that the entire invention of the need for a constructed social category known as 'gender' is the feminist desire to rewrite not only history but prehistory. "One of the greatest strengths of matriarchal myth from a feminist perspective—is that it gives historical rather than biological reasons for the dominance of men. And, at least in theory, matriarchal myth could also give us license to believe that what we think of as femininity and masculinity are not inborn traits but are the cultural constructs of a patriarchal system, and thus rooted no more deeply than this five-thousand-year-old social organization," Cynthia Eller, *The Myth of Matriarchal Prehistory: Why an Invented Past Won't Give Women a Future*, Boston: Beacon Press, 2000, pp. 5-9, p. 63, p. 85, p. 87, p. 175.

63. W.V. Quine makes this claim in *Quiddities: An Intermittently Philosophical Dictionary*. Cambridge, MA: Harvard University Press, 1987, pp. 78-82.

64. Catherine A. MacKinnon, *Sexual Harassment of Working Women: A Case of Sex Discrimination*. New Haven: Yale University Press, 1979, p. 151.

65. Lynn Hankinson Nelson, *Who Knows: From Quine to a Feminist Empiricism*. Philadelphia: Temple University Press, 1990, p. 320, n.11.

66. Kourany, Sterba, and Tong, eds., *Feminist Philosophies*, p. 434.

67. Steven G. Smith, *Gender Thinking*. Philadelphia: Temple University Press, 1992, p. 49-56.

68. Judith Butler, *Gender Trouble: Feminism and the Subversion of Identity*.

London: Routledge, 1990, p. 6.

69. Smith, *Gender Thinking*, p. 48.

70. Phillips, *The Sex-Change Society: Feminised Britian and the Neutered Ma*le, p. 159.

71. Smith, *Gender Thinking*, p. 53-56.

72. Rachel T. Hare-Mustin and Jeanne Marecek, "Gender and the Meaning of Difference: Postmodernism and Psychology," pp. 78-109, p. 101 in Anne C. Herrmann and Abigail J. Stewart, *Theorizing Feminism: Parallel Trends in the Humanities and Social Sciences*. Boulder: Westview, 2001.

73. Shannon Sullivan, *Living Across and Through Skins: Transactional Bodies, Pragmatism, and Feminism*. Bloomington, IN: Indiana University Press, 2001, Chapter Four.

74. "Morning Edition," *National Public Radio,* August 29, 1995.

75. Kourany, Sterba, and Tong, eds., *Feminist Philosophies*, p. 3.

76. Cited from Robert Bly, *Iron John: A Book About Men*. New York: Vintage Books, p. 234. As pointed out by one of my students, Ms. Cheryl Fitzgerald, this fact can be confirmed in most any biology textbook, see, for example, J. Dusheck and A. Tobin, *Asking About Life*. Fort Worth, TX: Saunder College Publishing, 1998.

77. See, for example, the work by Michael Levin, espeically "Maritime Policy for a Flat Earth," in James Sterba, ed., *Controversies in Feminism*. Lanham, MD: Rowman and Littlefield, 2001, p. 197-218; and the work by Peter Copeland and Dean Hamer, *Living With Our Genes: Why They Matter More Than You Think*. New York: Anchor Books, pp. 164-165.

78. See, for example, the case of David Reimer in John Colapinto's *As Nature Made Him: The Boy Who Was Raised as a Girl*, New York: Harper Collins, 2000. For this abuse of the gender construct see, especially, pages xiii, 44, 51, 55,66, 131, 135, 143, 176, 180, 204, 210, 213, 219, 233-234, 274.

79. John Colapinto's *As Nature Made Him: The Boy Who Was Raised as a Girl*, New York: Harper Collins, 2000, p. 176.

80. Kourany, Sterba, and Tong, eds., *Feminist Philosophies*, p. 3.

81. For more detail on this and some interesting photos, see E.R. Klein, *Gender Images: Voice or Vice," Zeitschrift Fuer Philosophie*, April-June, 1999, pp. 26-35.

82. "Uncut Heroines: Being Butch and being male are not the same identity but some women have felt forced to choose between their butch self and their female gender," *Diva Magazine*,

83. *Life Magazine*.

84. *Manifesta*, see especially p. 192 and 226.

85. Adrienne Rich, *Blood, Bread and Poetry: Selected Prose, 1979-1985*. New York: Norton, 1986, p. 461.

86. Rachel T. Hare-Mustin and Jeanne Marecek, "Gender and the Meaning of Difference: Postmodernism and Psychology," pp. 78-109, p. 101 in Anne C. Herrmann and Abigail J. Stewart, ed., *Theorizing Feminism: Parallel Trends*

in the Humanities and Social Sciences. Boulder: Westview, 2001, p. 79 and 99.

87. Cressida J. Heyes, *Line Drawings: Defining Women through Feminist Practice*. Ithaca: Cornell University Press, 2000, p. 124 where she agrees with and cites Carol Gilligan, *In a Different Voice: Psychological Theory and Women's Development*. Cambridge: Harvard University Press, 1993.

88. Young, *Ceasefire! Why Women and Men Must Join Forces to Achieve True Equality*, p. 41.

89. Bell Hooks, *Feminism is For Everybody: Passionate Politics*. Cambridge, MA: South End Press, 2000, p. 5.

90. Given the above analysis, and for the sake of simplicity, I will now use the term 'feminism' with a capital 'F' to mean any and/or all of the above construction.

91. Diemut Bubuck, "Feminism in Political Philosophy: Women's Difference," in Miranda Fricker and Jennifer Hornsby, eds., *The Oxford Companion to Feminism in Philosophy*. New York: Cambridge University Press, 2000, pp. 185-204, p. 185.

92. Frank A. Schubert, *Introduction to Law and the Legal System*. Boston: Houghton Mifflin, 2000, pp. 722-723. See, *Fed. R. Civ. p. 2*. "Historically, the courts of equity had a power of framing and adapting new remedies to particular cases, which the common law courts did not possess. In doing so, they allowed themselves latitude of construction and assumed, in certain matters such as trusts, a power of enforcing moral obligations which the courts of law did not admit or recognize," p. 723.

93. Sharon Fass Yates, ed., *The Reader's Digest Legal Question & Answer Book*. Pleasantville, NY: The Reader's Digest Association, Inc., 1992, p. 465.

94. Stanley I. Benn, "Egalitarianism and the Equal Consideration of Interests," in Richard E. Flathman, ed., *Concepts in Social & Political Philosophy*. New York: MacMillan, 1973, pp. 336-347, p. 337.

95. Aristotle, *Nichomachean Ethics*, Book V.

96 So called, for example, by Louis Pojman, "Equality: A Plethora of Theories," *Journal of Philosophical Research*, Vol. XXIV, 1999, pp. 193-245, pp. 195-198.

97. John Locke, *Second Treatise On Government*, sect. 149.

98. Jean-Jacques Rousseau, *Social Contract*.

99. For example, Madison's "The Federalist No. 41," in *The Federalist: A Commentary on the Constitution of the United States, eds.*, Alexander Hamilton, John Jay and James Madison. New York: Random House, 1941, pp. 259-270, p. 261.

100. Louis Pojman claims that the construct of "legal equality" is simply redundant, since what else could "equality" mean if not "equality under the law...giving the false appearance that equality is a separate and independent norm." Louis Pojman, "Equality: A Plethora of Theories," *Journal of Philosophical Research*, Vol. XXIV, 1999, pp. 193-245, pp. 201-203.

101. I call them "pre" since it wasn't until the poll tax was removed in 1964,

The Twenty Fourth Amendment, that true civil rights actually begun.

102. Alexis de Tocqueville, *Democracy in America*. New York: Alfred A. Knopf, 1972, p. 95.

103. Ibid., p. 96.

104. Arneil, *Politics & Feminism*, p. 135.

105. Ibid., p. 136.

106. Judith Lorber and Susan A. Farrell, eds., *The Social Construction of Gender*. Sage, 1991.

107.For an alternative account see Estelle B. Freedman, *No Turning Back: The History of Feminism and the Future of Women*. New York: Ballantine Books, 2002.

108. See the work of, for example, Paula Rothenberg, *Invisible Privilege: A Memoir about Race, Class, and Gender*. Lawrence, KS: University Press of Kansas, 2000.

109. As with feminism, the "men's movement" does not like to be viewed as a monolithic group of men or ideologies.

110. I use the term 'masculism' to mean the "men's movement" or what is spelled "masculinism."

Chapter Two

THE FIRST GENERATION

1. Anne-Marie Kappeli, "Feminist Scenes," Genevieve Fraisse and Michelle Perrot, eds., *A History of Women in the West: IV. Emerging Feminism from Revolution to World War*. Cambridge, MA: Harvard University Press, 1993, pp. 482-514, p. 482.

2. Olympe de Gouges, "Declaration of the Rights of Women," 1791, reprinted in Susan Alice Watkins, Marisa Rueda, and Marta Rodriguez, *Feminism for Beginners*. Cambridge, England: Icon Books, 1992, p. 24.

3. Eve Browning Cole, *Philosophy and Feminist Criticism: An Introduction*. New York: Paragon House, 1993, p. 3.

4. Zillah R. Eisenstein, *The Radical Future of Liberal Feminism*. Boston: Northeastern University Press, 1981, p. 92.

5. Mary Wollstonecraft, *A Vindication of the Rights of Woman* in Carol H. Poston, ed., *Mary Wollstonecraft, A Vindication of the Rights of Woman: An Authoritative Text, Backgrounds, The Wollstonecraft Debate, Criticism*. New York: W.W. Norton, 1988, p. 194.

6. Eisenstein, *The Radical Future of Liberal Feminism*, p. 7.

7. Wollstonecraft, *A Vindication of the Rights of Woman* in Carol H. Poston, ed., *Mary Wollstonecraft, A Vindication of the Rights of Woman: An Authoritative Text, Backgrounds, The Wollstonecraft Debate, Criticism*, p. 24.

8. Ibid., p. 177.

9. Ibid., p. 51.

10. Some scholars claim that these early feminists had their political views intimately tied in with the Unitarian religious organizations at the time. See, for example, Kathryn Gleadle, *The Early Feminists: Radical Unitarians and the Emergence of the Women's Rights Movement, 1831-51*. New York: St. Martin's Press, 1995.

11. Richard J. Evans, *The Feminists: Women's Emancipation Movements in Europe, America and Australasia 1840-1920*. New York: Barnes & Nobel Books, 1977, p. 14.

12. From England the arguments were similar but more legalistic. They usually centered on two points. "First, they pointed to the inconsistency that the head of the realm might be female, and yet women were not permitted even to choose members of parliament. Secondly, they railed against the injustice that propertied women were forced to pay taxes, but had no political representation. Kathryn Gleadle, *The Early Feminists: Radical Unitarians and the Emergence of the Women's Rights Movement, 1831-51*. New York: St. Martin's Press, 1995, p. 72.

13. Evans, *The Feminists: Women's Emancipation Movements in Europe, America and Australasia 1840-1920*, p. 13.

14. John Stuart Mill, *The Subjection of Women* in Sue Mansfield, ed., Arlington Heights, IL: Harlan Davidson, Inc., 1980.

15. Eisenstein, *The Radical Future of Liberal Feminism*, p. 113-114.

16. Mill, *The Subjection of Women*, p. 1.

17. Evans, *The Feminists: Women's Emancipation Movements in Europe, America and Australasia 1840-1920*, p. 20.

18. Eisenstein, *The Radical Future of Liberal Feminism*, p. 127.

19. Ibid., p. 128.

20. Stephane Michaud, "Artistic and Literary Idolatries," in Genevieve Fraisse and Michelle Perrot, eds., *A History of Women in the West: IV. Emerging Feminism from Revolution to World War*. Cambridge, MA: Harvard University Press, 1993, pp. 121-144, p. 121.

21. Eisenstein, *The Radical Future of Liberal Feminism*, p. 145.

22. Elizabeth Cady Stanton and Lucretia Mott, "Seneca Falls Declaration of Sentiments," reprinted in Susan Alice Watkins, Marisa Rueda, and Marta Rodriguez, *Feminism for Beginners*. Cambridge, England: Icon Books, 1992, p. 42.

23. Barbara Arneil, *Politics & Feminism*. Malden, MA: Blackwell, 1999, p. 159.

24. Theodore Stanton and Harriot Stanton Blatch, eds., *Elizabeth Cady Stanton*. New York: Arno and the New York Times, 1969, 2:105, reprinted in Zillah R. Eisenstein, *The Radical Future of Liberal Feminism*. Boston: Northeastern University Press, 1981, p. 148.

25. Elizabeth Cady Stanton, Susan B. Anthony, and Matilda Joslyn Gage, eds. *History of Woman Suffrage*. New York: Source Book Press, 1970, 3: 81, reprinted in Zillah R. Eisenstein, *The Radical Future of Liberal Feminism*.

Boston: Northeastern University Press, 1981, p. 149.

26. Eisenstein, *The Radical Future of Liberal Feminism*, p. 151.

27. Susan Alice Watkins, Marisa Rueda, and Marta Rodriguez, *Feminism for Beginners*. Cambridge, England: Icon Books, 1992, p. 47.

28. Donald Dale Jackson, *The Civil War: Twenty Million Yankees*. Alexandria, VA: Time-Life Books, 1985, p. 75.

29. Marli Frances Weiner, *Mistresses and Slaves: Plantation Women in South Carolina*. Urbana: University of Illinois Press, 1996.

30. Ibid., see especially p. 201 and 212.

31. Ibid., p. 232.

32. For brief histories on other interesting, delightful, deceitful, outrageous, and heroic women see Gemma Alexander, ed., *The Mammoth Book of Heroic & Outrageous Women*. New York: Caroll & Graff Publishers, 1999.

33. Wendy McElroy, "The Roots of Individualist Feminism in 19th-Century America," *Freedom, Feminism and the State*. The Independent Institute, 2000.

34. Quoted in William O'Neill, *Everyone was Brave: A History of Feminism in America*. New York: Quadrant Press, 1971, p. 17.

35. Elizabeth Cady Stanton speaking to *the International Council of Women*, 1888 reprinted in Miriam Schneir, ed., *Feminism: The Essential Historical Writings*. New York: Vintage Books, 1992, inside front cover.

36. Nicole Arnaud-Duc, "The Law's Contradictions," Genevieve Fraisse and Michelle Perrot, eds., *A History of Women in the West: IV. Emerging Feminism from Revolution to World War*. Cambridge, MA: Harvard University Press, 1993, pp. 80-113, p. 107.

37. Julia Kirk Blackwelder, *Now Hiring: The Feminization of Work in the United States, 1900-1995*. College Station: Texas A & M University Press, 1997, p. 5.

38. Miriam Schneir, ed., *Feminism: The Essential Historical Writings*. New York: Vintage Books, 1992, 255.

39. Ibid., p. 305.

40. Marxist socialism, which will later become the backbone of Feminist theorizing, was evident in the poem since it was Marx who said you cannot exact revolution when people are starving, so they must "have bread before roses." The poem used by marching women written by James Oppenheim, reprinted in Miriam Schneir, ed., *Feminism: The Essential Historical Writings*. New York: Vintage Books, 1992, pp. 306-307.

41. Blackwelder, *Now Hiring: The Feminization of Work in the United States, 1900-1995*, p. 61.

42. Helen L. Sumner, Volume IX of the report "History of Women in Industry in the United States," 1908-1911, reprinted in Miriam Schneir, ed., *Feminism: The Essential Historical Writings*. New York: Vintage Books, 1992, pp. 255-267.

43. Blackwelder, *Now Hiring: The Feminization of Work in the United*

States, 1900-1995, p. 61.

44. Dorothy M. Brown, *Setting a Course: American Women in the 1920s*. Boston: Twayne Publishers, 1987, p. 35.

45. Genevieve Fraisse, "A Philosophical History of Sexual Difference" in Genevieve Fraisse and Michelle Perrot, eds., *A History of Women in the West: IV. Emerging Feminism from Revolution to World War*. Cambridge, MA: Harvard University Press, 1993, pp. 48-79, p. 79.

46. Dorothy M. Brown, *Setting a Course: American Women in the 1920s*. Boston: Twayne Publishers, 1987, pp. 35-36.

47. Philip S. Foner, *Women and the American Labor Movement: From WWI to Present*. New York: The Free Press, 1980, pp. 1-2.

48. Ibid., p. 21.

49. Ibid., p. 5.

50. Brown, *Setting a Course: American Women in the 1920s*, p. 78.

51. Ibid., p. 79.

52. Ibid., p. 79.

53. The big names usually associated with this momentous event are Susan B. Anthony, Elizabeth Cady Stanton, Lucy Stone, and black woman activist Sojourner Truth.

54. Cole, *Philosophy and Feminist Criticism: An Introduction*, pp. 5-7.

55. Louis Pojman, "Equality: A Plethora of Theories," *Journal of Philosophical Research*, Vol. XXIV, 1999, pp. 193-245, pp. 195-198.

Chapter Three

THE SECOND GENERATION: ITS "FIRST WAVE"

1. Barbara Arneil, *Politics & Feminism*. Malden, MA: Blackwell, 1999, p. 101.

2. Ibid., p. 154.

3. Dorothy M. Brown, *Setting a Course: American Women in the 1920s*. Boston: Twayne Publishers, 1987, p. 1.

4. Preston W. Slosson, *The Great Crusade and After, 1914-1928*. New York: Macmillan, 1929, p. 157.

5. Brown, *Setting a Course: American Women in the 1920s*, p. 42.

6. Ibid., p. 52.

7. Ibid., p. 97.

8. Ibid., p. 164.

9. Ibid., p. 105

10. Estelle B. Freedman, *No Turning Back: The History of Feminism and the Future of Women*. New York: Ballantine Books, 2002, p. 149

11. Brown, *Setting a Course: American Women in the 1920s*. p. 141.

12. Ibid., p. 248.

13. Ibid., p. 248.

14. Ibid., p. 249.

15. Susan Ware, *Holding Their Own: American Women in the 1930s*. Boston: Twayne Publishers, 1982, p. 65.

16. Author of *The Yellow Wallpaper*. Dale M. Gilman, ed., New York: St. Martinus Press, 1999.

17. Charlotte Perkins Gilman, "The New Generation of Women," *Current History* 18, August, 1923, pp. 736-737.

18. Brown, *Setting a Course: American Women in the 1920s*, p. 249.

19. Ware, *Holding Their Own: American Women in the 1930s*, p. 14.

20. Ibid., p. 49.

21. Ibid., p. 21.

22. Ibid., 1982, p. 1.

23. Ibid., p. 29.

24. Ibid., p. 21

25. Freedman, *No Turning Back: The History of Feminism and the Future of Women*, p. 172.

26. Ware, *Holding Their Own: American Women in the 1930s*. Boston, p. 72.

27. Ibid., p. 200.

28. Ibid., p.xvii.

29. Ibid., p. 15.

30. Ibid., p. 87.

31. Ibid., p. 104.

32. Ibid., p. 107-108.

33. Susan M. Hartman, *The Home Front and Beyond: American Women in the 1940s*. Boston, Twayne Publishers, 1982, p. 21.

34. Miriam Schneir, *Feminism In Our Time: The Essential Writings, World War II to the Present*. New York: Vintage Books, 1994, p. 38.

35. Hartman, *The Home Front and Beyond: American Women in the 1940s*, p. 87.

36. Ibid., 1982, p. 23.

37. Schneir, *Feminism In Our Time: The Essential Writings, World War II to the Present*, p. 38.

38. Hartman, *The Home Front and Beyond: American Women in the 1940s*, p. 45.

39. Ibid., p. 45.

40. Eugenia Kaledin, *Mothers and More: American Women in the 1950s*. Boston: Twayne Publishers, 1984, p. 68.

41. ERA, 1923 version. "Men and women shall have equal rights throughout the United States and in every place subject to its jurisdiction. Congress shall have power to enforce this article by appropriate legislation."

42. Blanch Linden-Ward and Carol Hurd Green, *American Women in the 1960s: Changing the Future*. New York: Twayne Publishers, 1993, p. 1.

43. Hartman, *The Home Front and Beyond: American Women in the 1940s*,

p. 131-133.

44. Melanie Phillips, *The Sex-Change Society: Feminised Britian and the Neutered Ma*le. London: The Social Market Foundation, 1999, p. 82.

45. Hartman, *The Home Front and Beyond: American Women in the 1940s*, p. 12.

46. It has been argued that most women did not want to leave their jobs, see, for example, Eugenia Kaledin, *Mothers and More: American Women in the 1950s*. Boston: Twayne Publishers, 1984, p. 61.

47. Hartman, *The Home Front and Beyond: American Women in the 1940s*, p. 213.

48. Ibid., p. 79.

49. Phillips, *The Sex-Change Society: Feminised Britian and the Neutered Ma*le, p. 101.

50. Kaledin, *Mothers and More: American Women in the 1950s*, preface.

51. Ibid., p. 36.

52. Ibid., pp. 37-38.

53. Ibid., p. 71-72.

54. Ibid., p. 211.

55. The name was playing off of the "first generation" group of women known as the *Bluestockings*. "This group of women, which included Hannah More, Elizabeth Carter, Elizabeth Montagu, and Hester Chapone, gained some position in a male world through combining piety, seriousness, and learning," Moira Ferguson and Janett Todd, "Feminist Backgrounds and Argument of a *Vindication of the Rights of Woman*," in Carol H. Poston, ed., *Mary Wollstonecraft, A Vindication of the Rights of Woman: An Authoritative Text, Backgrounds, The Wollstonecraft Debate, Criticism*. New York: W.W. Norton, 1988, pp. 317-328, p. 318.

56. Linden-Ward and Green, *American Women in the 1960s: Changing the Future*, p. 436.

57. Winifred D. Wandersee, *On the Move: American Women in the 1970s*. Boston: Twayne Publishers, 1988, p. 62.

58. Linden-Ward, *American Women in the 1960's: Changing the Future*, p. 114.

59. And this held true throughout the seventies. "Feminists showed little interest in the 1970 White House Conference on Children because they knew that conservative 'delegates shared a prior consensus on what constituted an ideal family and what direction social policy should take'...parents of a third of the nation's preschool children worked outside the home...Nixon declared 'good public policy requires that we enhance rather than diminish both parental authority and parental involvement with children—particularly in those early years when social attitudes and conscience are formed.' Ironically, little reaction came from organized women's groups, which had given little attention to child care and other domestic concerns of women," Blanch Linden-Ward and Carol Hurd Green, *American Women in the 1960s: Changing the Future*. New York:

Twayne Publishers, 1993, p. 116.

60. Phillips, *The Sex-Change Society: Feminised Britain and the Neutered Male*, p. 128.

61. Betty Friedan, *The Feminine Mystique*. New York: W.W. Norton & Co., 1963, p. 15.

62. Schneir, *Feminism In Our Time: The Essential Writings, World War II to the Present*, pp. 48-50.

63. Friedan, *The Feminine Mystique*, p. 364.

64. Wandersee, *On the Move: American Women in the 1970s*, p. 62-62.

65. Linden-Ward and Green, *American Women in the 1960's: Changing the Future*, p. 91.

66. Ibid., p. 92.

67. Schneir, *Feminism In Our Time: The Essential Writings, World War II to the Present*, p. 71.

68. Executive Order 10980, December 14, 1961, in *American Women*. Washington D.C.: U.S. Government Printing Office, 1963, p. 76.

69. Schneir, *Feminism In Our Time: The Essential Writings, World War II to the Present*, p. 71.

70. Catherine A. MacKinnon, *Sexual Harassment of Working Women: A Case of Sex Discrimination*. New Haven: Yale University Press, 1979, p. 107.

71. Ibid., p. 107.

72. Schneir, *Feminism In Our Time: The Essential Writings, World War II to the Present*, pp. 71-72.

73. Excerpts from the *NOW 1966 Statement of Purpose* written by Betty Friedan and Dr. Pauli Murray.

74. Schneir, *Feminism In Our Time: The Essential Writings, World War II to the Present*, pp. 369-370.

75. Even today, despite all of Feminism's ups and downs, women who came of age during this decade are adamant about calling themselves, and still proud to be, Feminists.

76. Wandersee, *On the Move: American Women in the 1970s*, p.xii.

77. Linden-Ward and Green, *American Women in the 1960's: Changing the Future*, p. 417.

78. Schneir, *Feminism In Our Time: The Essential Writings, World War II to the Present*, p. 108.

79. Ibid., p. 245.

80. Ibid., p. 125.

81. Wandersee, *On the Move: American Women in the 1970s*, p. 3.

82. WITCH was born on Halloween 1968 in New York under the belief that witches were the first women to fight men's oppression. As an acronym it meant "Women Interested in Toppling Consumption Holidays," such as Mother's Day, which they believed was fundamentally oppressive. See, for example, Jane J. Mansbridge, *Why We Lost the ERA*. Chicago: University of Chicago Press, 1986, pp. 103 and 279. More radically, WITCH stands for "Women's

International Terrorist Conspiracy from Hell," in Winifred D. Wandersee, *On the Move: American Women in the 1970s*. Boston: Twayne Publishers, 1988, p. 1. It also stood for, at different political events including "Women Incenses at Telephone Company Harassment," "Women's Independent Taxpayers, Consumers, and Homemakers," and "Women Inspired to Commit Herstory," Robin Morgan, ed., *Sisterhood is Powerful: An Anthology of Writings from the Women's Liberation Movement*. New York: Random House, 1970, pp. 538-553.

83. Schneir, *Feminism In Our Time: The Essential Writings*, p. 126.

84. Shulamith Firestone, "The Redstocking Manifesto." Parts are reprinted in Robin Morgan, ed., *Sisterhood is Powerful: An Anthology of Writings from the Women's Liberation Movement*. New York: Random House, 1970, pp. 533-535. A full copy can be obtained on the internet. http://fsweb.berry.edu/academic/HASS/csnider/berry/hum2oo/redstockings.htm.

85. Wandersee, *On the Move: American Women in the 1970s*, p.xii.

86. Valerie Solanas, "The Scum Manifesto," reprinted in Blanch Linden-Ward and Carol Hurd Green, *American Women in the 1960's: Changing the Future*. New York: Twayne Publishers, 1993, p. 278.

87. Emma Rauschenbusch-Clough, "Mary Wollstonecraft's Demands for the Education of Woman," in Mary Wollstonecraft, *A Vindication of the Rights of Woman* in Carol H. Poston, ed., *Mary Wollstonecraft, A Vindication of the Rights of Woman: An Authoritative Text, Backgrounds, The Wollstonecraft Debate, Criticism*. New York: W.W. Norton, 1988, pp. 280-285, especially p. 281 and 284.

88. Phillips, *The Sex-Change Society: Feminised Britain and the Neutered Male*, p. 125.

Chapter Four

THE SECOND GENERATION: ITS "SECOND WAVE"

1. Blanch Linden-Ward and Carol Hurd Green, *American Women in the 1960's: Changing the Future*. New York: Twayne Publishers, 1993, p. 101.

2. Rosemarie Tong, "Confessions of a Winged Woman: Flying Free From a Constricting Cage," in, ed., James P. Sterba, *Controversies in Feminism*. Lanham, MD: Rowman & Littlefield, p. 227.

3. Barbara Arneil, *Politics & Feminism*. Malden, MA: Blackwell, 1999, p. 154.

4. Ibid., p. 101.

5. Ibid., p. 186-187.

6. This was soon to be made clear by the *Equal Employment Opportunity Act* of 1972, the 1972 amendments to the *Equal Pay Act* of 1963, amendments to the *Comprehensive Employment and Training Act* of 1973, as well as the *Women's Educational Equity Act* of 1974.

7. Miriam Schneir, *Feminism In Our Time: The Essential Writings, World*

War II to the Present. New York: Vintage Books, 1994, p. 344.

8. Ibid., p. 126.

9. Ibid., p. 229.

10. Interestingly, the withholding of sex from men in order to achieve political gains is as old as the Greeks, see, Aristophanes' *Lisistrata*, c. 400 B.C.

11. Schneir, *Feminism In Our Time: The Essential Writings, World War II to the Present*, p. 160-161.

12. Winifred D. Wandersee, *On the Move: American Women in the 1970s.* Boston: Twayne Publishers, 1988, p. 65.

13. Ibid., p. 54.

14. Ibid., p. 44.

15. Linden-Ward, *American Women in the 1960's: Changing the Future*, p. 431,

16. Wandersee, *On the Move: American Women in the 1970s*, p. 67.

17. Betty Friedan herself claims that the "lesbian issue" created a huge "stumbling block" for the women's movement. See Marcia Cohe, *The Sisterhood: The True Story of the Women Who Changed the World.* New York: Simon and Schuster, 1988, p. 382.

18. Lesbian influences in Feminism would, nonetheless, grow in the next decades. "Adrienne Rich's essay "Compulsory Heterosexuality and Lesbian Existence" was published in the journal *Signs* in 1980. It was created, she later explained, "to challenge the erasure of lesbian existence from so much of scholarly feminist literature" and "to encourage heterosexual feminists to examine heterosexuality as a political institution," Miriam Schneir, *Feminism In Our Time: The Essential Writings, World War II to the Present.* New York: Vintage Books, 1994, p. 311.

19. *Roe et al. v. Wade*, District Attorney of Dallas County, No.70-18, Supreme Court of the United States, argued December 13, 1971, decided January 22, 1973.

20. Wandersee, *On the Move: American Women in the 1970s*, p. 82.

21. Ibid., p. 83.

22. Schneir, *Feminism In Our Time: The Essential Writings, World War II to the Present*, p. 400.

23. Wandersee, *On the Move: American Women in the 1970s*, p. 84-87.

24. Marcia Cohen, *The Sisterhood: The True Story of the Women Who Changed the World.* New York: Simon and Schuster, 1988, p. 322.

25. Schneir, *Feminism In Our Time: The Essential Writings, World War II to the Present*, p. 408.

26. Wandersee, *On the Move: American Women in the 1970s*, p. 111.

27. Ibid., p. 199.

28. Zillah R. Eisenstein, *The Radical Future of Liberal Feminism.* Boston: Northeastern University Press, 1986, pp. 233-234.

29. Ibid., p. 234.

30. *General Electric Co. v. Gilbert, et al.*, No. 74-1589, Supreme Court,

December 1976.

31. Catherine A. MacKinnon, *Sexual Harassment of Working Women: A Case of Sex Discrimination*. New Haven: Yale University Press, 1979, p. 111.

32. The question of men ever being able to become pregnant, though technologically problematic at this time, is not logically impossible and so should not be ignored as frivolous when thinking about establishing law. Certainly the case of men having to behave in similar ways to pregnant women in terms of job security so that they can stay home with preemies or newborns is not unreasonable.

33. MacKinnon, *Sexual Harassment of Working Women: A Case of Sex Discrimination*, p. 118.

34. The actual issue concerning the funding of *Viagra* on health plans is quite similar.

35. Eisenstein, *The Radical Future of Liberal Feminism*, pp. 235.

36. MacKinnon, *Sexual Harassment of Working Women: A Case of Sex Discrimination*, p. 221.

37. Wandersee, *On the Move: American Women in the 1970s*, p. 175.

38. Ibid., p. 162.

39. Jane J. Mansbridge, *Why We Lost the ERA*. Chicago: University of Chicago Press, p. 8.

40. Ibid., p. 2.

41. Ibid., pp. 2-3.

42. This was a phrase used in the '70s by *Virginia Slims* cigarettes to sell cigarettes to the burgeoning new market of the "hip" woman. *Virginia Slims* sponsored the "fight" of the decade when Feminist Billie Jean King beat self-proclaimed "sexist" Bobbie Riggs in tennis. The phrase lived on long after to denote "liberated" women, p. 197.

43. Soon this capitalistic, consumer oriented and competitive woman will be turned on by Feminism for having "completely negated the true meaning and intent of feminism," in Winifred D. Wandersee, *On the Move: American Women in the 1970s*. Boston: Twayne Publishers, 1988, p. 173.

44. The "superwoman" was someone who becomes established in a career, 10 years later gets married and has children, all the while keeping herself beautiful and sexy for adventurous romantic nightlife throughout her life. This ideal, supported at one time by Feminism, was given up once the drudgery of real life set in and many women found this "having it all" ideology was just more rhetoric.

45. Wandersee, *On the Move: American Women in the 1970s*, p. 84-87.

46. Ibid., p. 120.

47. Miranda Fricker and Jennifer Hornsby, "Introduction," in Miranda Fricker and Jennifer Hornsby, ed., *The Cambridge Companion to Feminism in Philosophy*. New York: Cambridge University Press, 2000, pp. 1-9, p. 5.

48. Melanie Phillips, *The Sex-Change Society: Feminised Britian and the Neutered Ma*le. London: The Social Market Foundation, 1999, p. 120.

49. Cathy Young, *Ceasefire! Why Women and Men Must Join Forces to Achieve True Equality*. New York: The Free Press, 1999, p. 6.

50. Susan Moller Okin, "Gender Inequality and Cultural Differences," in *Political Theory*, Vol. 22, No.1, February, 1994, pp. 5-24, p. 12.

51. Moira Gatens, *Feminism and Philosophy: Perspectives on Difference and Equality*. Bloomingon, IN: Indiana University Press, 1991, p. 44-46.

52. Carol A. Whitehurst, *Women in America: The Oppressed Majority*. Santa Monica, CA: Goodyear Publishing Co., 1977, p. 71.

53. Young, *Ceasefire! Why Women and Men Must Join Forces to Achieve True Equality*, p. 57.

54. *The Man Show* on the *Comedy Channel* spoofs most of contemporary culture regarding the relationships between men and women. The episode I am referring to aired March 3, 2001 at 10:30 p.m.

55. Barbara Bergmann, *The Chronicle of Higher Education*, December 1, 1993, p.A9.

56. There are men who agree with this idea. See, for example, Hugh LaFollette, "Real Men," in Larry May and Robert A. Strikwerda, eds., *Rethinking Masculinity: Philosophical Explorations in Light of Feminism*. Lanham, MD: Rowman & Littlefield, 1992, p. 64.

57. Melanie Phillips, *The Sex-Change Society: Feminised Britian and the Neutered Ma*le. London: The Social Market Foundation, 1999, pp. 124-125.

58. For example, Louise M. Antony, "'Human Nature' and its Role in Feminist Theory," in Janet Kourany *Philosophy in a Feminist Voice*. Princeton: Princeton University Press, 1998, pp. 63-91, claims that "feminist theory needs to appeal to a universal human nature in order to articulate and defend its critical claims about the damage done to women under patriarchy, and also to ground its positive vision of equitable and sustainable human relationships," p. 67. And that "as long as women and men share certain morally relevant capacities—the capacity for rationally directed action, the capacity to form emotional attachments, the capacity to communicate—general norms of human flourishing will still apply equally to both," p. 86.

59. Arneil, *Politics & Feminism*, p. 193.

60. Young, *Ceasefire! Why Women and Men Must Join Forces to Achieve True Equality*, p. 5

61. Phillips, *The Sex-Change Society: Feminised Britian and the Neutered Ma*le, p. 159.

62. Carole Pateman, "Introduction," in Carole Pateman and Elizabeth Gross, eds., *Feminist Challenges: Social and Political Theory*. Boston: Northeastern University Press, 1987, pp. 7-8.

63. Susan Moller Okin, "Feminism and Political Theory," in Janet Kourany, ed., *Philosophy in a Feminist Voice*. Princeton: Princeton University Press, 1998, pp. 116-144, p. 123.

64. John Corry, "Dames at Sea," *American Spectator*, August 1996.

65. Warren Farrell, *The Myth of Male Power: Why Men are the Disposable*

Sex. New York: Simon and Schuster, 1993, p. 127-128.

66. Lionel Tiger, *The Decline of Males*. New York: Golden Books, 1999, p. 210.

67. Janet Radcliffe Richards, *The Skeptical Feminist*. Harmondsworth, United Kingdom: Pelican, 1982, p. 143.

68. Tiger, *The Decline of Males*, p. 211.

69. Laura Miller, "Feminism and the Exclusion of Army Women from Combat," *Olin Institute for Strategic Studies, Working Paper NO.2*, Harvard University, December 1995.

70. Tiger, *The Decline of Males*, p. 209.

71. Elizabeth Rappaprot, "Generalizing Gender: Reason and Essence in the Legal Thought of Catherine MacKinnon," in Louise M. Antony and Charlotte Witt, eds., *A Mind of One's Own: Feminist Essays on Reason and Objectivity*. Boulder: Westview Press, 1993, pp. 127-144, p. 128.

72. Farrell, *The Myth of Male Power: Why Men are the Disposable Sex*, p. 126.

73. *Manifesta,* p. 280.

74. Anna Simons, "In War Let Men Be Men: Why Combat Units Should Remain Male," *New York Times*, April 23, 1997.

75. Public Law 103-3, enacted on February 5, 1993.

76. FMLA, Findings #5.

77. Baumgardner and Richards, Manifest, pp. 278-281.

78. Statistics from Warren Farrell cited by Jack Kramer, "The Men's Rights Movement: 'Male' is Not a Four-Letter Word," in Janet Kouraney, James Sterba, and Rosemarie Tong, eds., *Feminist Philosophies*. Upper-Saddle, NJ: Prentice Hall, 1999, pp. 510-516, p. 515.

79. Young, *Ceasefire! Why Women and Men Must Join Forces to Achieve True Equality*, p. 134.

80. Cressida J. Heyes, *Line Drawings: Defining Women through Feminist Practice*. Ithaca: Cornell University Press, 200, p157.

81. Lee Vickers, "The Second Closet: Domestic Violence in Lesbian and Gay Relationships," *Murdoch University Electronic Journal of Law*, Vol.3, No.4, December 1996. In addition, it may be that "although men are often guilty of physical violence, women's tendency to use indirect aggression and to deny their competitive impulses can lead them to oppose each other in more destructive and wounding ways." Phyllis Chester, *Woman's Inhumanity to Women.* Cited by Deborah Tannen, "Dangerous Women." *The Washington Post Book World.* Sunday, March 10, 2002, pp. 1-3.

82. There are now dozens of studies which show that women are as violent towards their partners, if not more so, than men," pp. 134-136. Melanie Phillips, *The Sex-Change Society: Feminised Britian and the Neutered Ma*le. London: The Social Market Foundation, 1999.

83. Young, *Ceasefire! Why Women and Men Must Join Forces to Achieve True Equality*, p. 97.

84. Ibid., pp. 132-133.

85. Ibid., p. 128.

86. Ibid., p. 157.

87. Though such cases are supposedly "rare" (Linda Brookover Bourque, *Defining Rape*, Duke University Press, London: 1989, p. 105, and Andrea Parrot and Laurie Bechhofer, *Acquaintance Rape: The Hidden Crime*, John Wiley and Sons, New York: 1991, p. 313), and despite the claim made by J. Grano, "Free Speech v. The University of Michigan," *Academic Questions*, Spring, 1990, pp. 7-22, that the very idea of a false rape is a form of discriminatory harassment, there is nonetheless some evidence that this does occur. The first recorded case is in Genesis 39. It is interesting to note that Suzanne Scholz, *Rape Plots: A Feminist Cultural Study of Genesis 34*, New York: Peter Lang, 2000, never mentions Genesis 39 although she is sure that the Biblical story of Dinah's "rape" has seriously affected contemporary male culture, pp. 1; 8-9; 12; 44; 129; 150; 164-165; 169-169; 178), she completely ignores the fact that the Biblical story of the false charge of rape against Joseph may have affected female culture. In addition, there are "a number of very contemporary examples." (*Washington Post*, June 27, 1992, B1, B7.). Katie Roiphe cites several real life examples in "Antirape Activists Exaggerate the Threat of Rape," *Date Rape*, San Diego, CA: Greenhaven Press, 1998, pp. 39-47. In addition note the Ben Gose case, documented in "Students at Brown University Settle Dispute Over an Allegation of Date Rape," *The Chronicle of Higher Education*, 43(37), May 23, 1997, p. A49 where a young woman accused the Prince Faisal Ra'ad Zeid Al Hussein of rape after what he believed was a consensual sexual encounter. The case law on this issue is also quite interesting. See, for example, the "Model Penal Code of 1980" given in Susan Estrich, in *Real Rape*, Harvard University Press, Cambridge, MA: 1987, pp. 46-47. Finally, Randy Thornhill and Craig T. Palmer, *A Natural History of Rape: Biological Bases of Sexual Coercion*, Cambridge, MA: MIT Press, 2000, claim that "a careful study of 109 rape cases in the United States found that 41 percent of rape accusations to be false as evidenced by the women's own recantations," pp. 160-161.

88. Tana Dineed, *Manufacturing Victims: What the Psychology Industry is Doing to People*. Montreal: Robert Davies Multimedia Publishing, 1998, p. 88.

89. This law has recently been broadened to include statutory rape by women, however, such broadening did not come at the hands of Feminists.

90. Actually the fact of her illness is now in doubt. See, Cathy Young. *Ceasefire!: Why Women and Men Must Join Forces to Achieve True Equality*. New York: The Free Press, 1999, p. 157.

91. Farrell, *The Myth of Male Power: Why Men are the Disposable Sex*, p. 318; "Man Guilty in Sex Assault on Woman with 46 Identities," *The Los Angeles Times*, November 9, 1990; *State of Wisconsin vs. Dell F. Steadman*, 152 *Wis. 2d* 293, 1989 Wisconsin.

92. Catherine MacKinnon, "Difference and Dominance," in *Feminism*

Unmodified. Cambridge: Harvard University Press, 1987, p. 36.

93. Sally Haslanger, "On Being Objective and Being Objectified," in Louise M. Anthony and Charlotte Witt, eds., *A Mind of One's Own: Feminist Essays on Reason and Objectivity*. Boulder: Westview Press, pp. 85-125, p. 86.

94. Richard J. Ellis, *The Dark Side of the Left: Illiberal Egalitarianism in America*. Lawrence, KS: University Press of Kansas, 1998.

95. Elizabeth Grosz, "Philosophy," in Sneja Gunew, ed., *Feminist Knowledge: Critique and Construct*. New York: Routledge, 1990, pp. 147-174, pp. 158- 159.

96. Ibid., pp. 332-344, pp. 339-340.

97. Robyn Rowland and Renate D. Klein, "Radical Feminism: Critique and Construct," in Sneja Gunew, ed., *Feminist Knowledge: Critique and Construct*. New York: Routledge, 1990, pp. 271-303, p. 274.

98. Carol A. Whitehurst, *Women in America: The Oppressed Majority*. Santa Monica, CA: Goodyear Publishing Company, 1977, p. 99.

99. Ibid., p. 104.

100. Louise M. Antony, "Quine as Feminist: The Radical Import of Naturalized Epistemology," in Louise M. Antony and Charlotte Witt, eds., *A Mind of One's Own: Feminist Essays on Reason and Objectivity*. Boulder: Westview Press, 1993, pp. 185-225, p. 204.

101. Miranda Fricker and Jennifer Hornsby, "Introduction," in Miranda Fricker and Jennifer Hornsby, ed., *The Cambridge Companion to Feminism in Philosophy*. New York: Cambridge University Press, 2000, pp. 1-9, p. 2.

102. Miranda Fricker and Jennifer Hornsby, "Introduction," in Miranda Fricker and Jennifer Hornsby, ed., *The Cambridge Companion to Feminism in Philosophy*. New York: Cambridge University Press, 2000, pp. 1-9, p. 3. Interestingly Fricker and Hornsby site Lloyd as having demonstrated the essential male bias inherent in philosophy. For a serious critique see, E.R. Klein, "Sorry Virginia, There is No Feminist Science," in James P. Sterba, ed., *Controversies in Feminism*. Lanham, MD: Rowman and Littlefield, 2001, pp. 131-154.

103. "The replacement of time-honored universal values with a relativized system of morality in which values are individually designed and self-authenticated is a very recent phenomenon, but one which has become deeply embedded in the public mind," Don E. Eberly, ed., *The Content of America's Character: Recovering Civic Virtue*. New York: Madison Books, 1995, p.xi. E.R. Klein argues that the most fundamental problem with Feminism is that it has a deep-seated commitment to Relativism—the philosophical position that there simply cannot be any absolute truths. See, for example, "Can Feminism Be Rational?," *Journal of Interdisciplinary Studies*, Vol.X, No.1/2, September 1998, pp. 17-29.

104. Catherine MacKinnon, *Feminism Unmodified*. Cambridge: Harvard University Press, 1987, p. 50.

105. Allison Wylie, "Feminism in Philosophy of Science: Making Sense of Contingency and Constraint," in Miranda Fricker and Jennifer Hornsby, ed.,

The Cambridge Companion to Feminism in Philosophy. New York: Cambridge University Press, 2000, pp. 166-184. p. 166.

106. Susan James, "Feminism in Philosophy of Mind: The Question of Personal Identity," in Miranda Fricker and Jennifer Hornsby, ed., *The Cambridge Companion to Feminism in Philosophy*. New York: Cambridge University Press, 2000, pp. 29-48, p. 29.

107. Rae Langton, "Feminism in Epistemology: Exclusion and Objectification," in Miranda Fricker and Jennifer Hornsby, ed., *The Cambridge Companion to Feminism in Philosophy*. New York: Cambridge University Press, 2000, pp. 127-145, p. 142.

108. Wylie, "Feminism in Philosophy of Science: Making Sense of Contingency and Constraint," in *The Cambridge Companion to Feminism in Philosophy*, pp. 166-184. p. 179.

109. See, for example, Sandra Harding, *Whose Science? Whose Knowledge?* Ithaca, NY: Cornell University Press, 1991 and "Rethinking Standpoint Epistemology; 'What is Strong Objectivity?'," in ed. L. Alcoff and E. Potter, ed., *Feminist Epistemologies*. New York: Routledge, 1993, pp. 49-82. For a detailed critique of this position see E.R. Klein, "Criticizing the Feminist Critique of Objectivity," *Reason Papers,* 18, 1993, pp. 57-70.

110. Allison Wylie, "Feminism in Philosophy of Science: Making Sense of Contingency and Constraint," in Miranda Fricker and Jennifer Hornsby, ed., *The Cambridge Companion to Feminism in Philosophy*. New York: Cambridge University Press, 2000, pp. 166-184. p. 175 and 178.

111. Arneil, *Politics & Feminism*, p. 223.

112. Richard J. Evans, *The Feminists: Women's Emancipation Movements in Europe, America and Australasia 1840-1920*. New York: Barnes & Nobel Books, 1977, p. 236.

113. Friedrich Nietzsche, *The Gay Science*, 66. (Trans.) Walter Kaufman. New York: Vintage Books, 1974.

Chapter Five

THIRD GENERATION: LOOKING "BACK TO THE FUTURE"

1. Cathy Young, *Ceasefire! Why Women and Men Must Join Forces to Achieve True Equality*. New York: The Free Press, 1999, p. 7.

2. Richard J. Evans, *The Feminists: Women's Emancipation Movements in Europe, America and Australasia 1840-1920*. New York: Barnes & Nobel Books, 1977, p. 223.

3. Ibid., p. 223.

4. July 13, 2001.

5. Carol A. Whitehurst, *Women in America: The Oppressed Majority*. Santa Monica, CA: Goodyear Publishing Company, 1977, p. 77.

6. Christina Hoff-Sommers, *The War Against Boys: How Misguided Fem-*

inism Is Harming Our Young Men. New York: Simon and Schuster, 2000, pp. 175-176.

7. Naomi Wolf, *Fire With Fire: The New Female Power and How it Will Change the 21st Century*. New York: Random House, 1993, p. 62.

8. Whitehurst, *Women in America: The Oppressed Majority*, p. 5, 123, and 136 repsectively.

9. Naomi Wolf, *Fire With Fire: The New Female Power and How it Will Change the 21st Century*. New York: Random House, 1993, p. 135.

10. Melanie Phillips, *The Sex-Change Society: Feminised Britian and the Neutered Male*. London: The Social Market Foundation, 1999, pp. 134-136.

11. Ibid., p. 147.

12. Young, *Ceasefire! Why Women and Men Must Join Forces to Achieve True Equality*. New York: The Free Press, 1999, p. 87.

13. Wolf, *Fire With Fire: The New Female Power and How it Will Change the 21st Century*, 1993, p. 183.

14. Ibid., p. 144.

15. Young, *Ceasefire! Why Women and Men Must Join Forces to Achieve True Equality*, p. 78.

16. Sally Satel, *P.C. MD's: How Political Correctness is Destroying Medicine*. New York: Basic Books, 2001.

17. Tana Dineed, *Manufacturing Victims: What the Psychology Industry is Doing to People*. Montreal: Robert Davies Multimedia Publishing, 1998, p. 98-99.

18. Katie Rophie, "Antirape Activists Exaggerate the Threat of Rape," *Date Rape*, San Diego, CA: Greenhaven Press, 1998, pp. 39-47, p. 47.

19. Camille Paglia, "No Law in the Arena," in Linda LeMoncheck and James P. Sterba, *Sexual Harassment: Issues and Answers*. New York: Oxford University Press, 2001, pp. 260-264, p. 260.

20. Camille Paglia, "No Law in the Arena," in Linda LeMoncheck and James P. Sterba, *Sexual Harassment: Issues and Answers*. New York: Oxford University Press, 2001, pp. 260-264, p. 263.

21. Ibid., pp. 260-264, p. 262.

22. Hoff-Sommers, *The War Against Boys: How Misguided Feminism Is Harming Our Young Men*, pp. 63-64.

23. Paglia, "No Law in the Arena," in *Sexual Harassment: Issues and Answers*, pp. 260-264, p. 264.

24. Christina Hoff-Sommers, *Who Stole Feminism? How Women Have Betrayed Women*. New York: Simon and Schuster, 1994.

25. Eugenia Kaledin, *Mothers and More: American Women in the 1950s*. Boston: Twayne Publishers, 1984, p. 55.

26. Blanch Linden-Ward and Carol Hurd Green, *American Women in the 1960's: Changing the Future*. New York: Twayne Publishers, 1993, p. 87.

27. Linden-Ward, *American Women in the 1960's: Changing the Future*, 1993, p. 67.

28. For a very pointed attack on Feminism's position here see Diana Furchtgott-Roth and Christine Stolba, *The Feminist Dilemma: When Success is Not Enough*. Washington D.C.: AEI Press, 2002.

29. Linden-Ward, *American Women in the 1960's: Changing the Future*, pp. 82-83.

30. Whitehurst, *Women in America: The Oppressed Majority*. Santa Monica, p. 50.

31. Margo Culley, Arlyn Diamond, Lee Edwards, Sara Lennox, and Catherine Portuges, "The Politics of Nurturance," in *Gendered Subjects: The Dynamics of Feminist Teaching*. Boston: Routledge, 1985, p. 19.

32. Courtney Leatherman, "Free Speech or Harassment?," *The Chronicle of Higher Education*, September 28, 1994, A22.

33. Julianne Basinger, "Arizona State U's Stance on Academic Freedom Angers Faculty Group," *The Chronicle of Higher Education*, May 22, 1998, A15.

34. Hoff-Sommers, *Who Stole Feminism? How Women Have Betrayed Women*, p. 117.

35. *Title IX Education Amendments*, 1972, ensure that there is gender equity in educational settings.

36. Interestingly, there have been some attempts to answer the empirical questions of who actually calls oneself a feminist today, and what, exactly, such persons claim to be doing to support their beliefs. See, for example, Faye J. Crosby, Janet Todd and Judith Worell, "Have Feminists Abandoned Social Activism? Voices from the Academy," in, eds., Leo Montada and Melvin J. Lerner, *Current Societal Concerns About Justice*. New York: Plenum Press, 1996, pp. 85-102. More interestingly are the kinds of self-justifying and petty concerns that count as "activism," e.g., "participating on women's studies coordinating committees," p. 100-101.

37. Peter Monaghan, "Dropping Men's Teams To Comply With Title IX," *The Chronicle of Higher Education*, December 4, 1998, pp.A41-A42.

38. See Hoff-Sommers, *The War Against Boys: How Misguided Feminism Is Harming Our Young Men,* Simon and Schuster, 2001.

39. For example, see Nancy Frazier and Myra Sadker, *Sexism in School and Society*. New York: Harper & Row, 1973.

40. Carol Gilligan, *In a Different Voice*. Cambridge, MA: Harvard University Press, 1982.

41. For more details see E.R. Klein, *Feminism Under Fire*. Amherst, NY: Prometheus Books, 1996.

42. Marilyn Friedman, "Feminism in Ethics: Conceptions of Autonomy," Miranda Fricker and Jennifer Hornsby, ed., *The Cambridge Companion to Feminism in Philosophy*. New York: Cambridge University Press, 2000, pp. 205-224, p. 205 and pp. 210-211.

43. Hoff-Sommers, *The War Against Boys: How Misguided Feminism Is Harming Our Young Men*, p. 23.

44. Ibid., p. 133.

45. Ibid., p. 41.

46. See, for example, E.R. Klein, "Sorry Virginia, There is No Feminist Science," in James P. Sterba, ed., *Controversies in Feminism.* Lanham, MD: Rowman and Littlefield, 2001, pp. 131-153.

47. Hoff-Sommers, *The War Against Boys: How Misguided Feminism Is Harming Our Young Men*, p. 23.

48. Ibid., pp. 31-32.

49. *Quit It!* is designed to "render little boys less volatile, less competetive, and less aggressive." Christina Hoff-Sommers, *The War Against Boys: How Misguided Feminism Is Harming Our Young Men.* New York: Simon and Schuster, 2000, p. 52.

50. Hoff-Sommers, *The War Against Boys: How Misguided Feminism Is Harming Our Young Men*, p. 50.

51. Ibid., p. 71.

52. Ibid., pp. 207-208.

53. Miriam Schneir, *Feminism In Our Time: The Essential Writings, World War II to the Present.* New York: Vintage Books, 1994, p. 272.

54. Winifred D. Wandersee, *On the Move: American Women in the 1970s.* Boston: Twayne Publishers, 1988, p. 91

55. Ibid., p. 92.

56. Catherine A. MacKinnon, *Sexual Harassment of Working Women: A Case of Sex Discrimination.* New Haven: Yale University Press, 1979, p. 218.

57. Catherine MacKinnon on *NBC*, cited in Warren Farrell, *The Myth of Male Power: Why Men are the Disposable Sex.* New York: Simon and Schuster, 1993, p. 316.

58. Warren Farrell, *The Myth of Male Power: Why Men are the Disposable Sex.* New York: Simon and Schuster, 1993, p. 316.

59. Christina Hoff-Sommers, *Who Stole Feminism? How Women Have Betrayed Women.* NY: Simon and Schuster, 1994, Chapter Ten.

60. Dineed, *Manufacturing Victims: What the Psychology Industry is Doing to People*, p. 29.

61. See the case of the Brandeis University student who was accused of having raped his girlfriend of several months. She brought the charges to bear nearly a month after the couple broke up. ("All Things Considered," *National Public Radio* 12 May 2000); see also the Brown University student Mr. Adam Lack who was accused of having raped a woman whom he said "appeared sober and initiated the contact.... They talked for four hours afterward, and she gave him her phone number when she left his room the next morning.... A week later she told him she was drunk and didn't remember anything.... A month after that, in a complaint filed with the Office of Student Life, she accused him of rape." Ben Gose, *The Chronicle of Higher Education*, 43(7), October 11, 1996, pp. A53-A55; Ben Gose, *The Chronicle of Higher Education*, 43(35), May 9, 1997, pp. A43-A44. Christina Hoff-Sommers, *Who Stole Feminism?*

New York: Simon and Schuster, 1994, p. 44 cites cases in which several male students at Vassar were falsely accused of date rape.

62. *Time* magazine

63. David R. Carlin, "Claims of Date Rape Can Trivialize the Problem of Sexual Violence," *Date Rape*, San Diego, CA: Greenhaven Press, 1998, pp. 23-25, p. 24.

64. For more on date rape see, E.R. Klein, "Date Rape: The Feminist Construct That's Harmful to Women," *Contemporary Philosophy*. Vol XXIII, No. 1 and 2. Jan/Feb and Mar/Apr 2001, pp. 24-35.

65. Dineed, *Manufacturing Victims: What the Psychology Industry is Doing to People*, p. 62.

66. Internally, colleges and universities usually take action against men in such cases, for example, expulsion.

67. Schneir, *Feminism In Our Time: The Essential Writings, World War II to the Present*, p. 420.

68. Ibid., p. 420.

69. Catherine MacKinnon, *Feminism Unmodified: Discourses on Life and Law*. Cambridge, MA: Harvard University Press, 1987, p. 172.

70. Sally Haslanger, "On Being Objective and Being Objectified," in Louise M. Anthony and Charlotte Witt, eds., *A Mind of One's Own: Feminist Essays on Reason and Objectivity*. Boulder: Westview Press, pp. 85-125, p. 100.

71. See, for example, Stephanie Rothman's film, *Group Marriage*.

72. See, for example, "Men's Pornography: Gay vs. Straight," in Susan Dwyer, ed., *The Problem of Pornography*. New York: Wadsworth, 1995.

73. E.R. Klein, *Feminism Under Fire*. Amherst, NY: Prometheus Books, 1996, p. 17.

74. Haslanger, "On Being Objective and Being Objectified," *A Mind of One's Own: Feminist Essays on Reason and Objectivity*, pp. 85-125, p. 111.

75. If being "round" is sufficient for being a ball, it does not follow that all balls are round, e.g., a football. Therefore, if being an objectifier is "sufficient" for being a man, then all that follows is that only men can be objectifiers, not that all men are objectifiers.

76. A serious argument against this claim is given by Melinda Vadas, "A First Look at Pronography/Civil Rights Ordinance: Could Pornography Be the Subordination of Women?," *Journal of Philosophy* 89, No.4, 1987, pp. 487-511.

77. Phillips, *The Sex-Change Society: Feminised Britian and the Neutered Ma*le, p. 11.

78. Robert Bly, *Iron John: A Book About Men*. Reading, MA: Addison-Wesley, 1990, p. 93.

79. Which not only valorizes "men behaving badly" via a lot of beer and boobs, but offers some scathing criticisms of women—their stupidity (e.g., when they had women chanting "against any more suffrage for women" and insecurity about their physical appearance and desirability to men).

80. Which is basically a talk show "about breasts." Joel Stein, "Can We Talk a Little More About Breasts?," *Time*, July 23, 2001, p. 69.

81. Jack Zines (trans.) "Iron Hans," The Complete Fairy Tales of the Brothers Grimm. NY: Bantam Books, 1992, pp. 482-487.

82. Bly, *Iron John: A Book About Men*. Reading, p. 92.

83. Ibid., p. 93.

84. Ibid., p. 29.

85. Ibid., p. 147.

86. Rosemary Radford Ruether, "Patriarchy and the Men's Movement: Part of the Problem or Part of the Solution?," in Kay Leigh Hagan, ed., *Women Respond to the Men's Movement: A Feminist Collection*. San Francisco: Harper Collins, 1992, pp. 13-18, p. 17.

87. Margo Adair, "Will the Real Men's Movement Please Stand Up?," in Kay Leigh Hagan, ed., *Women Respond to the Men's Movement: A Feminist Collection*. San Francisco: Harper Collins, 1992, pp. 55-66, p. 55.

88. Jane Caputi and Gordene O. MacKenzie, "Pumping Iron John," in Kay Leigh Hagan, ed., *Women Respond to the Men's Movement: A Feminist Collection*. San Francisco: Harper Collins, 1992, pp. 69-81, p. 72.

89. Bly, *Iron John: A Book About Men*, p. 227.

90. Harriet Gill, "Men's Predicament: Male Supremacy," in Kay Leigh Hagan, ed., *Women Respond to the Men's Movement: A Feminist Collection*. San Francisco: Harper Collins, 1992, pp. 151-157, p. 152.

91. Harry Brod, The Profeminist Men's Movement: Fraternity, Equality, Liberty," in Janet Kouraney, James Sterba, and Rosemarie Tong, eds., *Feminist Philosophies*. Upper-Saddle, NJ: Prentice Hall, 1999, pp. 5-4-510.

92. Janet Kouraney, James Sterba, and Rosemarie Tong, "Toward Gender-Inclusive Feminism: Men's Responses to Feminism in Janet Kouraney, James Sterba, and Rosemarie Tong, eds., *Feminist Philosophies*. Upper-Saddle, NJ: Prentice Hall, 1999, p. 502.

93. Jack Kramer, "The Men's Rights Movement: 'Male' is Not a Four-Letter Word," in Janet Kouraney, James Sterba, and Rosemarie Tong, eds., *Feminist Philosophies*. Upper-Saddle, NJ: Prentice Hall, 1999, pp. 510-516, p. 515.

94. Kouraney, "Toward Gender-Inclusive Feminism: Men's Responses to Feminism" in *Feminist Philosophies*, p. 502.

95. Lionel Tiger, *The Decline of Males*. New York: Golden Books, 1999, p. 27.

96. Young, *Ceasefire! Why Women and Men Must Join Forces to Achieve True Equality*, p. 60.

97. Lionel Tiger, *The Decline of Males*. New York: Golden Books, 1999, p. 257.

98. Rich Zubaty, *Surviving the Feminization of America: How to Keep Women from Ruining Your Life*. Key West: Panther Press, 1993, p. 1.

99. Ibid., p. 410.

100. This is a phrase used by Tom Cruise's hypermasculine character in

the film *Magnolia*.

101. Zubaty, *Surviving the Feminization of America: How to Keep Women from Ruining Your Life*, p. 61.

102. Ibid., p. 68.

103. Ibid., back jacket flap.

104. Naomi Wolf, *Fire With Fire: The New Female Power and How it Will Change the 21st Century*. New York: Random House, 1993, p. 16.

105. Lionel Tiger, *The Decline of Males*. New York: Golden Books, 1999, p. 256.

106. Phillips, *The Sex-Change Society: Feminised Britian and the Neutered Mal*e, p. 13.

107. Wolf, *Fire With Fire: The New Female Power and How it Will Change the 21st Century*, p. 188.

Chapter Six

THE NEXT GENERATION

1. Barbara Arneil, *Politics & Feminism*. Malden, MA: Blackwell, 1999, p. 186.

2. Ibid., p. 212.

3. I trust that the book, *Feminism Under Fire*, has been helpful in pointing this out.

4. Naomi Wolf, *Fire With Fire: The New Female Power and How it Will Change the 21st Century*. New York: Random House, 1993, p. 54.

5. Alison Jaggar, "Feminism in Ethics: Moral Justification," in Miranda Fricker and Jennifer Hornsby, ed., *The Cambridge Companion to Feminism in Philosophy*. New York: Cambridge University Press, 2000, pp. 225-244, p. 242.

6. Susan Faludi, *Backlash: The Undeclared War Against American Women*. New York: Crown Publishers, Inc., 1991.

7. Marilyn French, *The War Against Women*. New York: Summit Books, 1992.

8. Faludi, *Backlash: The Undeclared War Against American Women*, p.xxii.

9. Ibid., p. 452.

10. Ibid., p. 459.

11. Ibid., p. 460.

12. Marilyn French, *The Women's Room*. NY: Ballantine Books, 1989.

13. Marilyn French, *The War Against Women*. New York: Summit Books, 1992, p. 18.

14. Ibid., p. 13.

15. Ibid., pp. 181-207.

16. Ibid., pp. 199.

17. Ibid., p. 26.

18. Cathy Young, *Ceasefire! Why Women and Men Must Join Forces to Achieve True Equality*. New York: The Free Press, 1999, p. 10.

19. Cressida J. Heyes, *Line Drawings: Defining Women Through Feminist Practice*. Ithaca: Cornell University Press, 2000, pp. 167-168.

20. Ibid., p169.

21. Leona Tanenbaum, *Slut! Growing up Female with a Bad Reputation*. New York: Perennial, 2000, p.xix.

22. Ibid., pp. 3-4.

23. Tanenbaum, *Slut! Growing up Female with a Bad Reputation*, p. 20.

24. One of the main arguments used against homosexual marriages—and therefore adoption rights—is their sexual promiscuity. See, for example, Laurence M. Thomas and Michael E. Levin, *Sexual Orientation & Human Rights*. Lanham, MD: Rowman and Littlefield, 1999.

25. Tanenbaum, *Slut! Growing up Female with a Bad Reputation*, p. 24.

26. Interestingly, Dorothy herself only wants to go home which offers up an interpretation that women are more interested in home and hearth than in personal spiritual adventure or global human excellence. The movie ends with Dorothy telling the old woman (Feminism?) that she was right: "There's no place like home!" I leave this story for another time.

27. Analogies can be drawn with *Next Generation*, *Deep Space Nine* and *Voyager* as well, albeit with a bit more work.

28. Marcelle Kays and Debbie Stoller, *The Bust: Guide to the New Girl Order*. New York: Penguin, 1999, pp. 2-3.

29. Jennifer Baumgardner and Amy Richards, *Manifesta: Young Women, Feminism, and the Future*. New York: Farrar, Straus and Giroux, 2000, p. 49.

30. Ibid., p. 57.

31. Ibid., p. 54.

32. Ibid., p. 61.

33. Ibid., pp. 62-63.

34. Ibid., p. 136.

35. Ibid., p. 115-116.

36. Ibid., p. 119.

37. Ibid., p. 215.

38. Ibid., p. 192.

39. Ibid., p. 83.

40. Ibid., p. 166.

41. Ibid., p. 56.

42. Katie Roiphe, *The Morning After: Sex, Fear and Feminism on Campus*. New York: Little Brown, 1993.

43. Baumgardner, *Manifesta: Young Women, Feminism, and the Future*, p. 241.

44. Although I have unmasked such beliefs (which propound in numerous "second wavers"), and discredited these claims on numerous occasions, they exist unabashedly and without response. Even today, the belief that science is

essentially male biased is neither uncommon nor passe in the Feminist community. See, for example Jane Kouraney, "No Need to Be Sorry Virginia," in James P. Sterba, ed., *Controversies in Feminism*. Lanham, MD: Rowman & Littlefield, 2001, pp. 161-172; Allison Wylie, "Feminism in Philosophy of Science: Making Sense of Contingency and Constraint," in Mirand Fricker and Jennifer Hornby, ed., *The Cambridge Companion to Feminism in Philosophy*. New York: Cambridge University Press, 2000, pp. 166-184.

45. Baumgardner, *Manifesta: Young Women, Feminism, and the Future*, p. 240.

46. Ibid., p. 262.

47. Ibid., p. 278.

48. Ibid., p. 278-281, my emphasis.

49. Kays, *The Bust: Guide to the New Girl Order*, pp. 7.

50. Elizabeth Wurtzel, *Bitch: In Praise of Difficult Women*. New York: Anchor, 1998, p. 395.

51. Ibid., p. 33.

52. Ibid., p. 34.

53. Jean Harris killed her lover Herbert Tarnhower, the author of the "Scarsdale Diet" for cheating on her.

54. Lorenna Bobbit cut off her husband's penis for cheating on her.

55. Wurtzel, *Bitch: In Praise of Difficult Women*, p. 3.

56. Inga Musico, *Cunt: Declaration of Independence*. Seattle: Seal Press, 1998.

57. Ibid., p. 223.

58. Ibid., p. 251.

59. Ibid., p. 203.

60. Ibid., author's note in preface.

61. Ibid., p. 9.

62. Ibid., pp. 232-233.

63. Ibid., p. 222.

64. Arneil, *Politics & Feminism*, p. 221.

65. Excerpts from the *1998 Declaration of Sentiments of NOW*, anonymous.

66. Excerpt from the *2000 Statement of Purpose Proposal from the 2000 National Conference of NOW*, anonymous.

67. See, for example, Judith Harlan, *Feminism: A Reference Handbook*. Denver, CO: ABC-CLIO Inc., 1998, p. 234-243.

68. Excerpt from the *2000 Statement of Purpose Proposal from the 2000 National Conference of NOW*, anonymous.

69. Genevieve Lloyd, for example, in her attempt to unearth the "maleness of Reason" inherent in the great works of Western philosophy, actually ends up only making the case not with Plato, or Aquinas, or Descartes, or even Kant, but with respect to the obscure work of the relatively unimportant philosopher, Philo. See, Lloyd, *The Man of Reason: "Male" & "Female" in Western Philosophy*.

Minneapolis: University of Minnesota Press, 1993. For how Feminists harp on this kind of trivia see E.R. Klein, "Sorry Virginia, There is No Feminist Science," in James P. Sterba, ed., *Controversies in Feminism.* Lanham, MD: Rowman and Littlefield, 2001, pp. 131-154; E.R. Klein, *Feminism Under Fire.* Amherst, NY: Prometheus Books, 1996.

70. Sojourner Truth, excerpt from "Ain't I a Woman? *1851 Women's Convention in Akron Ohio.*

71. Arneil, *Politics & Feminism*, p. 160.

72. Barbara Smith wrote this in her introduction to *Hoe Girls: A Black Feminist Anthology*, 1982 cited in Miriam Schneir, *Feminism In Our Time: The Essential Writings, World War II to the Present.* New York: Vintage Books, 1994, p. 176.

73. Maria Lugones and Elizabeth Spelman, "Have We Got a Theory for You! Feminist Theory, Cultural Imperialism and the Demand for 'The Woman's Voice'," in Janet A. Kourany, James P. Sterba, and Rosemarie Tong, eds., *Feminist Philosophies.* Upper Saddle River, NJ: Prentice Hall, 1999, pp. 474-486, p. 477.

74. Ibid., pp. 474-486, p. 478.

75. bell hooks, *Feminism is for Everybody: Passionate Politics.* Cambridge, MA: South End Press, 2000, pp. 44-45.

76. Anne Waters, "Language Matters: A Metaphysic of Non-Discreet Non-Binary Dualism," *APA Newsletters on American Indians.* Vol 01, No. 2, Spring 2002, pp. 5-13, p. 10.

77. Constance Hillard, "Feminists Abroad: Ugly Americans?" *USA Today*, Friday April 12, 2002.

78. hooks, *Feminism is for Everybody: Passionate Politics*, p. 45.

79. Ibid., p. 47.

80. Ibid., pp. 487-500, p. 500.

81. See, for example, Jane Flax, "On Encountering Incommensurability" Martha Nussbaum's Aristotelian Practice," in James Sterba, ed., *Controversies in Feminism.* Lanham, MD: Rowman and Littlefield, 2001, pp. 25-45.

82. Which is very interesting given that "Third World women are rushing, when they can, into small-business enterprises." Naomi Wolf, *Fire With Fire: The New Female Power and How it Will Change the 21st Century.* New York: Random House, 1993, p. 303-304.

83. Judith Harlan, *Feminism: A Reference Handbook.* Denver, CO: ABC-CLIO Inc., 1998, p. 85.

84. Reprinted in Linda LeMoncheck and James P. Sterba, *Sexual Harassment: Issues and Answers.* New York: Oxford University Press, 2001, pp. 391-398.

85. For a more sympathetic account of Global Feminism see Estelle B. Freedman, *No Turning Back: A History of Feminism and the Future of Women.* New York: Ballantine Books, 2002, Chapter Four.

Chapter Seven
IS FEMINISM DEAD?

1. Tamara Wilson, "Feminism—The Dead Horse Who's Still Alive and Kicking," *Lion's Tale*, October 2001, p. 2.

2. Naomi Wolf, *Fire With Fire: The New Female Power and How it Will Change the 21st Century*. New York: Random House, 1993, p. 320.

3. Feminism, especially through its overbearing stronghold in academic communities, has proven itself over and over again to be nothing less than self-serving. If one does not buy into the particular party line they personally are committed to, one is punished—called names in print, ignored as a scholar, pulled from important political committees, and perhaps even fired from one's job. This has been documented in numerous places including Paul Gross and Norman Levit, *Higher Superstition: The Academic Left and its Quarrels with Science*. Baltimore: Johns Hopkins University Press, 1994.

4. Opening epigraph from Tana Dineen, *Manufacturing Victims: What the Psychology Industry is Doing to People*. Montreal: Robert Davie Multimedia Publishing, 1998.

5. This list was taken by Gemma Alexander, ed., *The Mammoth Book of Heroic & Outrageous Women*. New York: Carroll & Graf Publishers, 1999, Chapter Four.

6. Note that the list does not continue into the post-"second wave" Feminist era.

7. This phrase came out of the Supreme Court case *Plessey vs. Ferguson*. It is important to note that this distinction didn't work for racism and it doesn't work for sexism.

8. Editorial, *The St. Petersburg Times*, July 10, 2001. This doesn't even mention the harm to "academic freedom" allowed by colleges and universities themselves.

9. Schopenhauer, DeWitt H. Parker (trans.) "On Women," *Schopenhauer Selections*. New York: Charles Scribner and Sons, 196, pp. 434-447, p. 442.

10. Freidrich Nietzsche, for example, talks about attempting this kind of truly noble life in *Beyond Good and Evil*, as does Jose Ortega y Gassett in *The Revolution of the Masses* where the emphasis is on "striving" and "effortful attempting."

11. See, for example, Michael Levin, "Maritime Policy for a Flat Earth," in James Sterba, ed., *Controversies in Feminism*. New York: Roman and Littlefield, 2001, pp. 197-218.

12. Plato, *The Republic*, Book V.

13. It is important to note that women of great wealth—such as queens (e.g., Catherine De Medici) and Hollywood movie stars (e.g., Madonna) may seem to be exceptions to this rule but in fact are not, since, although technically mothers, they easily had the financial means to hire 24-hour nannies, cooks, etc.

14. For example, Joan of Arc, Florence Nightengale, Jane Addams, Simone de Beauvoir, Susan B. Anthony, and Helen Keller. (These women were all chosen by *Time/Life Books* to be in the top 100 list of people relevant to the past millennium.)

15. For example, Grandma Moses.

16. Christina Hoff-Sommers, "The War Against Boys," *The Atlantic Monthly*, Vol 285, No. 5, May 2000, pp. 59-74.

17. Of the 2,561,294 teachers in private and public elementary schools in the USA, 694,098 are men and 1,867,195 are women. Source: *U.S. Department of Education, National Center for Education Statistics*, "Schools and Staffing Survey, 1993-1994," 1997.

18. An argument often given is that the life of the schoolteacher is an excellent life since someone has to prepare and train excellent human beings in all other areas of global competition. This however, is a fallacious argument. First, it presupposes that simply by having the opportunity to teach someone to be excellent you are excellent. Second, the argument only makes sense if we assume that raising excellent citizens means more than just raising them to go back into the classroom to raise more "excellent" citizens. Without an independent account of excellence, the claim is circular and hollow. Of course once we unpack the notion of excellence as something more substantive than simply being a teacher of excellence, it is easy to see that even if teachers were fundamentally responsible for their creations (which is itself problematic), such "excellence" qua taught someone to read who then grew up to be excellent, is not in league with having actually achieved excellence at a global level. (A similar and more damning argument can be given to the response that being a mother who then raises excellent children makes the mother excellent.) Finally, such a move is inherently sexist. Given that almost all primary care takers are women, the de facto outcome of the above argument is that women are excellent for having raised other women who will become excellent child rearers. This cycle continues without any substantive account of what it means to have human excellence unless it ends in the rearing of a man who, in some way or other, becomes world class.

19. Christina Hoff-Sommers recently argued that American schools actually favor girls in "The War Against Boys," *The Atlantic Monthly*, May 2000.

20. *National Public Radio*, "Morning Edition," January 11, 2000 claimed that there is a great deal of evidence that teachers of primary and secondary education are simply untrained and ill-equipped to teach. It was argued that the training needs to be made more demanding and rigorous.

21. The statistics used to understand why it is that women on average have a smaller retirement nest egg than men show that "women are likely to work part-time, in smaller firms, or in the industries that pay the lower wages.... And because women tend to move in and out of the labor force to care for their children or elderly relatives..." *TIAA-CREF Participant*, February, 2000, pp. 4-5.

22. Statistics show that aside from retirement age, more women leave the profession of teaching between the ages between 25 and 35 than at any other time during their teaching career. *U.S. Department of Education, National Center for Education Statistics* "The Condition of Education 1998, Supplemental Table 59-7."

23.A similar thesis is now being presented by Diana Furchgott-Roth and Christine Stolba, *The Feminist Dilemma: When Success in Not Enough*. Washington D.C.: AEI Press, 2002.

24. I realize that this is only a hypothetical case, but there are real cases of instances where women claim to have suffered "serious long-term discrimination" when the facts do not bear this out. See, for example, the work of Dr. Judith Kleinfeld in John Leo's "Gender Test at MIT: A Faculty Committee Report on Bias Seems Biased Itself," *U.S. News & World Report*, December 20, 1999, p. 14.

25. Actually some feminists are finally realizing the power of certain vilified male emotions such as anger. See Wendy Donner, "Feminist Ethics and Anger: A Feminist Buddhist Reflection," *APA Newsletter on Feminism*. Vol 01, No. 2, Spring 2002, pp. 67-70.

26. Jose Ortega y Gasset, *The Revolt of the Masses*. New York: W.W. Norton & Co., 1932, p. 14.

27. Even women's magazines such as *Ladies Home Journal*, in an article by Melina Gerosa, plead with women to "Diet Like a Man," Oct. 1998, pp. 106-107.

28. Friedrich Nietzsche, *Schopenhauer as Educator* (trans. James W. Hillesheim and Malcom R. Simpson). Chicago: Gateway Editions, 1965, p. 34.

29. Simon de Beauvoir, *The Second Sex*. (trans. H.M. Parshley) New York: Vintage Books, 1989.

30. Ibid., p. 45.

31. Ibid., p. 606.

32. Ibid., p. 133.

33. Ibid., p. 267.

34. Ibid., p. 732 (my emphasis).

35. Friedrich Nietzsche, *Schopenhauer as Educator* (trans. James W. Hillesheim and Malcom R. Simpson). Chicago: Gateway Editions, 1965, pp. 80-82.

36. It is important to note that when men get married and have children they are still expected (by themselves and society at large) to do something else, something in the public sphere as well. It is rarely the case that men assume the role of primary homemaker and caretaker. It is also important to note that Marie Curie is an exception to this rule. Not only did she work with her husband, she produced two female children one of whom went on to write her biography and the other to become a physicist, had a daughter who is alive today and is a physicist. Finally, Mary Wollstonecraft needs to be recognized for having been one of the first suffragettes, and one that purposely had a child

out of wedlock in order to challenge the social taboos of her time.

37. Though true that most people fail to achieve excellence, nonetheless, most women are not "urged, by interior necessity, to appeal from themselves to some standard beyond oneself, superior to oneself, whose service she freely accepts...the excellent man makes great [global] demands on themselves," Jose Ortega y Gasset, *The Revolt of the Masses*. New York: W.W. Norton & Company, 1932, p. 69.

38. This is not to say that women shouldn't have children but only to realize that in few cases is this act itself a serious part of the concept of global excellence.

39. Producing, creating, thinking, writing or saying something remarkable and enduring on a global scale as did, for example, Socrates, Plato, Aristotle, St. Augustine, Descartes, Rembrandt, Picasso, Gandhi, King, Siddhartha Gautama, Confucius, and Muhammad.

40. E.R. Klein, *Feminism Under Fire*. Amherst, NY: Prometheus Books, 1996.

41. See, for example, the numerous citations of those arguing against relativism in E.R. Klein. *Feminism Under Fire*. Prometheus Books, 1996.

42. "State University Library Bans American Pride Stichers," *News 10*, October 24, 2001.

43. *FIRE*, www.thefire.org.

44. Lou Marano, "School Warns Man Who Rebuked Saudis," *UPI*, October 25, 2001.

INDEX

abortion, 74, 75, 137, 139
academic feminism, 152, 205*n*3
Adam, Abigail, 29
Adam, John, 29
adultery, 43
advertising, 16
Against Our Will: Men, Women, and Rape (Brownmiller), 118
Ain't I a Woman? Network/PAC, 150
alcohol abuse, 42
Alcott, Louisa May, 37
Al Hussein, Prince Faisal Ra'ad Zeid, 193*n*87
Aliens II (film), 160
amendments, constitutional
  First, 86, 123, 124
  Fourth, 86
  Fifth, 77
  Thirteenth, 22, 38
  Fourteenth, 22, 38–39, 54, 61, 74, 76–77, 81, 90, 103
  Fifteenth, 22, 35, 39
  Nineteenth, 23, 24, 37, 44–45, 48, 54, 73
American Association of University Women (AAUW), 81–82, 114–15, 117
American Legion, 53
androgyny, 23
Anthony, Susan B., 34, 35–36, 39, 184*n*53
Antoinette, Marie, 161
Apology (Plato), 82
Aristotle, 20, 208*n*39
Arlington National Cemetery, 64
Army Air Forces (AAF), 53
Aron, Ruthann, 3
attacks, of September 11, 2001, 27, 171–72, 173
authority, 108–9

backlash, 134–39, 140, 146
Backlash (Faludi), 135–36
Baker, Josephine, 161
Barton, Clara, 37
battered women syndrome, 90–91
Bechhofer, Laurie, 193*n*87
beliefs, trio of exaggerated, 2
Benn, Stanley, 20
bias, workplace, 62
Bible, 193*n*87
birth control, 36, 87, 107, 139, 145, 164
bitch, 146–47, 157, 158
blacks, 35, 38–39, 62, 151–52, 153, 154. *See also* slaves, slavery
Bluestockings, 186*n*55
Bly, Robert, 125, 126, 127, 128
Boadicea, 161
Bobbit, Lorenna, 147
Booth, Heather, 64
Bourque, Linda Brookover, 193*n*87
Bowles, Mark, 3
bra burning, 65, 66, 106
Brandeis University, 198*n*61
Brod, Harry, 128
Brown, Helen Gurley, 59
Brownmiller, Susan, 6, 118
Brown University, 198*n*61

Bullard, Irving, 43
Burke, Edmund, 30, 31
Burning City, 72
butch, 179*n*82

Calvin Klein, 16
capitalism, 4, 5, 80, 83–85, 109, 112, 142, 154, 155, 158, 190*n*43
Capone, Al, 47
Carlyle, Belinda, 147
Carter, Elizabeth, 186*n*55
Carter, Rosalynn, 80
Cavanaugh, Christina, 161
Central Michigan University, 173
Chapone, Hester, 186*n*55
chauvinism, feminist, 107
Chicago Westside Group, 64
children, 2, 129, 130, 137, 142, 145, 170, 186*n*59, 208*n*38
Children's Bureau, 58
Civil Rights Act, 61–62, 76, 77–79, 80
Civil War, 36–37
Clift, Elayne, 3
Clinton, Bill, 176*n*24
"Clothesline Project, the," 3
CNN, 1
Comedy Channel, 125
Commission of Education, 110
Commission on the Status of Women, 60
Comprehensive Employment and Training Act, 188*n*6
condoms, 36
Congress, U.S. *See also* House of Representatives, U.S.
  on Civil Rights Act, 62
  on Equal Pay Act, 60–61
  on Equal Rights Amendment, 54, 63, 75, 81, 185*n*41
  on Family and and Medical Leave Act, 90
  on Gender Equity in Education Act, 116
  Rankin in, 43
  Women's Joint Congressional Committee, 48
consciousness, gender, 10–11, 58, 59–60, 67, 69, 72, 112, 127, 128, 143, 153
Constitution, U.S., 21, 22, 23, 24, 25, 29, 174. *See also* amendments, constitutional; Equal Rights Amendment (ERA)
Convention on the Elimination of All Forms of Discrimination Against Women (CEDAW), 155
Copernicus, Nicolaus, 130
Court of Appeals, U.S., 123
Coward, Rosalind, 131
Crawford, Joan, 147
cultural feminism, 8
cunt, 146, 147–48, 157, 158
Cunt (Muscio), 147, 148
Curie, Marie, 160, 207*n*36
custody, child, 129

Darwin, Charles, 129
date rape, 92, 106, 118, 120–22, 124, 193*n*87, 198–99*n*61
Davis, Caroline, 63
Davis, Katherine B., 43
Davis v. Monroe County Board of Education, 117
de Beauvoir, Simone, 7, 170
Declaration of Human Rights, 155
Declaration of Independence, The, 21
Declaration of the Rights of Women (de Gouges), 29
Decline of Males, The (Tiger), 128–29
de Gouges, Olympe, 29–30, 34
De Medici, Catherine, 160
Democracy in America (de Tocqueville), 22
Department of Education, U.S., 117
Department of Health, Education, and Welfare, U.S., 58
Department of Labor, U.S., 44

Depression, 50–52
de Tocqueville, Alexis, 22
Dialectic of Sex, The (Firestone), 71, 72
Dinah, 193*n*87
discrimination
  in education, 110–12
  sex, 61–62, 64, 76–79, 103, 137
  workplace, 89–90
divorce, 69, 127, 129, 135
DNA, 14
double standard, 139, 145
due process, 103, 124
Dunbar, Agnes, 161
Dworkin, Andrea, 6, 122

ecologicial feminism, 8
Edmonds, Sarah Emma, 37
education
  in early 1900s, 42, 43
  patriarchy's effect on, 2
  in 1920s, 48, 49, 50
  in 1930s, 51
  in 1940s, 53
  in 1950s, 57
  Sommers on, 110–17
Education Week, 115
Einstein, Albert, 164
Eisenhower, Dwight D., 57
Elizabeth I, 160
Elmeer, Diane, 162
Enlightenment, 29
Equal Employment Opportunity Act, 188*n*6
Equal Employment Opportunity Commission (EEOC), 62
Equal Pay Act, 60–61, 188*n*6
Equal Rights Amendment (ERA), 51, 54, 57, 63–64, 67, 75–81, 110, 143, 144, 145, 185*n*41
essentialism, 164–65
Estrich, Susan, 193*n*87
Excalibur (film), 126
excellence, global, 2, 163–71, 206*n*18, 208*nn* 37, 38
existentialist feminism, 6–7, 170

Faludi, Susan, 130, 135, 136
Family and Medical Leave Act (FMLA), 89–90
Federalist Papers, The, 21
Feeney v. The State of Massachusetts, 80
Female Eunuch, The (Greer), 71
Feminazis, 5, 6, 176*n*24
Feminine Mystique, The (Friedan), 59
Feminism and Masculism (course), xiv
Feminists, The, 65
Feminist Women's Health Center, 74–75
Ferry, Nicole, 162
Firestone, Laya, 64
Firestone, Shulamith, 64, 72
First National Women's Conference, 80
First National Women's Rights Convention, 36
flappers, 47, 48
Florida Gulf Coast University, 173
Ford, Maggie, 115
freedom, in existentialist feminism, 7
Freeman, Jo, 64
French, Marilyn, 135, 136–37
French Resistance, 161
Freud, Sigmund, 6, 42–43
Friedan, Betty, 59, 62, 63, 71, 73, 107, 189*n*17
fundamentalism, 137

Gandhi, Mohandas, 82, 208*n*39
gays, 17, 72–73, 106, 173, 202*n*24. *See also* lesbian feminism
Geduldig v. Aiello, 77
Gender Equity in Education Act, 116
gender feminism, 8, 9–19
gender norming, 87–88
General Electric Co. v. Martha Gilbert, et. al., 77–78
Generation X, 139–47, 157, 158–59

GI Bill, 53
Gilligan, Carol, 113–15
Gilman, Charlotte Perkins, 49
girlie, 2, 141–46, 147, 157, 158
Glamour, 16
glass ceiling, 109, 128, 137
global, 157
globalization, 150–51, 153
Goesaert v. United States, 55
Gone With the Wind (film), 36
Gose, Ben, 193*n*87, 198*n*61
Grano, J., 193*n*87
Green, Edith, 61
Greer, Germaine, 71–72
Griffin, Susan, 118–19
Grimm's Fairy Tales (Grimm), 126
Grosz, Elizabeth, 94–95
Gulf War, 80

Hanson, Katherine, 116–17
Harper's, 51
Harris, Jean, 147
Harvard University, 117, 143
health movement, women's, 75
heart disease, 107
hermaphrodites, 14, 15–16
Hippel, Theodor Gottlieb von, 32, 34
Hispanics, 151, 153
Hobbes, Thomas, 20, 21
Hoeth, Kathleen, 173
homosexuality, 202*n*24. *See also* gays; lesbian feminism
hooks, bell, 176*n*24
House of Representatives, U.S., 54, 111. *See also* Congress, U.S.
hysterectomies, 107
hysterical feminism, 162

In a Different Voice (Gilligan), 113
industrialization, 43–44
International Council of Women, 39
Internet, 6, 150
Iron Hans (Grimm), 126
Iron John (Bly), 126, 127

Jews, 20, 153
Joan of Arc, 159, 160
Johnson, Lyndon B., 62
Joseph, 193*n*87
Journal of the American Medical Association, 48

Kant, Immanuel, 32
Kennedy, John F., 60, 110
Kennedy Commission on the Status of Women, 110
Kesselman, Amy, 64
Kidman, Nicole, 16
King, Billie Jean, 190*n*42
Kleinfeld, Judith, 115
Koestner, Katie, 120, 121
Kramer, Jack, 128

labor movement, 40–41, 50, 52, 63
Lack, Adam, 198*n*61
Ladies Home Journal, 48
Latina PAC, 150
Lavender Menace, 72
law, liberal feminism on, 4
Lawrence, Dorothy, 161
League of Women's Voters, 55
lesbian feminism, 5, 6, 16, 72–74, 91, 142, 145, 173, 189*nn* 17, 18
liberal feminism, 4, 7, 45
Life, 17
lifestyle feminism, 8, 13, 65, 148
Liggett, James, 3
Limbaugh, Rush, 176*n*24
Lincoln, Abraham, 39
Little Women (Alcott), 37
Lloyd, Genevieve, 203*n*69
Locke, John, 20–21

MacKinnon, Catherine, 6, 93–94, 119, 122, 144
"MacKinnon/Dworkin" law, 124
man, wild, 126–27
Man Show, The (TV program), 125
marriage, homosexual, 202*n*24
Marx, Karl, 4, 5, 129, 147, 183*n*40
Marxist feminism, 4–5, 7
masculism, 125–30
Matrix (film), 126
McCarthyism, sexual, 176*n*24
McLean Center for Men, 117
Mead, Margaret, 13
media, 16
medicine, 107–8
men. *See also* gays; patriarchy
  acting like, 109
  child care by, 190*n*32
  hatred of, 6, 66–67, 146, 147
men's movement, 127–28, 181*nn* 109, 110
"Mental Traits of Sex, The" (Thompson), 42
military service, 2, 87, 88–89, 93, 101, 145, 172
Mill, John Stuart, 33–34
Millet, Kate, 72, 73, 110
Minneapolis City Council, 123
minorities, 116, 150–56
Miss America Pageant, 64–65
Mommie Dearest (film), 147
money, cunts on, 146, 147
Montagu, Elizabeth, 186*n*55
More, Hannah, 186*n*55
Morning After, The: Sex, Fear, and Feminism on Campus (Rophie), 143
Mott, Lucretia, 34
Moyer, Bill, 102
Ms. Magazine, 75, 142
multicultural feminism, 8
Murray, Pauli, 152

Naked Guy, 106, 108
National Abortion and Reproductive Rights Action League (NARAL), 150
National American Women's Suffrage Association, 39
National Conference on Day Care, 58
National Federation of Business and Professional Women, 57
National Organization of Women (NOW), 62–64
  on abortion, 75
  Declaration of Sentiments, 149
  Education Committee, 110
  on Equal Rights Amendment, 63–64, 67, 75, 110
  lesbianism in, 72–74
  National Conference 2000, 149
  Statement of Purpose, 152
National War Labor Board, 52
National Women's Party, 51, 55, 63
Native Americans, 154, 176*n*25
NBC, 119
"New Generation of Women, A" (Gilman), 49
Newsweek, 75
New York Radical Feminists, 64
New York Radical Women, 64, 65
New York Times, The, 115
Nick at Night (TV program), 56
Nietzsche, Friedrich Wilhelm, 100, 169
Nigger Lover (photo), 162
1995 United Nation's World Congress on Women, 13
Nixon, Richard M., 69, 186*n*59
Notes From the First Year (New York Radical Women), 64
Nurse and Spy in the Union Army (Edmonds), 37

objectivity, 97–99, 124, 134, 199*n*75
Old Testament, 20
On the Civil Improvement of Women (Kant), 32

"On Women" (Schopenhauer), 163
Opie & Anthony Show, The (radio program), 125
oppression, sexist male, 1, 72, 82, 104, 154, 157. *See also* patriarchy
Orbach, Susie, 131
Ortega y Gasset, Jose, 169

PAC feminism, 148–50, 157
Paglia, Camille, 102, 108–10, 118, 147, 161, 176*n*25
Palmer, Craig T., 193*n*87
Parkhurst, Genevieve, 51
Parks, Rosa, 82
Parrot, Andrea, 193*n*87
Pateman, Carole, 86
paternity, 2
patriarchy, 95. *See also* oppression, sexist male
  Brod on, 128
  in classical studies, 144
  cunts on, 147
  damage to women under, 2, 116, 169, 191*n*58
  freedom from, 142, 162
  French on, 137
  matriarchal myth and, 178*n*62
  men's movement and, 127
  Millet on, 72
  Paglia on, 109
  of philosophy, 194*n*102, 203*n*69
  sluts and, 139
  Sommers on, 112
  terrorism and, 172
Paul, Rue, 17
P.C. MDs: How Political Correctness is Destroying Medicine (Satel), 107
Peer Marriage (Schwartz), 84
penis envy, 6
Peterson, Mark, 93
phallologocentric thought, 8
Philo, 203*n*69
philosophy, patriarchy of, 96–100, 194*n*102, 203*n*69
Picasso, Pablo, 164, 208*n*39
Plato, 20, 82, 140, 164, 208*n*39
Playboy, 57, 75
Politically Incorrect (TV program), 102
pornography, 122–24
postfeminists, 81
postmodern feminism, 7–8, 9
power feminism, 105, 155, 158
pregnancy, 77–79, 89, 155, 165, 190*n*32
President's Commission on the Status of Women, 63
Princeton University, 144
prison reform, 42
Prohibition, 42, 48
promiscuity, 139–40
prostitution, 155
Proverbs, 20
Psalms, 20
psychoanalytic feminism, 6, 7

Quit It! (WEEA program), 117

radical feminism, 5–6, 7
Rankin, Jeanette, 43
rape, rapists, 118–22
  in Bible, 193*n*87
  exaggerated beliefs about, 2, 142
  false allegations of, 3, 91–93, 198–99*n*61
  Friedan on, 107
  of gay men, 106
  MacKinnon on, 144
  objectifiers and, 124
  radical feminism on, 6
  statutory, 92, 193*n*89
Rape: The Power of Consciousness (Griffin), 118–19
Reage, Pauline, 11
Reconstruction, 37
Red Cross, 44
Redstockings, 6, 58, 64, 65–66
Reflections of the Revolution in France (Burke), 30

Reimer case, 15–16
relativism, 172–74, 194*n*103
Republic, The (Plato), 140
Rich, Adrienne, 189*n*18
Riggs, Bobbie, 190*n*42
Robert the Bruce, 161
Roe v. Wade, 74
Roiphe, Katie, 143, 193*n*87
Rominski, Frank, 64
Rosie the Riveter, 52
Rossi, Alice, 111
Rousseau, Jean-Jacques, 21

Sakren v. Arizona State University, 113
San Diego State University, 173
Sandler, Bernice, 111
Sapho, 159
Sartre, Jean-Paul, 7
Satel, Sally, 107
Scholz, Suzanne, 193*n*87
schoolteachers, 206*nn* 18, 20, 207*n*22
Schopenhauer, Arthur, 163
Schwartz, Pepper, 84
science, 97, 202–3*n*44
Science News, 114
Second Congress to Unite Women, 72
Second Sex, The (de Beauvoir), 170
Senate, U.S., 54
Seneca Falls Declaration of Sentiments, 34–35
separation, 138
sex, 139–40. *See also* discrimination, sex
  Davis on, 43
  Freud on, 42–43
  gender and, 11–19
  hatred of men and, 67
  male oppression and, 82
  meaning of, 11
  political aspect of, 72
  in 1960s, 58, 59–60
  sluts and, 157–58
Sex and the Single Girl (Brown), 59
sexes, war between the, 68
sexism, reverse, 85
Sexual Politics (Millet), 71, 72
Shakespeare, William, 113
Signs, 189*n*18
Silva v. University of New Hampshire, 112–13
Simon & Schuster, 144
sisterhood, 75, 148, 150
slaves, slavery, 37, 38, 151–52
sluts, 139–40, 157
Smith, Howard W., 62
socialist feminism, 5, 183*n*40
Social Security Administration, 58
Society for Cutting Up Men (SCUM), 67
Socrates, 82, 208*n*39
Solanas, Valerie, 66–67, 147
Sommers, Christina Hoff-, 102, 110–13, 117, 118, 144, 147, 161, 166, 178*n*52, 198–99*n*61
sports, college, 113
standard, double, 138, 139
Stanton, Elizabeth Cady, 34, 35–36, 39–40, 184*n*53
Star Trek (TV program), 140
Star Wars (film), 126
Steinem, Gloria, 75, 142
Stone, Lucy, 184*n*53
Stone, Sharon, 16
Story of O, The (Reage), 11
Stowe, Harriet Beecher, 152
Strike for Equality, 73
Subjection of Women, The (Mill), 33–34
suffrage, 29, 34–35, 38, 39, 44–45, 144, 207–8*n*36
  National Women's Party and, 63
Sun Tsu, 161
"superwoman," 190*n*44
support, child, 2, 129, 137
Supreme Court, U.S., 54–55
  on Congress, 81
  on *Feeney v. The State of Massachusetts,* 80

on *Geduldig v. Aiello,* 77
on *General Electric Co. v. Martha Gilbert, et. al.,* 77–78
on military combat, 88–89
on *Roe v. Wade,* 74
on Virginia Military Institute, 103
Susan B. Anthony amendment, 45

"Take Back the Night" marches, 143
Taliban, 172, 174
Taylor, Harriet, 33, 34
teachers, 206*nn*18, 20, 207*n*22
Teresa of Avila, Saint, 160
That 70s Show (TV program), 69
Thompson, Helen, 42
Thornhill, Randy, 193*n*87
Tiger, Lionel, 128–29
Time magazine, 1, 121, 157
Title IX, 113
Title VII, 61–62, 76, 77–79, 80
Token Learning (Millet), 110
Tong, Rosemary, 4, 5
Triangle Shirtwaist Company, 40
Truth, Sojourner, 151–52, 184*n*53
Tubman, Harriet, 151
Tucci, Kathryn, 3
Tufts University, 117
twenties, roaring, 47–50, 51

Uncle Tom's Cabin (Stowe), 152
Underground Railroad, 151
United Auto Workers, Women's Department of the, 63
United Nations, 155
University of Alaska, 115
University of California, 106
University of Chicago, 42
University of Minnesota, 122
University of South Florida, 162

vagina, myths about, 176*n*25
Vanity Fair, 16
Vassar College, 199*n*61
Veterans of Foreign Wars, 53
victim feminism, 103–8, 109, 130
victim masculism, 127
Vietnam War, 69
Vindication of the Rights of Man, A (Wollstonecraft), 30
Vindication of the Rights of Woman, A (Wollstonecraft), 29, 30–31, 67, 186*n*55
violence
courts on, 137
domestic, 90–93, 105, 192*n*81
male, 131, 137
school, 127
Virginia Military Institute, 103
Virginia Slims, 190*n*42

Wake, Nancy, 161
Walpole, Charlotte, 161
War Against Boys, The (Sommers), 113, 144
War Against Women, The (French), 135, 136–37
Warhol, Andy, 66
War Manpower Commission, 52
War Production Board, The, 52
"warriors," 26–27, 141, 159–61
Washington, Derek, 162
Watergate scandal, 69
Weaver, Sigourney, 160
WEEA Equity Resource Center, 117
Weisstein, Naomi, 64
Weldon, Fay, 131
Wellesley College, 115, 117
West, Mae, 147
White House Conference on Children (1970), 186*n*59
Who Stole Feminism? (Sommers), 110
WITCH, 65, 187–88*n*82
Wizard of Oz, The Wonderful (Baum), 140, 202*n*26
Wolf, Naomi, 131

Wollstonecraft, Mary, 29, 30–32, 34, 67–68, 207–8*n*36
Women in Industry Service (WIS), 44
Women's Airforce Service Pilots (WASP), 53
Women's Bureau, 44, 58, 69
Women's Educational Equity Act (WEEA), 116–17, 188*n*6
Women's Equity Action League, 111
Women's Joint Congressional Committee (WJCC), 48
women's liberation, women's lib
  NOW on, 63, 64
  Redstockings on, 66
  in 1970s, 69–70
  Steinem and, 75
  women's movement
  equality centerpiece of, 32
  lesbian issue and, 189*n*17
  Mill on, 33–34
  origins of, 24, 29
  in 1920s, 47–50, 51
  in 1930s, 50–52
  in 1960s, 68
  in 1970s, 72, 73–74, 75, 80
Women's Room, The (French), 136
women's studies, 110, 112, 145, 197*n*36
Women's Trade Union League, 40
Women's Work in War Time (Bullard), 43
World Trade Center, 173
World War I, 43–44, 161
World War II, 52–56, 60, 80, 161
worth, comparable, 5

Xena, 160
X-Files, The (TV program), 167

Yound-Eisendrath, Polly, 131